R.   eral
Po   also
wo

'Ar   es
exce   he
wor   e
done

MACKENZIE'S MISSION

How one family turned tragedy into hope and love

Rachael Casella

With **Jonathan Casella**

ALLEN&UNWIN
SYDNEY•MELBOURNE•AUCKLAND•LONDON

First published in 2020
Copyright © Rachael Casella 2020

Allen & Unwin
83 Alexander Street
Crows Nest NSW 2065
Australia
Phone: (61 2) 8425 0100
Email: info@allenandunwin.com
Web: www.allenandunwin.com

A catalogue record for this book is available from the National Library of Australia

ISBN 978 1 76052 745 7

Set in 12.5/18 pt Granjon by Midland Typesetters, Australia
Printed and bound in Australia by Griffin Press, part of Ovato

10 9 8 7 6 5 4

The paper in this book is FSC® certified. FSC® promotes environmentally responsible, socially beneficial and economically viable management of the world's forests.

Contents

Foreword

By the lead investigators of Mackenzie's Mission

In August 2018, the Human Genetics Society of Australasia held its annual scientific meeting in Sydney. At one of the key events of the conference—a plenary session attended by most of the hundreds of scientists, genetic counsellors and clinical geneticists who took part in the meeting—the three of us took the stage to speak about the plans for Mackenzie's Mission, a national project to study how best to introduce genetic carrier screening in Australia. The project is named for Mackenzie Casella, who died, aged just seven months, of a genetic condition, spinal muscular atrophy (SMA). We were joined on stage by Rachael Casella, Mackenzie's mother, and, along with her husband Jonny, the author of this book.

Concerned that she might be overcome by emotion while talking about the events of her daughter's short life, Rachael had recorded a video message, telling Mackenzie's story and speaking about the importance of carrier screening. As it turned out, it was not Rachael who was overcome by emotion—her words moved everyone in the room deeply, many to tears.

Spinal muscular atrophy is one of thousands of different genetic conditions. Many of these are inherited from parents who are themselves healthy but who are genetic carriers: either both parents are carriers for an autosomal recessive condition or the mother is a carrier for an X-linked condition. In most cases, parents first learn they are carriers when a devastating diagnosis is made in their child. As genetics professionals, we have spent decades working with families affected by severe genetic conditions: two of us (Edwin and Martin) are clinicians who work directly with families, and the third (Nigel) is a scientist who has spent his career working to understand the causes of severe muscle and nerve conditions.

We recognised that there had to be a better way, that it should be possible to test prospective parents *before* the birth of an affected child, and each of us researched genetic screening. In recent years, rapid changes in genetic technology have made it possible to extend testing beyond a handful of the genes that are most commonly involved in childhood genetic disease. Now it is technically possible to screen for changes in hundreds, even thousands of genes in a single test. The goal of testing is to give couples choices—choices that they would not otherwise have. They might choose any of several options, including testing during a pregnancy to find out if the baby is affected. If they find out about their carrier status before a pregnancy there are some additional choices, one of which is using IVF and testing the embryos with the intention of choosing to implant an embryo that is not affected by the condition.

Tests had become available through the private sector, but most people did not know about them, and not everyone could afford to pay for them. Availability of any screening was better than none, but we were still far from where we need to be—screening should be freely available to all couples who wish to access it, with good-quality information available to all.

In 2017, frustrated by the pace of change in this area and saddened by the tragedies we had grown all too used to seeing, we wrote to the Australian federal government, explaining the possibilities and urging government action. It was a step we felt we had to take but one which seemed unlikely to meet a sympathetic ear—we were suggesting a large investment in an area which could not possibly seem as urgent to the health department as it did to us.

This was the point at which our lives intersected with Rachael and Jonny's. They, too, had decided that screening should be available to all, and that something should be done about it. They, too, went to the government seeking change. For them, that decision was prompted by the loss of a child, something no parents should have to go through. When Rachael and Jonny had learned that it would have been possible for them to use a simple test to find out that they were genetic carriers for SMA, the news shocked them and spurred them into action. They were determined to do everything they could to make sure that others would have the choices that they had not.

Their approach to the government had a unique power: it was driven by their personal story of love and loss. They told that story to everyone who would listen and eventually met with Australia's then-Minister for Health, Greg Hunt. From that meeting came a plan: we would conduct a study, funded by the government, aimed at developing a national program of carrier screening. There are many questions that need to be answered before such a program can be put in place, and we are working to answer them. How best should the test be set up? Will it be cost-effective? What will the social and ethical implications be, and how can we conduct screening in a way that does the most good and causes the least harm? The study is world-leading in a number of ways, particularly in its scale and its approach to testing. We hope that it will have an impact across the world.

Minister Hunt named the study after the child whose life had inspired it: Mackenzie's Mission.

There are many choices to be made when setting up a complex project such as this. As doctors and scientists, we know that there are some decisions that are technical and best made based on data. But there are other decisions that need input from those who will be most affected by them—for those, we often need to turn to a representative of the Australian couples whom the study is designed to help. Australian Genomics, the body that has been helping to coordinate and run Mackenzie's Mission, has a community advisory group that has helped. We have also sought advice from patient- and family-support groups centred on particular conditions, such as spinal muscular atrophy, fragile X syndrome and cystic fibrosis. But our key collaborator in this area has been Rachael Casella. Rachael is a member of our steering committee, the key group that oversees the entire project. She has also been a valued contributor to the education and engagement committee, responsible for preparing educational and communication material. And she played a critical role on the committee that chose the 1300 genes to be included in the screening test, which is to be offered to 10,000 Australian couples over the course of the project.

Throughout the two years we have been working on the project—from the earliest planning stages to enrolling of couples into the study—Rachael has never once wavered from her purpose. We have come to admire her deeply. Despite the pain it must cause her, she has never stopped speaking about Mackenzie and about the importance of screening, knowing that she has the ability to move others to action, knowing that her voice reaches far and wide.

This is a book about Mackenzie, but it also tells Rachael and Jonny's extraordinary story. Anyone can think that something needs to happen, but it takes exceptional people to go out and make it happen: to change the world. And that is precisely what this remarkable couple have done, and are doing. Through Mackenzie's Mission, we are working towards a long-held ambition that every Australian woman or couple planning or in the early stages of pregnancy has equitable access to genetic carrier screening should they wish it. When this happens, it will in no small part owe its genesis to Rachael and Jonny Casella.

Professor Edwin Kirk
Professor Martin Delatycki
Professor Nigel Laing AO

Prologue

'You can't change what happened to you but your story can change what happens to someone else.'

Tanya Markul

While writing this book I have tried to focus on the beauty in life and what love can accomplish, but I cannot share what we have learned on our journey without also sharing our loss, grief and the deepest depths of pain and heartache.

But please do not fear reading this book. Do not be scared of experiencing the sadness we have had in our lives or turn away from witnessing our pain, because I promise you that this is real life, and this pain happens every day, all around the world. It is horrible and it is tragic but rather than turning away, I encourage you to stay present, because experiencing someone's life is the greatest gift you can give them.

The sadness you may feel while reading sections of this book might, for a moment, take you to a place of discomfort, but remember that what you will feel in that moment is what we live with every single hour and day of our lives. What this has taught us is that to live the fullest of lives you need to experience all sides of it, so we hope to share with you the lessons we have learned along the way.

This book is primarily written from my perspective, however, I have managed to convince my husband, Jonathan, to write a chapter on his life and add his point of view throughout our book. Our parents add another perspective to give you a holistic understanding of our journey.

I hope what you take away from this book is not the pain that loss can bring but the beauty and strength that can come from love. We want to share the lessons that a special little girl taught us.

This book is about love.

I wouldn't wish this pain on our worst enemy, but I wish to give the perspective it has brought us to everyone.

Introduction

'Life is not what you expected it to be.'

Lauren Bacall

'I am sorry—she is gone.'

Those words still echo in my head.

I can still hear the doctor's voice, his tone. I can remember the look on his face. The sadness in his eyes. I remember the stillness of the room, like there was no air moving despite the click of the air conditioning, the only sound we could hear. I can still smell what remained of her scent mixed with the sterility of the hospital.

It is now over two years since I heard those words and I still struggle to understand them. Gone where? Where do we go? When will I see her again? How can she be gone? She was just here; I could still feel the warmth in her skin and the smell of my milk on her breath.

Mackenzie, our daughter, took her last breath on the morning of Sunday, 22 October 2017, at Sydney Children's Hospital, as she lay on a bed between me and my husband, Jonathan. I saw the fall of her chest, but I never saw it rise again. The doctor stepped towards us with his stethoscope to listen for a heartbeat. It felt like he searched for hours, but really it was probably only a couple of minutes. For just a second I let myself think that maybe she was still with us and this had all been a mistake. But then he said those words: 'I am sorry—she is gone.'

Despite seeing her no longer living, feeling her slowly becoming cold in our arms and living through the last two years without her, I still can't comprehend what happened to her. It shocks me every day. I am a mother without a child.

My child died.

Mackenzie is dead.

I hate that word, dead. I do everything I can to avoid using it. I tell people we lost her, or she passed away. Anything but that word.

I have always been drawn to reading biographies, specifically books about regular people overcoming the adversity they had been thrown in life. I admire their resilience, their persistence, their authenticity and their raw honesty. I always felt a need to understand the pain and courage of real lives. I never really wanted to read fantasy, though I can understand wanting to be whisked away to a foreign place; for me, everyday life held more incredible stories than could ever be made up.

Despite this, I never thought I would be sitting here at 36 years old writing a book about the tragedy that has become my life.

Understandably, most people turn away from tragedy. They are too scared to look, worried that if they get too close something might happen to them too, like tragedy could be contagious.

Life is easier to comprehend and compartmentalise when sadness doesn't exist. Since we became 'tragedy people' ourselves we have experienced this firsthand, but you can never predict who will walk away and who will come closer.

What the ones who walk away don't realise is that while the heartache around tragedy is overwhelming and can be beyond comprehension at times, beauty can also follow tragedy if you are strong enough to stay around it. If you are able to sit, watch and listen to a person's tragedy, then your life can be injected with a perspective that brings fulfilment at a level you didn't know before. Life will seem like you have opened both eyes instead of looking at the world through one blurry eye. You will see and experience personal post-traumatic growth, perspective, kindness, compassion and friendship like never before.

When I was a little girl I told people that I wanted to be a criminal lawyer by day and a rock star by night. As I got older I used to smile to myself when I remembered this, but recently I realised it was me and my beliefs shining through at a young age.

As a criminal lawyer I wanted to protect the victims of the world, making things right and putting things in an understandable order. The world was supposed to be fair; good things happened to good people and bad things happened to bad people.

As a rock star I wanted to change the world, to be creative and influence others through my words. Plus, being famous, rich and glamorous looked like a recipe for a good life, like money could create happiness.

This isn't exactly how my life ended up, but I can see some parallels in what the young me was aiming for.

Instead of being a criminal lawyer I am a police officer—an investigator, to be precise—so I suppose my strong moral compass and desire to right wrongs did manifest itself in the end.

I am nowhere close to being a rock star, however: I have zero musical abilities and I hate direct attention, so being on stage sounds like a nightmare. But I have found a passion and a release in writing and it has become a part of my every day, although I have no formal training. Maybe writing to express myself is my adult version of being a rock star.

When picturing my future as I child, I never once thought I would be a grieving mother. I never thought I would be a 36-year-old woman who has been pregnant at least four times, but who is writing a book on her couch with no babies climbing all over her. But we have tried hard to make sure that our daughter's life and memory is not just another sad story, even though it isn't the first tragedy in the world and it won't be the last. Instead, we have begun spending our lives honouring her name, celebrating her, creating a legacy that will hopefully spare others the pain we have felt and making sure that we experience post-traumatic growth.

Our family, our daughter and her message are more than a sad story.

Rachael

'Work on being in love with the person in the mirror who has been through so much but is still standing.'

Unknown

Trying to summarise a life is a daunting task. In fact, the idea of writing a book at all feels scary and quite self-indulgent. I am also suffering severe imposter syndrome: do I have something important enough to say that others will want to listen to?

I guess time will tell, but where to begin?

There are two of me: there is the me before my daughter Mackenzie was born and the me after. Most parents say that their life changed when they had children and I don't doubt them, but I know in my case this change was extreme and not the normal family story.

My life before Mackenzie was simple, happy and carefree. It was not better back then, not by any means, it was just very different. Looking back, it was like I was living at half my capacity, with one eye closed. At the time I thought I knew it all. I thought

I knew what stress was. Naïve does not even come close to an adequate description.

I was born in Nambour, Queensland, to a Canadian mother, Wendy, and an English dad, David. My parents both came to Australia in their late teens, although in very different ways. Dad first arrived in Australia in the 1970s when his merchant navy ship docked. He was still a young boy, but he had already experienced so much, including a stint in the British army. He jumped ship chasing some woman (not my mum), but when that fizzled he returned aboard with his tail between his legs—only to jump ship again the next time it docked in Australia. This time he stayed for good.

My mum was dragged here by her parents, who were looking for a warmer life than Canada could give, prompted by the ailing health of my grandmother. Mum was seventeen and not happy about being taken away from her life in Canada and from her brother, who remained in Canada, but eventually she adjusted and learned to love what Australia could offer her.

My parents were in their mid-twenties when they were set up on a blind date by two friends. It was a work function for my dad, whose workmate's wife worked with my mum. The dinner was at Lowenbrau Keller, a restaurant in Sydney's Rocks which is still there today, albeit renamed. The German meat house caused a few issues for my mum, who was vegetarian at the time; back then a couple of lettuce leaves and some carrot sticks were deemed a suitable vegetarian alternative. Dad offered her his side salad and it was love. They married shortly afterwards and moved to Queensland to start a life together. My older brother, Chris, was born, and three years later I followed.

I don't remember much of my life in Queensland apart from it being a simple and happy time, but I know that it was filled with financial stresses for my parents. Both worked hard while also managing two young children. My dad juggled working as a carpenter during the day and looking after us at night while also studying computing. Mum looked after us during the day then worked as a telephonist at night. It was a lonely time for them both as they had very few friends and no family nearby, which led to my mum suffering from postnatal depression following the birth of my brother.

Luckily, our family was given a chance to move forwards. My dad did such a good job while studying that he was offered a spot in a graduate program in Canberra. So, when I was around five, my parents moved us to Canberra, believing the public service would give our family a comfortable and stable life. It was a gamble and it took all their remaining money to get us there and set us up, but it paid off. Both of my parents had long and successful careers within the Australian public service.

Not long after starting his graduate program, his senior manager saw my dad's potential and recommended that he drop out of the program, offering him a better paying position. Struggling to raise a family on a graduate trainee's salary, my dad quickly agreed. After that, in my eyes, there was nothing that could stop him. He steadily moved through a range of positions and promotions to eventually become Agriculture, Fisheries and Forestry Australia's first chief information officer, a role for which he received a Public Service Medal from the governor-general a few years ago. Following this were many successful years working in various government departments as chief operations officer. I know it wasn't the career he would have picked if he got to choose to do anything in the world—in fact, he probably would have been a police officer too—but he did it for his family. I couldn't be more proud of him.

My mum is just as remarkable. When we moved to Canberra she continued as a telephonist for a while and managed to get her Science degree while juggling full-time work and two children. She worked at the CSIRO and then the federal health department. She somehow managed to strike the perfect balance between being a mum and showing us that women could also have a successful career. She later went back to university to study writing and is a talented writer and painter, as well as an all-round wealth of knowledge (both she and Dad are really good to have on a quiz team). Like Dad, I know Mum would have wanted other careers, particularly as a teacher, but also like Dad she did what she had to do to make us comfortable and provide for our future.

I could not be prouder of my parents and all they have achieved, especially when they started with practically nothing. They showed Chris and I how to balance life. They had a strong work ethic, but it was clear that family came first. They also taught us how to strive to do your best and be a strong person while showing kindness—it was never one or the other with them. Being a good person and being true to yourself was what mattered in life. Not to mention having a sense of humour—our family was always laughing.

My parents taught me to be kind and caring to everyone, to never see people based on their gender, ethnicity, religion (or lack of), skin colour or sexual orientation. I was taught that people are all the same and it was only a person's personality that could make them less worthy of my respect, nothing else. You were either a kind person or you were a dickhead—the other stuff didn't matter. They taught me empathy and to use words to solve problems.

Conversations were important in our family, even the uncomfortable ones. We didn't let feelings sit unsaid—we told each other when we were hurt, sad, upset and happy. We didn't stew over fights, either; we had our arguments and then said 'I love you'. It taught me communication skills and allowed me to develop emotional maturity.

While my mum was big on feelings, my dad's focus was more facts and the importance of humour. Dad is one of the funniest people I have ever known, and both my parents have a good sense of humour, a shared quality that brought them together. Growing up, Dad also had a strong focus on teaching us to not care what other people thought of us. If someone didn't like you, well, that was okay, and it didn't affect your worth as a person.

My brother and I had a very happy and carefree childhood, and while our parents didn't earn much when we were younger, Chris and I certainly didn't know about it. We wanted for nothing. We camped, we hiked, we played and we had fun.

One of many favourite memories, and one that will give you an idea of my childhood, is of being at home with Dad, who must have picked us up from school after work. We were waiting for Mum to get home and Dad devised a plan for us to strategically hide around the garage armed with super soakers and water balloons. My poor mum, aka 'the target', got home, stepped out of the car dressed in her suit and was bombarded with water from all angles. She took it like a champ. This was not an unusual incident. We had a fun, loving childhood. We were lucky.

My relationship with my parents has always been close; honestly, unless they lived next door, we couldn't be closer. Like most families we occasionally get on each other's nerves but overall, they are my best friends, my heroes and my biggest cheerleaders. Every time I need advice I go to them and they are standing there at the ready, never wavering in their support.

They are also so in love! Their love for each other also taught me how to love and what true love looks like. I always knew I was lucky to have them growing up. I am thankful for them every day.

Mum is happy and bubbly—she'd talk your ear off if you sat still long enough. She is super smart and has an opinion on everything and believes she always has the answer (I guess in some respects the apple doesn't fall far from the tree). No one can make me feel better when I am sick or need looking after than my mum; she has healing hands, a calming voice and so much love to give. Sadly, Mum lost both her parents almost thirty years ago, when she was just a new mum herself. I wish she had had more time with them, and that she lived closer to her brother, because her heart is so big and she has so much love to share. She absolutely should have worked with children, but she can be proud that she did what she needed to do to make her family safe and financially secure. She loves her children and her grandchildren, and she is the centre of all our worlds. She is the perfect mum.

I definitely have some of Mum's qualities, however, most people say I am a mini version of my dad, David. He is my hero and the person I aspire to be like. If I need advice on what to do or how to act, I know I can trust his advice and that he has my back. He is ridiculously smart, the only person I know who reads about physics for fun. While Dad cares deeply about others, he legitimately doesn't care what people think of him. While my mum chats, my dad listens. Actually, that isn't always true, as while he is quiet and therefore gives the appearance of listening, instead he is off in his own world. Dad has a wicked sense of humour and will listen quietly to a conversation before slipping in a hilarious comment, then sit back in his chair waiting for his next act. Between him and Mum I have my number-one fan club. He is the perfect dad.

My brother, Chris, and I are chalk and cheese in a lot of ways. Growing up, we had a love-hate relationship. We would often play together happily but then it would inevitably turn into an argument. I put it all down to my brother, but no doubt he would beg to differ. Over the years we have become much closer; I think he eventually realised that I was a reasonably okay person and not just an annoying little sister!

Chris wouldn't want you to know it but deep down he is a total sweetheart: smart, funny and an all-round good guy. He can be a bit of a grumpy goose but ultimately, he loves his life and he is a dedicated family man. If you asked me what he does for work I would say he is a consultant working with computers, and that's it ... As soon as I hear computers my brain switches off! Chris married a gorgeous woman named Alison, a business analyst. Ali and Chris have two beautiful children, Alara and Henry. Geez, they are cute little kids. They are a great family and I am lucky to have them.

While my family life has always been happy, my upbringing wasn't always easy. Like a lot of children, I suffered from bullying at times and often had tumultuous relationships at school. My friends would be like my sisters one moment but then could turn their backs and be cruel the next. You were either on the in or the out. I felt like I was a confident person in my first few years of primary school but then got put back in my box through some tough bullying in late primary school and high school. But I developed resilience and the ability to rise above adversity.

My parents often commented that I was drawn to 'broken' people who needed fixing, which they said I seemed to make my personal mission. I don't know whether they were right—I was young and all I knew was that they were my friends and I would be there if they needed me—but it did come at a cost. My parents also say this showed my compassionate and caring side. Like I said, it was some tough years, but ultimately I got through it and became who I am today.

In Canberra I went to public schools and I turned out fine! I say this because I am a strong believer that private and religion-based schools should not exist. I think it is wrong that a child may get a better education because of the money their parents make or the religion they are told they are when they are born. Education should be equal for every child and school should not be the first taste of status and segregation. I understand why some people choose private schools in our current education system, because they want the best for their children. They are making a choice based on what we have, but what I don't agree with is the system.

You may be getting the idea that I am quite an opinionated and strong-willed person, and throughout this book you will hear my thoughts and opinions. Some of the topics I discuss are divisive but I'm going to be honest because, well, this is probably the only book I will get to write, so I want to take the opportunity I have been given. I am aware that some people won't agree with me, and that is okay. I am not here to change others' views but simply to express my own in order for people to know who I am and understand our journey.

Anyway, back to my childhood. I had a part-time job from fourteen years old. In hindsight it taught me valuable lessons, but at the time I just wanted my own money. I primarily worked in cafes and restaurants as a waitress but for years I also worked and managed a solarium, back when they were popular. This would come to bite me on the arse later in life.

In Year Eleven, I began playing around with career ideas. One of the classes that interested me the most was psychology, and it was also the class where I met my lifelong best friend, Kath. My first impressions of Kath were of a beautiful and elegant girl in designer clothes who was ridiculously smart. Ours would be one of the most important friendships in my life.

Growing up I was interested in many career paths. In high school I became fascinated with human emotion and human actions, but I also had a strong interest in crime, so I decided to study psychology at university, wanting to become a forensic psychologist—but not before a year off first. During my gap year I travelled to Canada and Europe. In England I worked in a pub, met a boy and enjoyed my freedom as I tried to discover who I was.

Once my year off was done, I dragged myself back home and went to university. I received my Bachelor of Science (Psychology) with a major in Anthropology and Forensics from the Australian National University (ANU).

Towards the end of my time at the ANU I started to become interested in the police force, with much encouragement from my dad. While I was in university Dad asked one of the guys he knew in the Australian Federal Police (AFP) to talk to me. I didn't know it at the time but his 'friend' was the then commissioner of the AFP, Mick Palmer. Commissioner Palmer told me that the AFP liked their recruits to have some life experience first, so when I finished university I went to the Australian Border Force (ABF) to work as an intelligence analyst, specialising in the analysis of drug imports. After four years with the ABF I moved from Canberra to Sydney and became an intelligence analyst with the Australian Crime Commission.

During these years I also did a lot of travelling. I loved exploring new places, learning about new cultures and living every minute to the fullest. While I was working full-time I nearly always had a part-time job on the side as a waitress just to pay for my annual trips overseas.

The move to Sydney was one of my most challenging and life-changing decisions. I was leaving my family, friends and my long-term boyfriend, whom I had brought back from England with me. I was walking away from it all but I was doing it because it wasn't working for me anymore: I needed a change and a challenge. I only knew two people who lived in Sydney but they were both in relationships at the time, so every step I made had to be on my own. I learned how to stand on my own two feet and began to truly discover who I was.

Since moving to Sydney in 2008, I have met some beautiful

friends who changed my life forever, including Dimi. She was from Temora in south-west New South Wales but had been living in London. We didn't know each other but had mutual friends who also knew of an available place—we both needed a place to live and the pieces just fit. Our new life together in Sydney was basically handed to us.

Dimi and I lived together in the beachside suburb of Coogee for around eight years. I look back on those times with such fondness. Dimi is the nicest person you will ever meet, not to mention stunning. Imagine a beautiful Sri Lankan Disney princess who can cook and style any event to be Instagram-worthy. She has more talent and creativity in her pinky than most people have in their whole bodies. She is the type of person who will buy presents for people coming to her birthday party and then write everyone thankyou notes for attending.

Dimi basically became the sister I never had. We navigated our twenties together, establishing our careers and trying to visualise the future we wanted. Dimi taught me about vision boards and manifesting, while I taught her about walking away from negative people and learning to say no. We would sit in our PJs and bounce ideas off each other over wine and cheese and share every detail of our lives. She was exactly what I needed and the rainbow in my life for those years.

Not long after moving to Sydney, I was having a regular skin check-up and my dermatologist identified what she thought might be a basal cell carcinoma. It looked like a pimple rather than a mole and it was smack bang in the middle of my forehead. The dermatologist biopsied a piece and stitched me up, and off I went feeling slightly self-conscious.

A week later I was back waiting to get the stitch out but instead I was taken to a small side room. The dermatologist told me I had cancer, a malignant melanoma. I was told I needed to have urgent surgery the next day and I should call my parents to travel up from Canberra to support me. I still remember that call; I was shocked and panicked. Immediately my close friend John came around to comfort me, and I wailed into his shoulder about not wanting to lose my hair or my life.

The next day, with my parents by my side, I went to see the specialist, a professor who specialised both in skin cancer and plastic surgery. There was a possibility that the cancer may have spread so they were going to remove the melanoma as well as two of my lymph nodes to check them for signs of cancer. He explained that I would wake from surgery with three scars, one down each side of my neck for the lymph nodes and one horizontally down the full length of my forehead. It sounded like I would look like Frankenstein. I remember asking how bad the scars would be and he said, 'You should be more concerned if you will live or not.' Great bedside manner, doc. Yes, I was very scared about whether I would live or not, but I was also a girl in her twenties.

I was lucky. During the surgery it looked like it hadn't spread so I only ended up with one scar on my forehead, although that scar still torments me in every photo to this day. That was a scary time, and looking back I can see that it gave me perspective on the fragility of life.

While working as an intelligence analyst I decided I needed a further challenge, so I started a postgraduate diploma in forensic science via correspondence with the University of Canberra.

I had a fascination with forensics and crime scenes, in particular blood spatter distribution patterns (much to my mum's dismay).

As I plugged away with work and study, I still never lost sight of becoming a police officer. I knew I wanted to join the AFP rather than state police so I kept my eye on applications, but sadly there was a recruiting freeze for federal agents and my desire went unanswered. In 2012, applications finally opened. After going through the recruitment testing barriers I was deemed suitable and in May 2013 I was walking through the door of the Australian Federal Police College in Canberra to train for six months as a recruit—excited, determined and nervous.

Six months of intensive training followed, and I loved every minute. It helped that my group of recruits (shout-out to FPDP 5/2013) were brilliant people. Us four girls and 33 boys were the best bunch I could have imagined going through that journey with, and I made some lifelong friends among them 'my girls': Emma, Nicole, Amelia and Liz. We tackled tasks I never imagined doing, let alone doing well at some, including legislation, marching, driver training, shooting, defensive tactics, scenarios and obstacle courses, just to name a few.

I probably could have had more fun at college, but I had wanted to be there for so long that my focus was on knowing that I gave it my all. In the end my hard work paid off and I received the Commissioner's Award at our attestation (graduation), which is for the hardest working student. I was finally a police officer, Constable Rachael Banham.

Jonathan

Written by Mackenzie's father, Jonathan.

The idea of helping to write a book on my experiences as a parent and compiling a chapter on my life makes me uncomfortable. Not because I'm embarrassed or an overly private person, but because I consider myself and my family to be quite unremarkable. I don't feel that my actions, beliefs or story are any more special than anyone else's, but then our lives were permanently changed through the death of our beautiful baby, Mackenzie. So here I am.

Those who know me understand that I like to find the funny side in almost any situation. It's the way I survive as a police officer, as a parent who lost a child, and just in my daily life. My humour isn't always pretty, it can be quite dark, but when the chips are down and those around me are starting to struggle, I'll often make a joke, as inappropriate as it may be.

I had a good childhood, happy and carefree. Most of the events

of my early and teenage years took place within twenty kilo-
metres of where I grew up in Canberra. For three years I was my
parents' one and only until my sister, Rachel, was born.

My parents, Ross and Linda, were both from Cairns, North
Queensland. They met in church when they were around fifteen,
dated, got married, and then in the mid-seventies moved to
Canberra when Dad got a job with the Commonwealth Police.
For two rural kids in the seventies, I can imagine how difficult it
must have been for them to move so far away from their families
and friends.

My dad's family background is Italian. Sicilian, to be precise.
From a young age Dad worked hard as a police officer, originally
for the Commonwealth Police before it became the Australian
Federal Police. I was always so proud of his job, but the nature
of his work meant he travelled a lot and I missed him. It wasn't
uncommon for Dad to be away for weeks at a time, back for
maybe a week, then gone for another month. As I've gotten older
I understand the sacrifice he made in being away for such long
periods to provide for his family.

When Dad retired from the AFP, he became bored and went
back to work as Governor-General Quentin Bryce's driver,
followed by a stint with Peter Cosgrove. When he left the
position, Dad retired once more only to get bored again. He now
works at Parliament House.

How to describe my dad? He is one of the kindest, most
genuine and friendly guys you will ever meet. He loves to be
around people and can chat with the best of them. He is also
the king of dad jokes, not so much because they are funny,
although quite a few of them land, but because they are frequent.

His energy is infectious and he will do anything for you if he can. He loves his family dearly.

My mum's family background is Danish, German and English. Mum started her career as a bank teller before deciding to go back to school in her thirties in hope of bigger and better things. After completing Year 12 and university, Mum started working as an accountant. This career eventually led her to jobs overseas in war-torn countries like Iraq. Her story really deserves its own book, and we've often joked about the working title, 'Hardcore Accounting'.

On meeting my mum she appears to be gentle, sweet and timid, and she is all those things. But scratch the surface and you find a very strong, educated and determined woman who is full of surprises. Just like my dad, Mum lives for her family. She is kind, caring and so compassionate.

In our youth, my sister and I didn't always see eye to eye, pretty typically of most sibling relationships, but now I consider her one of my best friends. Rachel—yes, my sister has the same name as my wife—is kind, funny, a talented photographer and an amazing mum to her three children, Ethan, Sienna and Sophia. Her husband, Michael, is a top guy and every bit the gentleman.

Rachel and I went to a small local Anglican school, and I was a shy and nervous kid. Despite this, I found myself in a small group of good friends who I stuck with for most of my schooling.

Unsure if I really wanted to follow in Dad's footsteps and be a police officer, in 2004 I joined the security side of the AFP as a protective service officer, to dip my toes in and see if policing was something I was interested in. I was originally assigned to the

Diplomatic Protection Unit in Canberra where I worked for a little over a year. I quickly decided I would apply to the police, however before doing so I was given the opportunity to deploy on a peacekeeping mission called RAMSI, the Regional Assistance Mission to the Solomon Islands.

From within my area, RAMSI was spoken about like a three-month dash-for-cash. It was supposedly a low-risk mission where members could go on short-term deployments, make a difference in other people's lives and earn great money. My decision to deploy would not only change my life forever but without it you would certainly not be reading this book, and Mackenzie's Mission would never have come into existence, due to the chain of events that followed over the next decade of my life.

Upon arrival in Honiara, I quickly realised the magnitude of an overseas deployment: I was now in a developing country in relative poverty and working with police from Australia and other countries within our region.

On the morning of 18 April 2006, I finished a twelve-hour night shift and went to bed in preparation for another shift that night. After what could only have been a couple of hours, my roommate woke me and said I was required to go back on duty as there were mass protests at the parliament building in the city, and some of our members had been injured.

I quickly put on my uniform and attended the station, where I put on a ballistic vest and a combat helmet before jumping into a troop carrier with other members and heading into town. The islanders were protesting because the winner of a recent election, Snyder Rini, was widely believed to be corrupt, a pawn of the many Chinese business owners in the country.

On arrival at the protest, I was ushered towards a cordon of police and other protective service officers who were holding back the protesters. There were rocks all over the ground, police everywhere, a cameraman filming, and members of the Operational Response Group dressed all in black with long shields and tear gas canisters.

I quickly took a position within the cordon and began trying to calm down the obviously upset locals around me, but the crowd was getting louder and louder. Someone came up behind me and said that guns had just been spotted within the crowd and that people were walking around with backpacks full of rocks, so we should be careful and notify them if we saw something.

Within seconds, something changed. The people I had been trying to communicate with started to yell and I saw a couple of rocks skim over the heads of the police to my right. And then I got hit.

I remember a flash of white light and a loud ringing in my ears. My jaw felt heavy, and all I could feel in my mouth was warm flesh. I brought my hand up and caught four teeth and blood.

Convinced I had been shot and feeling the weight of my jaw hanging, I moved towards the building behind me and saw a member of the tactical team, who yelled at me to get back to my post. In hindsight, I'm sure he hadn't seen what happened, and couldn't see the blood due to a mix of adrenalin and the dark colour of my vest.

In a daze, I turned back towards the crowd and started walking back to my post when another member who had seen me get struck grabbed me under the arm and led me back into the relative safety of the parliament building.

Inside many Solomon Island politicians and a couple of higher-ranking members of the AFP were standing in the foyer. As I walked past someone I assumed was a politician, I overheard him complain that I was getting blood on the carpet and someone would have to pay for the cleaning. I was taken to a bench where a field bandage was pushed into my face to stem the bleeding.

The next forty-five minutes were a blur. I recall the sound of tear gas being fired into the crowd, and rocks smashing into the glass doors and police shields. There were other injured officers, some gagging and coughing from the tear gas. Eventually I was loaded into a four-wheel drive vehicle and taken back to the relative safety of our base outside Honiara. It would turn out I had a broken jaw, fractured cheekbone and had lost seven teeth. I was operated on and stabilised in our medical facility.

The next day, the AFP arranged a Learjet and a nurse to take me back to Brisbane for more surgery. As we departed the Solomon Islands, the full extent of the riot became clear: from the plane window the entire town seemed to have been burnt to the ground. The air was thick with smoke, and several landmark buildings were now ash.

The flight passed quickly, even as I slurped a chocolate milk morosely while watching the nurse tuck into the delicious food prepared by the flight charter company. I arrived in Brisbane around 9 p.m. and my sister was waiting for me. As I passed through customs and was asked if I had anything to declare, I said, 'Yes, don't go to the Solomon Islands.' An ambulance transported me to the hospital where I was operated on again that night, and I spent another two weeks in Brisbane before being allowed to fly. That was the beginning of what would turn out to be a long process, years in fact, of repairing the damage caused to my face.

My time in the Solomon Islands can be difficult to talk about. Being away from those I cared about, the culture shock and, of course, the riot, all played pivotal roles in my life.

My return from the Solomon Islands also gave me my fifteen seconds of fame. I was on the front page of most Australian newspapers, did interviews for the news, and even appeared on the breakfast television show *Today*. The riots dominated the news cycle for a few days before being replaced by the Beaconsfield mine collapse. In interviews, the Australian press asked me if I considered my actions in the islands to be heroic, and that gave me a once in a lifetime opportunity to answer, 'I'm not a hero, I was just doing my job,' which I think is a bucket list item for everyone.

The years after the riots were some of the most difficult I'd had up until that point in my life. I found myself with very regular dental and orthodontic appointments along with multiple facial surgeries, most of which I went into not knowing what I'd look like afterwards. As a result I was diagnosed with post-traumatic stress disorder (PTSD) and had to find a way to balance that with my job and social life.

A few years after the incident, in 2008, I started dating a woman I'll refer to in this book as H, who I met in the office of one of my surgeons. We quickly moved in together and in 2012 I proposed, and we planned a wedding for October 2013. To say I had doubts in the lead-up to that wedding would be putting it mildly. I lay awake at night, found myself struggling with unhappiness, and was uninterested in most things in my personal life.

If I'm totally honest, I knew right from the start of the relationship that it was not going to work, but for whatever reason I continued on a failing course of action. Truthfully, I was suffering from PTSD that was not being properly treated and I may also have been depressed.

It took meeting Rachael to realise the fog that I had been in. I regret any hurt I caused H but without everything I had been through and experienced I wouldn't have ever met or appreciated Rachael.

Our love story

'One day someone will walk into your life and make you see why it never worked with anyone else.'

Unknown

One morning in May 2013, I woke up in my small bedroom at the Australian Federal Police College, ready to start my policing career. I was excited but incredibly nervous. I dressed in my suit, as we hadn't yet received our uniforms, and went to the theatrette where we would be introduced to our training teams.

One of these teams was Operational Safety Training (OST), where we would learn about firearms and defensive tactics. As the trainers stood up there explaining what they expected of us, I noticed one was incredibly cute. He was introduced as Jonathan Casella, or Senior Casella as we were all supposed to call him.

From that moment I developed a pretty substantial crush, but I was there to work so I tried to push him out of my mind. It was a hard task given he was so attractive, so it was probably a blessing that those OST classes were spread out, which meant that I wouldn't see him for weeks at a time. I suppose that helped me concentrate.

One hurdle we had to face as recruits was being sprayed with oleoresin capsicum spray (OC, or some might know it as pepper spray). One by one we lined up to be exposed to OC and then undergo a series of tasks before we were decontaminated (aka head dumped into a sink of water). I drew the short straw and had to go second last, which meant I had to watch everyone before me experience the pain, making the wait worse.

Finally it was my turn, and unluckily for me, Jonny was there supervising. How does one try to look hot while being OC'd? Note to others, waterproof mascara is not the key. From memory, I took the OC pretty well, didn't yell and managed to under-take the tasks with minimal struggle. Finally, my head could be dunked into the sink (goodbye mascara, hello panda eyes). Not long afterwards, as I sat facing a fan with my fingers prying open my red eyes so the air could hit them and give them just a second of relief, I heard Jonny's voice in my ear: 'How are you going, Rachael?' My response: 'Fuck off.' Smooth, Rachael . . .

It felt like every time we saw each other we exchanged love eyes. I made it pretty clear I liked him, and I was fairly sure he liked me too, but given we were not allowed to date I think we both knew to keep those 'love eyes' to ourselves. So you can imagine how devastated I was when I found out he was actually engaged and due to be married in a matter of weeks.

I remember my heart dropping. It was not something he had tried to hide, it just hadn't come up—apart from occasionally walking to get coffee together in the breaks, we were never alone. Learning that information shattered me, but what could I do?

He was taken and my crush had to stop. Next thing I knew he was taking two weeks off to get married and, with that, the one and only crush I had had in years was over.

Two weeks later Jonny returned from his 'holiday' and I remember looking down at his hand to see the ring, but it wasn't there. I didn't get excited; not wearing a ring isn't unusual for people in OST for safety reasons. A bunch of the recruits were all sitting around listening to what he was saying—he had a way of grabbing attention—and I stepped closer to hear.

He had called off his wedding. My heart skipped a beat but then made up for it by instantly beating faster. He sat there looking quite broken, explaining he felt awful but had to be true to himself. He had known for some time she wasn't the one for him and shouldn't have let it get so far. I was in shock; this stuff only happens in movies, doesn't it?

For the rest of the course nothing was said between Jonny and me. During this time I got extremely sick, though; I didn't know what was wrong with me but I was eventually diagnosed with shingles and acute labyrinthitis, an inner ear issue. I had put everything I had into the recruit course and my body couldn't cope anymore. The labyrinthitis meant I had vertigo and threw up with any visual stimulus—not ideal as a police recruit and it didn't make the last few weeks of the course very easy on me. But as per our course motto: Improvise, Adapt and Overcome.

On the day of attestation, I sat in the front row in my ceremonial suit and hat feeling so sick, worried I would faint or throw up at any time. Eventually, each recruit stood one by one to shake the commissioner's hand and receive warrant cards, our badges. When it was my turn I thought about finally getting what I had wanted for so many years as I walked up and received my badge with pride—and managed to not throw up (bonus points).

A few minutes later the commissioner introduced the Commissioner's Award for Excellence, given to the person who topped the course. When my name was called I looked up at my family cheering loudly, with Jonny sitting in the seat in front of them smiling widely back at me. At that time, it was the proudest moment of my life. I managed to push away the nausea in order to stand up and receive my award.

About ten minutes later, all the new constables, the recruit trainers and the proud family members were standing around in the commissioner's dining room, celebrating our new status. I looked up to see Jonny standing next to me. In front of a number of other recruits, and in particular one of my closest friends, Nicole, he mumbled a few words that sounded like, 'I was wondering if you wanted to go out with me sometime.' Nicole looked at him, stunned, then looked at me, clearly trying to comprehend what was happening. I saw realisation of the private nature of the conversation flash across her face and she tried to spin around. As I started to say 'Yes', Jonny said, 'Great, I'll call you sometime,' and ran away. Although when you hear his version he will probably say he bravely asked me out and then 'tactfully disengaged'.

Jonathan: In May 2013, I was working as a trainer at the AFP College and was allocated a new group. After conducting my usual introductory lecture to a group of around sixty fresh-faced and attentive recruits, one of them approached me and asked a series of questions before introducing herself—Rachael Banham.

Over the six-month course, I found myself thinking about Rachael often and enjoying every conversation we had. I started to find ways to interact with the group even when they weren't my responsibility in the hope of seeing her and having a chat.

The first opportunity I had, which was on her graduation day, I asked her out in front of one of her good friends from the course before tactically disengaging back to my office to breathe a sigh of relief that she'd actually said yes.

I'm not proud of my behaviour in calling off my engagement and the possible long-term effect it had on H, but in part meeting Rachael helped me do something about the situation I was in. Up until then I hadn't realised just how wrong it would have been. So in October 2013, just two weeks before the scheduled wedding, I ended the relationship with H. I didn't do it for Rachael, but I knew I shouldn't have felt the way I did about Rachael two weeks before my wedding.

I can honestly say that when Rachael and I got married in 2016, I couldn't have been more excited and confident in the lead-up to the day.

On our first date, Jonny asked me how upset I had been on finding out he was engaged, to which I replied, 'Gutted.' Can you believe the confidence of him?

For the next year Jonny and I had a long-distance relationship between Canberra and Sydney, where I was still living with Dimi in Coogee. We were determined to make it work. For our two months of dating I was still quite sick, and every time he came to visit I could barely leave the house for throwing up, which created some anxiety issues for me and made my first few months as a police officer nerve-wracking and hard. I had to push through the anxiety, the sickness and the nerves of my new job just to get through each day. I was surprised that he hung around, but he did.

During the first few weeks of our relationship we had some pretty heavy conversations. Given we were both in our thirties and living in different cities, we didn't want to waste any time by not truly understanding each other's values and dreams for the future. We discussed our views on family and marriage, religion, raising children, education and money. While we didn't know it at the time, these conversations gave us a strong platform for some hard conversations later.

After a year of long distance, Jonny was finally transferred to Sydney and our life together could properly start. This meant that I had to leave my safety net with Dimi and move into another Coogee apartment with Jonny. I was scared to take this leap, but I did and it was the start of a beautiful life.

Our time in Coogee is now fondly referred to as the 'simple days'. We spent our time walking along the coastline, lying on the beach, eating, drinking and developing a life together in Sydney. During this time, we also rescued a little tortie tabby kitten from the Cat Protection Society whom we named Kaylee, and she would bring us much joy.

We had already decided to travel as much as we could, and in the following years we went to Bali, Cairns, Tasmania, England, Italy, Scotland and France, to name a few. The trip to Europe was particularly special.

Jonathan: In 2015, I was given the opportunity to participate in the Trois Etapes bike race across the Dolomite Mountains in northern Italy. The team was organised through the charity Soldier On and consisted primarily of

Australian Defence Force members who had served overseas and had been injured in some way. We also had Australian comedian Hamish Blake and cycling royalty Cadel Evans joining the team. It was a three-day event consisting of multiple timed stages up some of Italy's better known and more difficult climbs.

The call to go to Italy was unexpected. I didn't own a bicycle and, to be honest, I hadn't ridden one since being hit by a car in 1994 when I rode across a busy intersection without looking. So I was certainly no cyclist and agreed to do it without knowing the full extent of the challenge I was about to undertake. The AFP had decided to participate and needed a member who had been injured overseas, was willing to talk about their injuries or PTSD, and was young and fit enough to take part. As you can probingly imagine, the list of AFP members fitting the requirements consisted basically of me. I had around six months to prepare from accepting the offer, so I needed to get a bike and start training.

I turned up to the first training camp with a new bike and no idea what to expect. My teammates were slim, fit and professional-looking, with expensive bikes and all the gear. They had clearly been riding for years and I was definitely out of my depth. We took off on a sixty-kilometre ride and I quickly fell behind the pack. Scott Sunderland, our team coach and a respected professional cyclist, stayed with me and offered advice on how to best use my energy and improve my technique. During that ride I had my first taste of a real hill climb, and the magnitude of the challenge finally started to dawn on me.

Over the next six months I trained daily. I rode to work, joined group rides, and did thousands of laps around Centennial Park in Sydney. We had several training camps where I could see huge improvement in my fitness each time I caught up with the team. Even though I was getting fitter and lighter, I realised the challenge of a three-day race consisting only of climbing, and it would be a stretch for me even to finish.

A few months before Rachael and I went to Italy, I chose a day she was working and drove down to Canberra to get her father's permission to ask her to marry me. He was surprised to see me in his office but immediately said yes (although it could be argued he traded his daughter for the bottle of Scotch I had brought of him). So while packing for Europe, I tied an engagement ring inside one of my shoes, stuffed it with socks and hoped Rachael wouldn't go snooping.

We arrived in Italy about five days before the event and I went for long rides each day in the lead-up to acclimatise. My nerves were totally destroyed when I failed to complete the climb to the top of Passo Giau a day before the event. Passo Giau is a famous 10-kilometre ride which climbs over a thousand metres in altitude and would be the final stage of the event.

I had never been more terrified than on my first day of the race. My heart rate was over 130 beats per minute before I'd even touched my bike. Rachael had been an invaluable asset since arriving in Italy, making sure I had everything I needed, keeping me calm, and giving me support when I needed it the most, even running beside my bike at times to egg me on.

The first two days were brutal. The climbs were steeper and longer than I could have imagined, and the pace of the other riders was fast. Nevertheless I managed to finish all stages and didn't even finish last in a few. The highlight was being peppered by a hailstorm on the final climb of day two, complete with high winds and freezing temperatures. My confidence was growing after each stage, however I knew I still had to tackle Passo Giau the next day in a timed stage. My legs were showing signs of fatigue after a week of solid training and riding and were not bouncing back in the morning the way they had a few days earlier.

The third day started with a ride through the hills, stopping for photos overlooking a beautiful valley before the timed stage began. When it did, as usual I watched my teammates and most of the other competitors disappear up the mountain ahead of me. Being very careful of my heart rate, and consuming energy gels, I eventually made it to the top of Passo Giau to finish the stage and the event. I will never forget the moment I crossed that line. Rachael and I were both in tears. I had completed something I would never have thought possible for me.

The next day, the whole team travelled by bus to Venice, where Rachael and I stayed on after the group had left. Our first night alone, we had a beautiful meal overlooking the Grand Canal, after which I proposed on a small Venetian street overlooking what Rachael romantically described as a gondola graveyard, and brothel. She obviously said yes, and the rest is history.

The day after we said goodbye to the Soldier On team in Venice, we had a gorgeous dinner beside a canal. Champagne, views of the canal and exquisite food—the works! After dinner we went for a walk and it was then that Jonny got down on one knee and proposed to me with the most perfect Tiffany ring. I was so shocked that all I could manage to say initially was 'Fuck off', as in, 'Are you serious?' It doesn't get any more romantic. I wish I had said something better, but Jonny thinks it was perfect because it means I was surprised.

The next few weeks travelling around Europe with my fiancé are memories that bring nothing but pure joy to my heart. It was one of the happiest times of my life.

We had a quick engagement—by then I was 32 and Jonny was 38, so we weren't wasting any time—but one thing we did before getting married was see a couple's counsellor. This might seem odd to some but to us it was important to make sure that our life values matched.

On 12 February 2016, in the beautiful garden at The Grounds of Alexandria, we had our fairytale wedding.

I have never met a better man than Jonny. He has everything: looks, wit, intelligence, optimism and emotional maturity. I am generally a Type A personality who is determined (and usually stressed) in everything I do, but Jonny balances me. He is pure perfection. I spent years wondering if I would ever meet someone who would make me happy, who I would be happy to settle down with, but instead the universe did me one better and gave me my soulmate. He makes me laugh, challenges me and, most importantly, can handle my strong personality. He shows me such kindness and every single day lets me know I am loved.

When people ask me how Jonny is, usually I smile cheekily and say he is perfect. I am addicted to him.

Making Mackenzie

'One day there will be little mes running around, half me and half the person I love, and thinking of that makes me happy.'

Unknown

In the six months after Jonny proposed, as we were planning our wedding, I was also planning our pregnancy. Being a Type A, I didn't want to leave anything to chance, so the year before I had taken myself off the pill to allow my body time to regulate. I also organised private health insurance to give us the option of having our child in a private hospital if we wanted to.

In the months before the wedding, Jonny and I both undertook all the pre-pregnancy blood tests the doctor recommended. The tests ranged from checking our iron levels and looking for illnesses to checking immunity to hepatitis, measles, rubella and chickenpox. We had our vaccines updated, our blood pressure tested, and our medications checked. Everything looked good.

We tried to improve our general health as well by eating more salads and vegetables, reducing alcohol intake and exercising more. We both took prenatal vitamins and started acupuncture and taking Chinese herbs to help to balance our hormones because I was prone to elevated oestrogen levels.

After all this, I even organised us to have basic fertility tests, all before we had even started trying. Poor Jonny. In these checks, Jonny's sperm was tested for motility, morphology and count. Meanwhile, I had my anti-Mullerian hormone (AMH) levels checked, which looks at a woman's egg reserves. Jonny was healthy and just needed to spend some time off his bicycle following his Soldier On ride in Italy (heat, pressure and lycra are not the best mix for sperm health). My AMH came back low, but all that really meant was for us to not wait five years to start trying, which we had no intention of doing anyway.

Based on the results we changed a few habits, but overall everything looked good. So from the honeymoon it was go time! I was even ovulating on our honeymoon, so the timing was perfect.

But in the first two months we didn't get pregnant. This isn't a long time to be trying but it felt like it to me. To get assistance and some answers we went to Genea fertility clinic in Sydney. Along with some other IVF clinics in Australia, Genea offers free ovulation tracking, which Medicare covers for three months. By doing blood tests over a few specific days in my cycle, we discovered we had been wrong in our ovulation calculation. While most women ovulate on day fourteen of their cycle, I was ovulating much earlier, on day eight, meaning that we had been trying a week late for the past two months.

With this new information, we got pregnant the very next month. On seeing those two lines, it felt like I was in a movie: I had the perfect career, the perfect man, the perfect family, the perfect wedding and now I was pregnant. We were over the moon. I started doing pregnancy tests almost every day. I became addicted to watching the line getting darker, reassuring me each time that everything was okay. I was excited and so happy!

We decided to tell our parents around week five, not long after the first positive test. We found what we thought was the cutest way to tell them: a little brown box containing a tiny pair of knitted booties and a note saying 'Coming soon'. Everyone was ecstatic.

At six weeks I woke up one morning at 5 a.m. feeling odd. Jonny was on a night shift, so I was alone in the apartment. I looked down my pyjama pants and thought I saw blood, but the room was dark so I couldn't tell. I threw off the doona and ran to the bathroom, pulled down my pyjamas and saw what I feared: bright red blood was trickling down my legs. I remember saying out loud 'no, no, no, no, no, no' on repeat. Panicking, I rang Jonny. We agreed I would drive to Prince of Wales emergency and he would meet me there.

The whole drive in I was terrified. What was happening? Was our baby okay?

I was lucky, I guess, as there was only one other person waiting in the emergency department. I sat on the plastic chairs trying to focus on my breathing and was soon seen by a nice young female doctor. She ordered a blood test to check my pregnancy hormone, or human chorionic gonadotropin (HCG).

I lay on the hospital bed in the small examination room waiting for the results and willed myself not to cry. I was trying not to let my head run away from me but my gut knew that something was wrong. I felt scared and alone.

Jonny arrived, out of breath and pale. He had been out on search warrants and was still in his work clothes, including his gun. The doctor came back saying that my HCG had dropped and she believed I was suffering a miscarriage. To be sure, she had scheduled an ultrasound.

We walked to the Early Pregnancy Centre in the nearby Royal Hospital for Women and sat in the waiting room, surrounded by pregnant women and babies. I was crying, almost hysterical. After a while, a lovely midwife named Felicity took pity on us and we were led to a private room where she gave us a calming hug. It would not be the last time we met Felicity on our journey.

Finally it was time for the ultrasound. I lay in the dark room looking at the screen in desperation, hoping to see the little flicker of a heartbeat. But there was nothing. The sonographer looked at us with sadness in her eyes.

We were devastated by our loss. I felt empty and crushed and all I could do was cry. We sat in the hospital cafe crying, surrounded by tiny newborns in their clear plastic cribs, parents looking down at them adoringly. We knew we had to call our families but I couldn't bring myself to say the words. In the end Jonny did it, as always my rock.

The hospital staff had explained that we could wait for my body to naturally finish miscarrying the baby, which would mean me bleeding for a week or so, or I could have a small procedure called a dilatation and curettage (D&C), an operation to scrape away the womb lining. It sounded horrible, but we were told that if we chose to let it happen naturally there was a chance we would still need a D&C, as some women retained 'product'. Product: what an awful, clinical term for losing a baby. We chose the D&C

as I couldn't imagine watching myself slowly lose the baby bit by bit each day, and Jonny was adamant that he didn't want that for me either.

The D&C is done as day surgery. I arrived in the morning and signed some forms then sat and waited, struggling not to focus on the details of what was about to happen. When it was my turn, I was wheeled into a prep room before theatre.

My anaesthetist was so lovely. As I lay there crying while he began to sedate me, he told me that he would see me one day soon when I was having a baby, and he would give me a discount on an epidural. It was so sweet of him to make me smile between the tears and then I was asleep.

I woke up in recovery no longer pregnant. That was it, our baby was gone.

Jonathan: I was near the end of a night shift when Rachael called and said, 'I think the baby has gone.' Caught way out in western Sydney, I was at least two hours from the hospital in Randwick but I dropped everything and made the slow trek east through Sydney traffic. Eventually I got to the hospital where I found Rachael crying in a small room off the emergency department. She looked so small and scared.

After watching the impact the miscarriage had on her, I felt the best way to help us move forwards and heal from what at the time felt very traumatic (my perspective on trauma has shifted somewhat since then) was to give the baby a name, so we could always refer to it as an individual. I named the baby Hope, as it would serve as a reminder to both of us that even in what we feel is our darkest time, we should always hold on to our optimism and hope. I had no idea then what the next few years would bring, but I like to think Hope was the very early building block of the resilience we would need to survive.

Approximately 20 per cent of pregnancies end in miscarriage. Most women don't even know they have miscarried, especially if they aren't trying for a baby and they don't take a pregnancy test early on. So when a miscarriage happens in the first few weeks, many probably think it is just a late and heavy period.

But for those who do know, everyone deals with the grief of miscarriage differently, and there is of course no 'correct' way to do so. Some need time to mourn the loss of their little one and can't bring themselves to try again for months. Others, like us, decide to start trying again as soon as possible.

While we were devastated, through my research I knew we weren't alone. We had to look at it logically and be thankful that we had at least got pregnant so easily.

Jonny and I decided to be honest with those around us about our miscarriage. We felt it was important to talk about it. Miscarriages are so common but seem to be often overlooked, with the grief sometimes minimised by others. People tend to ask how many weeks you were, with the number seeming to help them decide on their level of sympathy and, in turn, your acceptable level of grief. As we spoke about our miscarriage, many people around us revealed their own too.

There is sometimes an unwarranted shame surrounding miscarriage, as if the mother was somehow responsible. In my research I discovered that most miscarriages occur because of a chromosomal problem that makes an embryo incompatible with life, so it's the body's way of saying something isn't right. If you think about it, that makes sense: women around 30 years old have about a 28 per cent chance of producing an abnormal embryo and the miscarriage rate is around 20 per cent, so it stands to reason that most miscarriages are due to abnormalities.

A month after we lost baby Hope we went to Nhulunbuy in the Northern Territory to visit a friend. While we were there I was ovulating, and one day I less than delicately explained that Jonny and I needed some alone time. Our friend immediately went for a run. When she walked back through the door an hour later, Jonny and I were sitting on the couch watching *Keeping Up with the Kardashians*. We joked that she hadn't had to run that far as it was all business—even a slow jog to the mailbox and back would have done it.

Two weeks later we got the magic pink lines. Mackenzie was conceived in the Northern Territory—we like to say she was made 'Territory Tough'.

Naturally, losing baby Hope made us petrified for the first three months that we would miscarry again. So during our pregnancy we did every test we were offered to check our baby was okay. We had the usual blood tests and ultrasound scans, but we also paid for the GeneSyte test from Genea, also known as a non-invasive prenatal test (NIPT). At the time costing around $450, it was usually conducted after ten weeks and in combination with the twelve-week ultrasound. An NIPT examines the embryo to make sure there aren't any issues at a chromosome level, such as Down syndrome.

Luckily, all these checks showed we were low risk. Everything was looking okay so, while still nervous, around twelve weeks we began letting ourselves get excited and announced our news to the world.

I got so lucky with my pregnancy. I *loved* being pregnant. I never had morning sickness, I craved fruit salad and mostly gained weight in my bump. Yes, it would have been nice to have put on a few less kilograms, but what are you going to do? I was by no means a pregnant unicorn (you know, those women who are stunning during pregnancy and only gain the weight of their baby then are back to normal within two weeks) but I knew I was lucky for feeling so happy; not everyone is so lucky and I knew it. Even my chronic back pain got better.

Sometimes I felt guilty about how easy it was for me, especially when I knew people who really struggled, like my friend Kath, who had hyperemesis gravidarum (severe nausea and vomiting) and a myriad of other issues. I think that what happens around babies is mostly luck and a bit of genetics. Everyone has their hurdles in some form.

The only real pregnancy-related pain I had was with my feet, which had ballooned up to twice their size making thongs my only footwear option. And they hurt! Jonny rubbed them each night and somehow was still able to think that I was sexy. What a guy.

One of my favourite things about being pregnant was feeling her moving around. She was very energetic, twirling, kicking and spinning. I could have spent hours watching my stomach move, and in fact sometimes did.

I loved dressing my bump too, once there actually was a bump. Like most women, I didn't love the in-between stage where I just looked tubby. I never wear tight clothes normally but when I was clearly pregnant that all changed—I was pregnant and proud!

Every week I took a progress shot of my bump and wrote in a diary. I am so thankful that I documented those memories as I wouldn't realise until later how important they would become.

Every night Jonny and I lay in bed with a mobile phone resting on my belly playing a beautiful soft version of 'Sweet Child of

Mine'. As the song played, we would watch Kenzie react to the music, making the phone bounce around as she danced. Sometimes Jonny switched up the night-time playlist with Johnny Cash, which usually resulted in Kenzie bumping the phone completely off my belly. Did she like it or was she trying to push the phone away?

Mackenzie moved around like crazy. It was so beautifully distracting. Often something could happen right in front of me but I wasn't paying attention, so focused was I on feeling her turn, talking to her, being with her. I would sometimes be sitting in a meeting at work and there would be a ripple over my stomach, like that famous scene from *Alien*! I was a little worried I would freak out the men on my team.

Around 32 weeks we started doing our prenatal courses. I was so excited to start them; it felt like a rite of passage. We had chosen to do a private course taught over four consecutive weeks by one of the midwives at the Royal Hospital for Women. Every Tuesday night for a month we gathered at the midwife's house, who turned out to be Felicity, the woman who had been so nice to us when we lost baby Hope. Everything had come full circle.

The course and the couples who joined us were wonderful. It was so interesting hearing such different views on the same journey. It was also the first time I became aware of mother guilt. At one stage we were asked about our birth plans, and every person was set on having a natural birth to the point of considering an epidural or a caesarean a failure. I was quite blown away by this. Jonny and I had discussed our birth plan and, like most, we hoped for a natural birth with limited drugs, but we also knew that there was a strong chance that wasn't going to happen.

You can't plan everything in life and certainly not a birth. The baby will come how they come, and as long as they are safe and happy, that is what matters. To me, wanting or expecting everything to be perfect and getting depressed when it isn't is just unrealistic, egotistical and doesn't keep in mind how dangerous childbirth can be.

We agreed that while it was good to have an idea of our ideal birth, we should be open to whatever needed to happen. Writing yourself into a mental corner of what is acceptable would just lead to depression if it didn't go to plan. I strongly believe women shouldn't put guilt on themselves and on others about birth plans and, come to think of it, just being a mother as a whole.

I am so thankful for my pregnancy with Kenzie and look back on it with fondness. It was like we were our own little universe. I used to almost strut around with my pregnant belly, like I was finally special and part of something bigger.

The day a star was born

'No one else will ever know the strength of my love for you. After all, you're the only one who knows what my heart sounds like from the inside.'

Kristen Proby

Mackenzie's birth is something that will be with me for life. It is a memory I hold so very dear. It wasn't the easiest or smoothest birth, but it was *her* birth. The universe didn't let me keep her, but it can't take away that day.

At 39 weeks I experienced some reduced foetal movement. Because Mackenzie had always a big mover, we were naturally concerned when she stopped being so active. We know now that spinal muscular atrophy often causes reduced movement in the third trimester of pregnancy, but no one could have anticipated that this was the reason in our case. It was hard experiencing the reduced movement, especially as a first-time mum. You second-guess yourself. How much did she move before? Is it really less movement now? Am I going crazy and being paranoid?

We remembered that our midwife had told us that it is always better to be safe, so in my last week of pregnancy with Mackenzie we went to the hospital twice to check. Each time one of the midwives did all the necessary checks on Mackenzie and me. Each time the heart-monitoring belt was around my waist, Mackenzie began kicking about like crazy, making a total liar out of me. The midwives were lovely and told us we did the right thing coming in, saying it happened all the time.

The second time we went in to check we were advised to start the induction process the next day. While all the checks showed she was healthy, sometimes reduced foetal movement was the baby trying to say something was wrong, something they couldn't measure on all their machines. The next day we were going to be exactly full-term at 40 weeks anyway, so just to be cautious they suggested I be induced, and we agreed to do it. I know a lot of people try to avoid induction and I really do understand why, but when a medical professional is saying we need to do it for the baby then I am all for it. We had said from the start that while we had a plan of how we wanted the birth to happen and an induction wasn't on it, we would always do what the doctors recommended for a safe delivery.

Driving home from the hospital knowing this would be our last night together alone was surreal. We were so nervous but very excited. While writing this section I asked Jonny what he remembered doing the night before we went to the hospital and he said, 'I think we basically just went home and shat ourselves.' Seems like an accurate description, thanks, babe.

After a fitful night, the next morning, 9 March 2017, Jonny and I woke up early and had a final cuddle in bed. It would have been a peaceful moment but the cockatoo squawking just outside our window had other ideas. It was time to get going.

The drive to the hospital is imprinted in my memory for life. We arrived early and waited anxiously in the cafe for a room to become available. We had chosen to go with the midwife program at the Royal Hospital for Women, which meant I wouldn't see a doctor unless things didn't go to plan.

Once we were comfortable in a room, a midwife checked me over. I was one centimetre dilated but this wasn't enough to break my waters and start the induction. At midday, the midwife put in a cervix softener called Cervidil. It is basically a gel put on a vaginal insert that helps the cervix dilate and open. It was a slightly uncomfortable feeling at first but slowly the small contractions started. My friend Kath turned up and took me for a coffee as I walked around, trying to get things going. Hours later Jonny got us Thai food for dinner, and we watched *Gogglebox* as I sat with a heat pack on me. The midwives checked on me at midnight but I was still only one centimetre dilated, so I needed more time with the Cervidil I had been given. It wasn't the best sleep, as you can imagine, trying to sleep through contractions.

At 6 a.m. the next day a midwife checked me again and I was finally two centimetres dilated, and we were told that now my waters could be broken manually. I was taken downstairs to the delivery room. Such a crazy thing, to walk into the room where you know your baby will be born (well, that's what I thought).

However, after another internal examination they noticed Mackenzie had popped back out of my pelvis, which meant a doctor had to break my waters instead of the midwife. The concern was that when my waters were broken the rush of fluid may mean Mackenzie would fall back into my pelvis but with the umbilical cord in front of her face, cutting off her oxygen. They had an operating theatre on stand-by just in case that happened.

At 10.30 a.m. a doctor broke my waters with an implement that looked like a sewing needle with a hook on the end. I was expecting it to hurt but hardly felt a thing, just a giant rush of fluid. The umbilical cord did not fall in front of her face, however, the waters contained meconium, a baby's first bowel movement. While this is relatively common it can mean the baby is in distress, so it was decided that rather than leaving me to go into labour naturally following my waters being broken, I would be put on an oxytocin drip to cause the uterus to contract. They started this around 11.30 a.m.

My parents came into delivery room around 11.45 a.m. to say hi to us and to see how I was going—and they never left. Around noon my contractions were coming very hard and fast, which is the problem with the drip, so this meant my parents got stuck helping Jonny manage my pain. The midwife had warned us that an induction can increase the need for pain medication because the pain doesn't build slowly like in normal labour.

For the next six hours I moved between the floor, the bed and bending over an exercise ball. My dad held my hand and gave me the gas, my mum worked the TENS (transcutaneous electrical nerve stimulation) machine on my back while Jonny pressed down on my hips to give me relief. It was such a team effort. The contractions were coming so fast there was hardly any time between them and I could feel myself falling into a panicked state.

All the while we had RNB Friday playing on the radio— 'Shoop' and 'No Diggity' helped me through. Between our tunes and the lollies and chocolate we had brought for the midwives, our room was the happening place to be in the hospital.

After a while, the pain got too much and I asked for a morphine injection. I remember them giving it to me but it didn't take away a single ounce of pain. I asked Jonny to put on my relaxing labour music thinking it might help, but after one 'soothing' song I was yelling for RNB Friday again. It turns out I was not in a relaxing mood.

By about 6 p.m. I was six centimetres dilated and I couldn't take any more and asked for an epidural. Next thing I remember I was hunched over on the bed ready for the injection, going in and out of being mentally present. Mum and Dad had stepped outside the room. Jonny isn't a huge fan of needles but he stood by ready to support me. However, when the midwife and anaesthetist saw the look on his face on seeing the needle, they asked him to lie on the floor, concerned that if he fainted or was sick I would move. So he lay on the ground and I got into the zone. I don't know how I was able to stay still through a contraction while they injected me in the back but I just did.

The epidural was *amazing*! After 30 hours of contractions, six of those intense, the relief was huge. Finally I was going to be able to get some sleep, but before I did Jonny thought it was safe to take some selfies with me, jokingly complaining about how much his feet hurt. My husband the comedian.

The epidural allowed my poor parents and Jonny to take some time off. They went out for dinner, wine and, for Dad and Jonny, a whisky each, at a cafe in Randwick before popping home for a shower and change of clothes. I suppose they had earned it.

I had two favourite midwives who looked after me in my

pregnancy, Cat and Gemma. Cat hadn't been on shift since I had come in to be induced but when I was sleeping Gemma started her shift. She is someone who would easily have been our friend if we met outside of this process, so it was great to have her around.

About 11 p.m., Gemma told me I was 10 centimetres and it was time to push. I pushed as hard as I could, three pushes per contraction. I pushed so hard I felt like I would snap something inside. I did this for two long hours until we realised it wasn't working and she wasn't any further out.

Dr Giselle Crawford arrived. After examining me, she said Mackenzie was now in the posterior position, her back facing my back and her head facing up rather than her chin being tucked under. I had spent two hours pushing her head into my pelvis, the poor little girl. They explained that they would need to use forceps to get her out or I had to have a caesarean. At this point Dad left the room. He had been standing in the corner up at the 'no view' end in a tiny safe space but, at this point, it all got too much for him. Mum and Jonny remained, holding my hands.

For a second I started crying. I couldn't imagine being able to push any more, which would be needed for the forceps to work, but I was also unhappy about the idea of a caesarean after all this effort. It felt like I was so close. I had been labouring for almost forty hours at this point and was in so much pain as the epidural had worn off. Suddenly, I could hear a loud buzzing noise and the sound of Mum and Jonny talking became distant. I knew I was passing out but it seemed that no one around me could tell.

I came to again as they wheeled me into the theatre where they would either use the forceps or perform the caesarean, depending on what was needed. I remember seeing Mum as I was rushed by her, and poor Dad, who was standing outside and had no idea what was happening. Jonny stopped to explain before running to catch up and get into a surgery gown.

I am forever thankful to my parents for being there for us. It makes the memories so much more special—my dream team, although I am fairly certain my Dad is traumatised.

In the theatre they did another exam and decided that forceps wouldn't work: it was to be a caesarean after all. It was just after 2 a.m. when my epidural was topped up and, with Jonny by my side, they started. I felt the tugs and pulls but I kept focused on whispering a mantra to myself: 'Healthy baby, healthy baby'. Then suddenly I saw Jonny stand up and begin taking photos, and in that second I heard the most perfect and beautiful cry.

That sound signalled my relief. She was crying. She was healthy. She was okay. I could rest now.

Mackenzie was born at 2.44 a.m. on Saturday, 11 March 2017, weighing 3.89 kilograms and measuring 54 centimetres long.

Jonathan: The birth of Mackenzie was a whirlwind. Despite weeks of prenatal classes, stories from mates and watching that episode of *Friends* where Rachel has her baby, I was not prepared for what lay ahead of me. Within a few short minutes of starting the IV drip to induce labour, Rachael was doubled over in pain from the suddenly intense and regular contractions.

When I think back to that time in the birthing suite, the image that always comes to mind first is the fear in Rachael's eyes when she could feel another contraction coming. I knew it wasn't anything she couldn't handle, but as the labour intensified she began hyperventilating during contractions and even started to panic. Eventually we gave the nod for the doctors to give an epidural.

I will never know how she managed to stay still for the doctors as they inserted the needle into her spine. Halfway through the procedure she had a contraction, which meant the doctors had to pause, gigantic needle in hand. I'm only a little ashamed to admit that I needed to lie down so as not to pass out at the thought of the massive needle going into her spine while she was in such pain.

Thankfully, the epidural took almost immediate effect, which totally changed the atmosphere in the room. Rachael was exhausted and needed a nap. So her parents and I went to the bar for a well-earned whisky.

I'll be forever grateful to Rachael's parents for being the rest of her support crew during the labour. They helped with the gas, held her hand and operated the TENS machine during contractions. Between the three of us we filled the role of one capable support person.

Mackenzie was taken into the resuscitation room for standard checks and Jonny went with her. I tried desperately to keep my eyes on them but by this point I was so tired and kept falling in and out of sleep, no matter how hard I tried not to. I was also shivering, which is a side effect of the epidural. They bundled Mackenzie up and Gemma brought her to me while Jonny filmed. She was beautiful. Pure perfection. We just stared at her in amazement and wonder. I reached my hand out to carefully touch her, but I was so tired I couldn't judge distance properly, so in the video I look like I am moving in slow motion. I couldn't hold her yet as I was so weak and worried I would drop her. Meanwhile the doctors were delivering the placenta and stitching me up, but I was hardly aware of it.

Around 3.30 a.m. I was taken to recovery and Jonny took Mackenzie down to the delivery suite waiting room where all four of her grandparents were waiting to meet her. They tell me she was wide awake and quiet, staring at them all with her big eyes, taking it all in. Their excited chatter on seeing her slowly quieted as they looked down at her, and she gazed up at them. There was a lot of love in the room right then. They all naturally wanted to hold her, but my protective husband said no since I hadn't held her yet.

At 4.30 a.m. I was taken from recovery to my room in the post-natal ward. I remember waiting for what felt like ages, looking at the door, waiting for Jonny and Mackenzie to walk into the room. I wanted so much to see her, to touch her; I missed her already. Finally, they came in with Gemma and I gave Mackenzie her first breastfeed. I have never felt so at peace, so complete. Jonny and I looked at her and decided at that moment on her name. We had picked Mackenzie early on but we wanted to meet her and be sure it suited. We felt the name was strong and beautiful, just like her.

The three of us stayed in hospital for the next six nights, five to recover from the caesarean and one extra due to my blood pressure being elevated. All up we were in hospital for eight nights but we didn't mind. We were in our own little bubble in our private room, just enjoying learning this new life. During that time we went to bathing and breastfeeding classes and learned how to look after our little human.

Eventually we were able to leave with our baby girl, our new family.

While her birth was not ideal or how I'd imagined, I wouldn't change it for anything. I now have a beautiful permanent scar on me. It isn't pretty—it is raised, chunky and still red—but it is a sign of Mackenzie's entrance into this world. It is a scar that Jonny will often now tenderly kiss to feel close to Kenzie. I am so proud of her birth.

What just happened?

'Everything can change in an instant. Everything. And then there is only before and after.'

Phyllis Reynolds Naylor

Jonny and I had ten blissful weeks with Mackenzie before our world fell apart. In those weeks we learned a lot and, if I can say so, I think we nailed the parenting gig.

For us it was important to learn how to take her out of the house as early as possible. We mastered the car seat, the pram, breastfeeding in public, using the car for nappy changes and the baby carrier. We found our little groove. We were a family and we were blissfully happy.

Jonny had eight weeks off work which allowed us to really bond as a family. I loved seeing her in his arms—he was just a natural dad, always on hand to entertain and soothe. I think he felt a really special connection early on, and because of the caesarean I wasn't able to carry her as easily, so Jonny relished being needed. He was better at changing her nappy and swaddling her than I was initially, and he loved it.

When Mackenzie was eight weeks old, Jonny grudgingly went back to work, leaving little M and me alone. At first it was a bit daunting but on day one I made sure I headed out to Centennial Park and met my mother's group. I didn't want to get trapped into staying at home and felt like the longer I put it off, the more 'stuck' I would feel.

For a couple of weeks we cruised around, just the two of us. Our days started with me trying to sleep in as long as I could. I would bring her into bed with me in the morning after Jonny had left and we would just smile and stare at each other. I would juggle trying to get us both ready, usually with her strapped into her bouncer chair on the floor of the bathroom while I sang to her and quickly showered myself before she got upset. I took particular delight in picking an outfit for her each day: stylin' my baby was one of my new favourite pastimes, often with a little photo shoot before we headed out for the day. Usually we went to Centennial Park for a walk and a coffee. I loved being a mum and walked with a bit of a proud swagger, like I had finally been let into a secret club.

When Mackenzie was around nine weeks old, she began to cry at the end of each feed. She would feed beautifully and was putting on weight, but instead of just becoming full and pulling off she would cry. After a week of this, I decided to take her to one of the free lactation consultations at the local hospital. I messaged Jonny telling him my plan and off I went to make sure I was doing everything right.

When I arrived at the hospital, I told the consultant my concerns. Once Kenzie woke up from her nap I began feeding her to show the consultant. Like the times when I presented for reduced movement in the womb, she made me look silly and fed beautifully. As I was about to give up and leave, the consultant said that there was no problem with her feeding but that she seemed 'floppy'. I initially felt defensive but then the lactation nurse pointed to a baby boy on the change mat next to Kenzie and said, 'He is about ten weeks old and that is what she should be doing.' The baby boy was on his tummy and had pushed his chest off the ground with his forearms. My stomach sank. Kenzie didn't do that; she had never done that. She hated tummy time like a lot of babies, but she had never shown that strength.

I told the consultant I would look into it as I bundled Mackenzie up and quickly ran out the door, cuddling her close to my chest. She just needed more practice with tummy time, that was it. 'It will be okay,' I told myself, but as I said it my heart rate increased and my palms began to sweat.

I drove out of the hospital car park but pulled over to the side of the road as soon as I got a chance. Panicked, I rang Jonny, who calmed me down and said we needed to know more. He is forever the calm, level head, but I could hear the concern in his voice.

We had just moved to a new house down in south Sydney and didn't know any of the doctors in the area so I drove to the nearest medical centre and made an appointment. I sat in the waiting area, nervous and surrounded by people coughing near my new baby. When we finally got in to see the doctor, she did not ease my concerns. After checking Mackenzie over for a few minutes, she began calling around, trying to find a paediatrician. The very fact that she was trying so hard to get an appointment made me even more concerned. She couldn't find anywhere that could take us in under two weeks.

Walking back to the car, I was almost hyperventilating. I couldn't wait two weeks and ended up calling another paediatrician I had heard about. Like all the others there was a long wait and I burst into tears on the phone. The kind receptionist told me that the other paediatrician in the office could squeeze us in two days later.

For the next two days we watched Mackenzie carefully, justifying each movement she made. We practised swatting with her hands and forced her to do the tummy time she hated so much. She cried every time, with her face in the blanket. Jonny convinced himself that it was our fault that she was so floppy and weak—we hadn't done enough tummy time with her. I hoped it was just a developmental delay.

Even two days was too long, so in the meantime we met with our normal doctor, the one who had been with us throughout the pregnancy. She wasn't able to alleviate our fears either, but she was at least able to give us some hope that maybe it wasn't as serious as we feared: Mackenzie had had a cold in the week prior so she thought it was possible she was suffering from a transient muscle delay. She researched with vigour while we were there, clearly shaken, clearly worried that something was wrong. We were so confused because just four weeks earlier she had seen Mackenzie for her six-week check-up where everything had seemed fine.

Those two days of waiting were pure torture but it was nothing compared to what was coming. Not for a second did we believe it was something that would actually take Mackenzie from us.

On 24 May 2017, just two days later, we walked into a paediatrician's office. I have never been so nervous in my life. I felt nauseous, weak, my whole body tingled and my palms were sweaty. I wanted to be anywhere but there and felt like I might faint at any minute. Jonny wasn't much better. Mackenzie, meanwhile, just looked at us and smiled.

The paediatrician was a gruff older man. No doubt there are some very hard aspects of his job, but his bedside manner was a bit off. He asked a few questions and then told us to undress Mackenzie, down to her nappy. On the examination table he moved her around, watching how she reacted. I too was watching her closely. This was my baby. Surely she would be fine. We would just have to do more tummy time.

After two short minutes, he turned to us and said that he believed she had spinal muscular atrophy type 1. Just like that. He said it fast, with little feeling. We had never heard of it so didn't know how to react, but even the sound of it wasn't good. Just having your child diagnosed with anything is scary, but since he told us with such little show of emotion or even sympathy, we felt there must be a solution. So we asked the obvious question: what is the cure?

He said flatly, 'There is none. It is terminal.'

Terminal. Terminal. Terminal. Terminal. The word echoed in my mind.

Just like that, our world fell away. I couldn't believe what I was hearing.

I felt my whole body begin to shut down. Everything went blurry, sounds were muffled, and I felt like I would collapse. I stood over her as she lay quietly in her nappy on the bench, holding her hands as she stared up at me. We locked eyes but she knew nothing of the knife that had just torn through my heart. She lay there, thankfully oblivious to our turmoil. I went to pick her up but my legs were shaking so badly that I hesitated, worried I would pass out and drop her.

Instead I leaned over the bench, gasping for air, shaking my head to wake up. I looked at Jonny. I saw panic in his eyes. He started firing off questions to the doctor, straight into work mode and wanting to know all the details. I didn't hear a word of what was said.

My mind kept saying, 'This isn't happening, this isn't happening. He is wrong.' But somewhere a small part of me knew it was the truth.

Slowly I dressed her, picked her up and rocked her, and myself.

I finally sat down next to Jonny as the doctor made a call to the neurologist he said we needed to see. I turned to Jonny and looked desperately into his eyes and said, 'What just happened?' Jonny had no answers; he sat in shock.

Panicked, I began trying to find a loophole while trying to understand what SMA was. Asking the doctor what was next, I remember him saying, 'Calm down, missy.' He called me 'missy'!

I turned to him and said, 'You have just told me my daughter will die.' As I said, he didn't have the best bedside manner.

The paediatrician explained that SMA was a motor neuron disease which would see Mackenzie unable to use her muscles. She would waste away, losing her ability to swallow and eventually being unable to breathe and would pass away. How does something so cruel even exist? It was too much for me to take in.

The paediatrician said a new clinical trial was showing good results. It was only four months old, but some were calling it a 'miracle' treatment. We clung to that hope as we left his office with a referral to a neurologist for the next day.

We had walked into his office hoping we just were lagging in her tummy time, that it was a simple developmental delay. And walked out in shock. How was this happening? It wasn't really. Was it? I wanted to scream.

We stood at reception in a daze and paid an enormous amount of money for being told our child would potentially die. Without a single word exchanged between us, Jonny and I carried our baby out of the office and down the street. We held hands, clinging to each other. All around us people carried on in their 'normal' worlds, like nothing had changed. Cars drove by, people got their takeaway coffees.

I remember a guy sitting on the corner drinking a bottle of wine. I had seen him there plenty of times, but this time I wanted to snatch the bottle out of his hand and scream at him: 'How can you wreck your body when my daughter doesn't even get a chance at life? *My baby will die.* Fuck you! You don't deserve this life.' But instead we kept walking. People bumped into us; the world wouldn't stop for our pain. At the car we placed Mackenzie in her seat then got in ourselves and just sat there, tears running down our faces.

At home we called our parents to tell them what the paediatrician had said. I don't know how we made those calls; I barely remember them. I was half crying, half stunned, still in disbelief. They were shocked. One thing I do recall, though, were their cries of anguish when we told them. No one knew what to say. What was there to say?

Jonathan: There are moments in life that you look back on as a major turning point. It may be when you met your partner, got a new job, or had a rock smash you in the face. For me, the moment the paediatrician said the words 'Mackenzie has spinal muscular atrophy—it is terminal' was the biggest turning point in my life. Suddenly I saw all my dreams—watching her first steps, her first day at school or even walking her down the aisle—evaporate into nothingness, and an intense darkness settled into my life. I saw Rachael shut down and cease to function, and I felt like the world was about to swallow me up, like I was viewing the scene from a distance, almost hovering over it. Above all, I could see a beautiful baby girl lying on the paediatrician's examination table looking up and smiling at us, completely unaware she'd just been handed a death sentence.

Driving home from the paediatrician's office, Rachael sat in the back with Mackenzie while I was lost in a wash of a thousand thoughts, hardly able to grab hold of any one of them. The only thing I remember saying that day was that we had to fight together, we needed this horrible situation to bring us closer together as a couple. It would be so incredibly easy for this to end a marriage and we couldn't let that happen. Otherwise, what's the point?

Our appointment with the neurologist was the next day. That night we felt lost at home, like sitting there was wrong, so we bundled Mackenzie up and drove to a dark area of Sydney where we could view the stars. I don't know why we did that; it wasn't something we did regularly but it felt like something we needed. Back at home we could not sleep. I cried all night and watched her little face, holding her hand and whispering to her, loving her. Willing this to be a mistake and for it all to go away the next day.

We kept repeating to each other, 'This isn't happening, this isn't happening. We are good people. We are police officers, we pay taxes, we give to charity, we planned for her, she is here, she is perfect. This doesn't happen to people like us. We are nothing, we aren't special.'

I am not religious but I started bargaining with someone, anyone, out there. Any god, any higher power or spirit that would listen. 'Please . . .'

The next day, 25 May 2017, we drove to the neurologist's office at the Bright Alliance building off the Sydney Children's Hospital, silent and terrified. We walked stiff and heavy, like we were trudging through mud.

Dr Michelle Farrar was an exceptionally gentle and kind woman. She had a warm smile and a lovely demeanour, but even that couldn't calm us. In her office Kenzie was again put through some movement tests. After a few minutes, Dr Farrar— or Michelle, as we soon referred to her—turned to us and said that she was 95 per cent sure that Mackenzie had SMA type 1, but it would need to be confirmed by a blood test.

The same feeling as the day before hit me: I shook, I cried and I rocked myself. This can't be happening. My wish for the paediatrician to be wrong had gone unanswered.

Michelle explained that SMA was a rare neuromuscular disorder characterised by loss of motor neurons and progressive muscle wasting, often leading to early death. It is the childhood version of motor neuron disease. In essence, a baby with SMA will first lose the ability to move their limbs and then their internal organs will be affected, showing itself in an inability to swallow and eventually to breathe. It is one of the cruellest diseases I have ever heard described to me. Michelle explained that most babies with SMA type 1 often didn't see their first birthday.

The wind was literally knocked out of me and I gasped for air.

Naturally we wanted to know more about the 'miracle' trial that the paediatrician had mentioned. But Michelle explained that there was no cure, only something that may give us more time. A clinical trial of a new medication called nusinersen (marketed as Spinraza) was being undertaken on SMA type 1 babies, an injection given as a lumbar puncture four times a year. It was currently the most expensive drug in the world and would cost patients over half a million dollars per year for life, though there were attempts being made to get it onto the government-subsidised Pharmaceutical Benefits Scheme (PBS). Michelle explained that we could go on the trial for free but if the government didn't accept nusinersen onto the PBS we would eventually have to pay for the treatment. Meaning we would have to take Mackenzie off it, because no one can afford that.

While nusinersen was a huge medical advancement, it did not guarantee results. All it did was stop the disease from progressing as quickly. In our research we learned that it worked to a varying degree of success for about 60 per cent of patients, and that degree of success could range significantly. A few babies might react well, meaning their symptoms would become similar to the less severe SMA type 2, but they would still never walk, would still have multiple serious hospital visits a year, would need significant breathing assistance and would still eventually pass away at a young age. Having only been introduced in 2016, experts still didn't know the full extent of what it could do, how long the body would accept it or its side effects. Some babies were being taken off it because of a bad reaction or no reaction at all. It provided hope but it was up to each family to determine whether to take the chance and determine what they believed was quality of life.

Michelle told us to have a think about whether we would like to put Mackenzie on the trial. She was careful to not sway us either way but to give us the facts alone. The words 'no cure' spun around in my mind.

We became aware that the room had slowly started to fill up with people. There was a nurse, an assistant, a geneticist, a social worker . . . The seriousness of our situation was becoming clear. We were thrown information left, right and centre about Kenzie, her prognosis, treatment options and palliative care. We also discussed the need for a resuscitation plan for her. In two days, we had come to a resuscitation plan . . .

We couldn't believe what we were hearing: not only would our baby pass away but we had to make these huge decisions for her, including whether we wanted to put her on drugs that might give us more time, but at what quality of life for her?

We learned that Mackenzie was quite advanced in her symptoms; she had shown signs of SMA early. The average age for an SMA type 1 baby to pass away at was eight months, with the oldest being two years. We were also told that for Mackenzie it was likely to be months, not years, and this information would have an effect on whether she would be suited for nusinersen. Michelle explained that because SMA was a motor neuron disease, once a physical function was gone it could not be repaired—the horse had bolted. So whatever she had already lost would not be regained through nusinersen, it would only potentially stop her from getting worse.

We asked what losing her would look like. Michelle explained that there were normally three ways that SMA babies died. Firstly, some SMA babies had a slow decline, going in and out of hospital and basically dying slowly and somewhat painfully, given the inability to breathe and swallow. Secondly, some developed a cold which then led to a fast decline in hospital. Thirdly, there were a few cases where the baby seemed healthy one day and just didn't wake up the next. We had to be prepared for any of those scenarios, although I couldn't see how we could ever prepare for the possibility that one day we might wake up and look in her bassinet to find that she had passed away in the night.

After all this, we were taken to speak with a genetic counsellor. There we had a basic lesson in biology. The genetic counsellor explained to us that SMA was a recessive genetic disorder—more on this later—but basically, it meant that most likely both Jonny and I unknowingly carried SMA in our DNA. Meaning we gave this to our baby.

They explained to us that if we were carriers not all of our children would be affected, but with each pregnancy there would be a one in four chance. I felt relief that there was a chance we could have more kids because having that ripped away from us as well as Mackenzie seemed too much to cope with. But then I felt immediately sick with guilt that I had found any relief in this horrific situation.

We headed downstairs for blood tests to confirm that Mackenzie had SMA and that we were indeed both carriers. And then we were asked to come back when we had made our decision about whether to put her on the clinical trial.

Walking away from the hospital that day, it felt like we had entered a living nightmare that we couldn't wake up from. We haven't really woken up from it since.

After

'Where you used to be, there is a hole in the world, which I find myself constantly walking around in the daytime, and falling in at night.'

Edna St Vincent Millay

The days following Mackenzie's diagnosis passed in a daze. I stopped eating, and essentially stopped speaking. I sat on the couch staring at and holding my baby. All I wanted to do was hold Kenzie close, feed her, touch her, tend to her and talk to her. I wanted to attach her to me, in the hope that my body would combine with hers and maybe I could protect her. I felt like Mackenzie was tied to a railroad track in front of an oncoming train but there was nothing I could do to stop it.

Jonny went the opposite way. He found comfort in emotionally eating and talking to people. He paced up and down on the balcony on the phone to whoever needed to be spoken to: family, friends or medical specialists. I feel he did what I couldn't, and I think I did what he couldn't.

I spent hours staring at Mackenzie in complete disbelief. At times, I felt myself looking at her with such determined concentration that I realised I was subconsciously trying to swap with her. I would have given up my life in a second if it meant she could have the life she deserved.

The day after Mackenzie was diagnosed, both our parents rushed from Canberra to Sydney to be with us. I cannot describe the pain of a household with six parents filled with grief over their children, all terrified of the pain that they feared their children would have to go through, feeling helpless. For our parents the pain was intensified as they were scared and worried for their children as well as for their grandchild. The suffering in our house was palpable.

It must have been a day or two after and Mackenzie was asleep or with one of her grandparents when Jonny came to hold me in the living room. Between the silent tears, Jonny held my hands, looked into my eyes and said calmly and carefully, 'We have been given the worst hurdle a couple can face. We have to do this together. We can't let this break us.' Then he said just one word to me with such intensity: 'Together.' This would become our motto. Whenever we felt it needed to be said we would turn to each other and say the word 'together'.

Jonathan: Later in our journey I was watching Rachael record a 'No Filter' podcast with Mia Freedman and she asked Rachael how we were able to grieve a baby who was still alive. It was a good question and one I wouldn't have been able to give an answer to. From where I stood, I didn't have the luxury to really grieve while Mackenzie was still with us. After being told of Mackenzie's SMA, Rachael completely shut down and focused all her energy on Mackenzie. She needed the opportunity to process the information in order to heal and give Mackenzie the best and happiest life possible in the short time we had with her. Rachael's response was as you would expect: a complex mix of confusion, debilitating sadness and a raging anger at the world. As a result, I turned my attention to Rachael. I did everything I could to help her process the grief and look after the beautiful baby who was still in our arms. I did what I could to give her space to be angry when needed and held her when she needed to be held. Her emotions were extreme, and they needed to process in a safe and non-judgemental place. That's not to say I didn't cry or have an emotional response—quite the opposite. I cried and felt destroyed, but Rachael had to take priority as Mackenzie's mother, so I can't say I really grieved while Mackenzie was still alive.

The way our family rallied around us cannot be adequately expressed in words. They have been everything we needed in every second of every day. They have never failed us, especially our parents. As we put our arms around Kenzie and cared for her, our parents put their arms around us. They fed us, cared for us, cleaned the house for us and gave us their love. Most importantly, they gave Kenzie love, especially when we needed to cry. Everything we learned about being parents we learned from them. Better people you will not find.

None of us knew how to comprehend what was happening, and at first we didn't even believe it. We continually said to each other, 'This can't be happening.' Each of us hoped to wake up from this nightmare.

But every night we would go to sleep only to wake up and remember each morning. In one moment we'd be lost in laughter, playing with Kenzie, loving her smile, only to remember in the next moment. The pain would hit us like a truck. At all times it seemed that there was someone breaking down and crying as we took turns to feel the pain.

Slowly we started to pull ourselves out of our sad fog, and as we did we realised we needed to be something else, something more for Kenzie. She needed more from us because while we were in intense emotional pain, Mackenzie wasn't. She was so young, only ten weeks old at the time of her diagnosis, and still just a happy, healthy little baby. We knew that, for her, we needed to live, and live beautifully.

Our first job was to learn everything we could about SMA and how long we would have her, and how best to care for her in that time. And then there was the daunting task of deciding whether or not we wanted to put her on the new clinical trial.

In some ways whether or not to go on the trial was a hard decision, but in other ways it wasn't. Jonny and I knew that these awful conversations needed to be had in a safe place, a place where we could both share our thoughts, feelings and concerns—good, bad and ugly—without fear of reprimand or resentment. Once our safe place was established, we both revealed our initial reservations about the clinical trial. We spoke at length about the positives, negatives and unknowns. Once we came to our decision, we discussed it with our parents, the doctors we knew, Michelle and close friends like Kath. Every single one of us felt the same.

We decided not to put her on the trial.

We are lucky in a lot of ways that the people we surrounded ourselves with had the same values and views on life quality over quantity. But make no mistake, this was a soul-shattering decision to make, and one of many that could have destroyed our relationship.

Most people we have spoken to understand our reasoning and agree with us, including a number of medical professionals. Some people, especially those families who chose to put their child on nusinersen, don't understand our reasons, and probably never will. That's okay, they don't have to. Each family has to be at peace with the decision they made, knowing that it was the best for their child. The aim was to make a decision you would not regret and could stand by, which we did.

Whether or not to go on the clinical trial is such a personal choice, and one that no one can ever really guess at until forced to make such a decision. I do not believe there is a right or wrong answer, but it is a decision people need to make with all the available information as relevant to your own child. You need to look at all angles, including how progressed your child is with SMA as you cannot gain back any physical function that has been lost. In our case, Mackenzie was quite progressed in her symptoms, so nusinersen would have had less effect on her.

It is also important to look at all examples of children on nusinersen, not just the good ones that the drug company or the media choose to show. We know of a couple of children who have thrived on the drug and their parents are happy and cannot understand why everyone wouldn't give their child nusinersen. However, we also know parents who chose the drug but found it didn't work for their child and others who have had serious side effects, making their child's life worse. We also know of children for whom it worked for a little while but then stopped working. We knew at best it turned a SMA type 1 to an SMA type 2, which for us was still not a life we would choose for Mackenzie.

It was very confronting for us to research SMA and what Mackenzie's future might look like. We saw parents, especially in the United States, who had put their child on life support. They were trapped in their own body, unable to move, swallow or breathe, but their parents said they were thriving, purely because they were alive. For us that wasn't the life we believed she deserved.

We knew the drug would give us more time with her, which we were desperate for. Selfishly, we wanted that time, but we knew we wouldn't get it without a price. We might get an extra few weeks, months or even years, but by then she would know what was happening and those years wouldn't be easy for her. The only comfort we took in her diagnosis was her young age: if we lost her around eight months old then she would never be conscious of what had been given to her and what she had lost. She would never know pain, she would never suffer, and she would never know anything was wrong with her. She would always be perfect. For us it was quality over quantity.

In the time since we had to make this decision, nusinersen has been put on the PBS, thank goodness. This means that patients for whom nusinersen works can now afford it. Another option has now been developed, which shows great promise, but which was not available to us at the time: a gene therapy drug called Zolgensma, which is now available in some countries but costs over $3 million, making it the world's most expensive drug. Can you imagine knowing there was a drug that could potentially save your child, but it cost $3 million dollars?

Jonny and I began thinking of nusinersen as a drug for the parents, to give *them* more time. We accept the reasons why some parents have chosen to give their children nusinersen; we understand the desire to try anything that might keep your child with you, truly we do. We also hope that they respect our decision and that of other parents who decided to say no to nusinersen.

But not everyone has been kind. Some SMA families and related organisations have stepped back from us due to our choice; I guess they saw us as not being supportive of the drug they believed in. That was quite heartbreaking and left us feeling alone, a feeling we know other families in the same position as us also feel.

After that terrible decision was made there were multiple appointments at Sydney Children's Hospital in Randwick with our wonderful team, including Michelle. We met physiotherapists, social workers, psychologists, nutritionists, occupational therapists and more, all there to support us and make Kenzie as happy as possible for as long as possible. While this was comforting, it was also a reminder of the seriousness of our situation. As some people might know, when the shit hits the fan you can be looking around for the responsible adult to make the decision, but then you realise that person is you.

Every appointment meant walking through a hospital filled with sick children, and the sadness and heartbreak we witnessed will stay with us forever—life is so cruel and unfair. What makes it worse is walking outside to the 'real' world, where people are spending money on expensive handbags or complaining about the red lights they got on the way to work. It all seems so wrong.

Sitting outside Michelle's office waiting for our appointment we would see children in wheelchairs, unable to move at all. Trapped in their bodies. It was so devastating, both for those families and for us to see what Mackenzie's future could be—that is, if she was 'lucky'.

Because we chose not to put Mackenzie on the clinical trial, the only option open to us was palliative care, to make her as comfortable as possible when the time came. We had horrible meetings with lovely people who we never wanted to meet. With the local palliative care team in our area, we discussed through tears what we hoped for when it came to Mackenzie's end of life. Can you even imagine that, knowing you would lose your child so planning the 'best' way for it to happen? Every action and decision was filled with pain, but it was the life we were forced to now live. We sat with the teams and planned Mackenzie's resuscitation plan if an ambulance was ever called and at what point they should stop. We decided in what circumstances we wanted them to assist her and in what circumstances we would choose pain relief instead of action. It was pure torture.

Our plan was that we would want her to be resuscitated or treated if she was struggling through something she could return from, such as giving her antibiotics for a flu or a virus. But if assistance meant she would end up on life support then we didn't want them to prolong her life. We reiterated hundreds of times that Mackenzie's comfort and avoidance of pain was our primary concern. We said yes to pain medication being administered if and when she needed it.

One of our meetings was with a health professional who I would later ask to not be involved in Mackenzie's care. She sat Jonny and I down and said that she would go over what death was like, to prepare us. She explained that while death could be a peaceful leaving of this world, it is often similar to entering it, and sometimes there was blood, screaming and pain. I wanted to punch her. I don't know what she thought this conversation would accomplish but I never wanted to see or speak to her again. Apart from that one instance, I applaud and admire the teams that work in children's hospitals and palliative care. To watch children die on a regular basis must be truly awful, and it takes a special person to want to be there for children when they need adults the most.

We were told Mackenzie could either die at home, in hospital or, if we had notice, we could take her to pass away at Bear Cottage, a baby and children's hospice in the northern beachside suburb of Manly. Driving to Bear Cottage with Mackenzie in the back to 'scout out' the possible scene of her death felt so wrong, but I knew it was something we had to do. We broke down as we walked through the door of the place where our daughter could possibly take her last breath. Bear Cottage was a magical place filled with exceptionally special people, but places like this should not exist.

I cannot even begin to describe what each of these actions felt like. Every meeting, every visit and every decision took all our strength, but every time we did it for her. I wouldn't wish that pain on anyone. Our only comfort was that Mackenzie was too young to know what was going on.

Soon after Mackenzie's diagnosis we started seeing a psychologist, and she and our GP recommended we both go on a low-dose antidepressant, not only to deal with her diagnosis but in preparation for what was to come. It is something I am now so thankful we did. It never took away our pain or dulled it but it helped me handle the anxiety, calming my mind enough to manage my thoughts and responsibilities. I don't like the automatically negative connotations people have about antidepressants. Before this I had had no personal experience with antidepressants and initially I only told a couple of people, including a good friend who had also previously been on them, so it felt safe to talk to her about it. I was surprised by her negative response—I mean, if you can't share the need for help under these circumstances, when can you? To me, antidepressants are not an easy way out and in fact people who go on them are strong because they are being honest in acknowledging that they need help. If you broke your foot you would use crutches, right? I was more cautious in telling people after that reaction, though eventually I realised that there was nothing to be ashamed of.

Learning about the cruel disease that is SMA was heartbreaking, to say the least. Jonny and I often cried, screamed and begged each other to make the pain stop. However, we made it a rule to never break down in front of Kenzie. She was such a smart little girl, and very aware of everything around her. All she knew was what she could read in our faces, so every moment she was awake, no matter where we were or what we were doing, we smiled. We smiled at her, danced with her, sang to her. We were determined that she would never pick up on our sadness. She would only know love and light.

This is where friends and family saved us, especially in those early days—that, and the love of a beautiful baby girl. How lucky we were to have her.

SMA and genetic testing

'Could your worst enemy be your best teacher?'

Unknown

From 25 May 2017, the day Mackenzie was diagnosed, we threw ourselves into learning about SMA. In the process our eyes were opened to a whole new world—a terrifying, unfair, brutal world that didn't make any sense at all, but also a world that affects more people than we all realise. We learned about the world of genetics, recessive disorders, chromosome abnormalities, preimplantation genetic diagnosis, carrier testing, the statistics of childhood deaths and more. It was hard not to fall into a hole of depression and never claw our way out. But knowledge is power.

We had planned so carefully for a healthy baby. For six months we made sure our bodies were in the best condition they could be, and we did every blood test, scan or screen we were offered, both before and after we were pregnant, including the non-invasive prenatal test (NIPT). What we didn't know at the time is that this test is only assessing a baby's chromosomes, not the whole

DNA. We had had no idea that there was so much more that could go wrong and that within the supposedly perfect chromosomes that Kenzie had was DNA with a tiny glitch. A tiny glitch that would change all our worlds.

Remember the ice bucket challenge? It was a phenomenon that went viral in 2014 where people around the world threw a bucket of ice water over themselves to raise awareness and money for amyotrophic lateral sclerosis (ALS), the motor neuron disease made 'famous' by Stephen Hawking. Motor neurons exist in the brain and the spinal cord and control the muscles that allow us to move, speak, breathe and swallow. With motor neuron disease, muscles weaken, waste away and die.

Spinal muscular atrophy (SMA) type 1—otherwise known as Werdnig-Hoffmann disease—is a form of motor neuron disease affecting the lower motor neurons in the spinal cord. When the motor neurons stop sending messages properly to the muscles, the affected person loses the ability to move and their muscles slowly waste away due to inactivity. The muscles closest to the trunk are the first to be affected, including the upper arms, shoulders, hips, back and upper legs. Next the person struggles to swallow, making eating difficult. They have difficulty coughing and cannot move any mucus from their chest, so colds are a serious issue that can lead to life-threatening pneumonia. Eventually the person loses the ability to breathe. They become trapped inside their bodies.

It is the cruellest, most devastating disease, both to experience and to watch.

Feelings and sensations are not affected and those with SMA can feel tickles, hugs and the air on their skin. Their intellect is not affected at all, and in fact most people with SMA are thought to have a higher intelligence and are bright and sociable. A baby with SMA is as intelligent as any other baby, and you can see so much expression and emotion through their eyes.

There are a number of 'types' of SMA, categorised by age of onset and the rate of progression.

Type 0 is rare and severe, and most babies born with type 0 die upon birth or in the first month or two of life.

Type 1 is what Mackenzie was diagnosed with. It is the most common and is severe and lethal. Babies born with type 1 are usually diagnosed before six months old and the average life expectancy is eight months, with most passing away before two years unless interventions are made, such as feeding tubes, breathing tubes or new medications that slow progression.

Type 2 is usually diagnosed between six and eighteen months of age. It varies in symptoms and severity but usually children can sit but not walk or stand. They are prone to severe chest infections and usually pass away by early adolescence.

Type 3 is usually diagnosed between two and seventeen years old. It varies in symptoms and severity but usually results in difficulty climbing and running and causes a tremor. People can live a full life with therapy and treatment.

Type 4 is adult onset and can lead to tremor and difficulty moving.

I haven't seen many people with SMA types 0, 3 or 4. Type 1 is the most common, with type 2 the next.

SMA type 1 is a cruel and devastating condition—it is just so wrong to see a baby waste away and suffer. Of course, all forms of SMA are cruel and horrible, however, I try not to comment on anything other than our own journey with SMA as every story is different. But what I do know is that our journey with SMA type 1 was soul destroying.

We learned that SMA is the number-one genetic killer in babies under two. Despite this mind-blowing fact, it is largely unknown, even among healthcare professionals. I assume this is because babies tend to pass away so young and those with SMA are automatically referred to specialists, meaning few general practitioners regularly look after those affected by SMA.

SMA is a recessive genetic disorder, which meant that Mackenzie carried the inherited genes for it within her DNA. Jonny and I had no idea that we were both carriers of SMA and had inadvertently passed this horrible condition on to her.

Here's my Genetics 101 rundown. Humans are made up of cells. In these cells we have chromosomes, and those chromosomes are made up of DNA and genes. Humans have 23 pairs of chromosomes. Half of these chromosomes come from one parent and half come from the other parent. Issues can occur when we have too few or too many chromosomes, as is the case in conditions like Down syndrome. A chromosome issue occurs at the point an embryo is made and is not usually something that is passed on by a parent. These conditions can be picked up during pregnancy by the non-invasive pregnancy test (NIPT), which looks at the baby's DNA through the mother's blood. Whilst this NIPT testing falls under the umbrella of genetic testing, it is not the same test that looks at issues parents may carry—which is known as the genetic carrier testing.

The genetic reproductive carrier test we talk about throughout this book scans the DNA found within prospective parents' genes—rather than their baby's genes. Like chromosomes, genes come in pairs. Each of your parents has two sets of each of their genes: you get a copy of one of these genes from each parent.

A person is a 'carrier' of a genetic condition when they have inherited one copy of a faulty gene (a gene mutation) associated with a genetic condition, but their other gene, given to them by their other parent, is normal so it can take over the work. This means they won't be affected by the genetic condition themselves, but will be a 'carrier' of the condition. A carrier can pass on their faulty genes to their children. When a child is given the faulty gene associated with a genetic condition by both parents, they will be affected by the genetic condition as they have two faulty genes and no healthy copy to take over. On average, each and every one of us carries three genetic disorders in our DNA that could be passed onto our children. Yes—every one of us, even you! Isn't that scary?

There are a few ways genetic conditions can be passed on, including dominant genetic disorders, X-linked genetic disorders and recessive genetic disorders.

A dominant genetic disorder means only one faulty gene needs to be inherited in order to be affected by the disorder, so both parents do not need to be carriers. When only one parent is a carrier there is a 50 per cent chance that the condition will be passed on to a child. Huntington's disease is an example of a dominant genetic disorder.

Conditions known as X-linked, such as fragile X syndrome (FXS), are caused by a faulty gene on the X chromosome. Women have two X chromosomes and men have one X and one Y. Usually boys and men are more severely affected by X-linked conditions than girls and women—women may be healthy carriers showing no signs of the conditions or may have symptoms that are typically milder than those seen in boys and men. There is a 50 per cent chance that the condition may be passed on to the children of a woman who carries an X-linked condition, and typically this means a one in four chance of giving birth to a boy with a severe condition.

Spinal muscular atrophy is an example of a recessive genetic condition—it is the most common form. If a woman and man both carry a fault in a gene for the same condition, when they have a child there are a few possible outcomes. Firstly, there is a one in four (25 per cent) chance that their child will inherit faulty recessive copies of the gene from both parents, and therefore have the genetic condition. Secondly, there's a 25 per cent chance that the child will inherit two normal dominant genes copies and will be unaffected. And thirdly, there's a 50 per cent chance that the child will inherit one faulty recessive gene and one normal dominant gene from each parent and also be a carrier.

There are thousands of genetic disorders. Most people haven't heard of SMA, but you may have heard of cystic fibrosis (CF). Some genetic conditions are severe or lethal, while others can be mild and you can live with them or even have treatment. Like many illnesses, genetic conditions range from tolerable to life-shattering. It's a scary world.

But while the world of genetics can be scary, there is actually something simple we can do to know our own individual genetic faults and the chances of passing them on to our children: a genetic carrier screening test, also known as reproductive genetic screening. Without this testing or a family history, most people will never know they carry a genetic condition until they have—or a relative has—an affected child, as happened to us.

Autosomal Recessive Inheritance Pattern

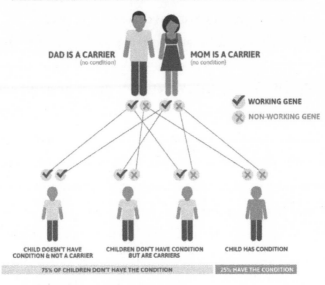

Image courtesy of the Genetic Support Foundation

If knowing that we all carry genetic disorders we can pass on doesn't scare you, think about this: new research published by Victorian Clinical Genetics Services (VCGS) has shown that when you combine the number of children affected by CF, FXS and SMA, it is the same number of children affected by Down syndrome. We routinely test for Down syndrome so why would we not routinely offer genetic carrier screening?

The more we learned, the angrier we got.

We discovered that a simple blood or saliva test that has been available for some time can reveal if you are a carrier of some genetic disorders. Yes, it costs a bit, making it inaccessible to some, but it exists. In fact, there are currently dozens of tests, each looking at a variety of genetic conditions and ranging in cost from $380 to $1500. Some look at just the top three genetic conditions while others can look for hundreds. The test can be taken in preparation for trying for a baby or in the first trimester, though currently most testing is done during pregnancy, even for planned pregnancies, because often people are only then made aware of the availability of the test. A genetic counsellor can look at your results to see if there is a risk that you could pass something on to your children.

With all this new information, we could have screamed in frustration. If we had done a genetic test when we were preparing for a baby or even when we were pregnant with Mackenzie, we would have found out that both Jonny and I carry the SMA genetic mutation. We would have learned there was a one in four risk of our beautiful child being afflicted by SMA. Why had we not been made aware of this genetic test? Mackenzie's suffering could have been avoided.

However, we also learned that not only do few GPs know about SMA, they also don't know about genetic testing. The GPs, obstetricians and IVF clinics that *do* know about genetic testing often only refer patients for carrier testing when there is a known family history of a genetic disorder. However, more than 95 per cent of babies born with a genetic disorder have no known family history, like us. This means the medical practice of only testing those with a family history of genetic conditions is ineffective, flawed and, quite frankly, dangerous.

In my opinion, genetic testing is one of the most important things you can do when preparing to have a child. It allows you to make sure you are not at risk of passing on something that could make the child's life painful or, in some circumstances, even kill them.

Even already having a healthy child does not mean you are

not a carrier and couldn't pass on a genetic disorder to future children. We know couples who have had one or even two healthy children then their next has been affected. They just got lucky the first times.

In 2018, the American College of Obstetricians and Gynaecologists released a paper recommending such a test for all potential parents. And the Royal Australian and New Zealand College of Obstetricians and Gynaecologists has recently changed its previous stance to now recommend: 'Information on carrier screening for other genetic conditions should be offered to all women planning a pregnancy or in the first trimester of pregnancy. Options for carrier screening include screening with a panel for a limited selection of the most frequent conditions (e.g. cystic fibrosis, spinal muscular atrophy and fragile X syndrome) or screening with an expanded panel that contains many disorders (up to hundreds).'

If genetic testing reveals one or both parents are carriers of a genetic disorder and are at risk of passing it on to a child, there are options.

The first thing that will happen is a discussion with your doctor or genetic counsellor to talk about what the condition is, if there are treatment options and the condition's severity. It may be a less serious genetic condition which, as a family, you decide whether you can live with after considering your family support, finances, treatment options, values, religion and so on. Hopefully it is a genetic condition that has a treatment or, even better, a cure. If you choose to proceed with a natural pregnancy and there is a treatment option then this knowledge is so important, as the sooner treatments are started the better in most circumstances.

If, however, the testing reveals the possibility of a severe, serious or life-threatening genetic disorder with limited or no treatment, or you simply want to be reassured that your child will not have the genetic condition passed on to them at all, around eleven weeks into the pregnancy and beyond it is considered safe to have a either a chorionic villus sampling (CVS) test, which takes a sample of placental tissue, or an amniocentesis test, which takes a sample of the amniotic fluid. These tests can show whether a baby has a genetic or chromosomal disorder, and depending on the results a decision can be made on whether to continue with the pregnancy or have a medical interruption. This is a very scary option and people will feel differently depending on their beliefs, but for some people this is the only way to have a healthy child who will not be born just to pass away, or to live in pain with a severe and chronic illness.

In-vitro fertilisation (IVF) is another option for ensuring a baby does not possess the possible genetic condition. In IVF, a fertility specialist can test embryos for any genetic conditions so only healthy, unaffected embryos will be implanted in the uterus; this is called preimplantation genetic diagnosis (PGD).

If we had had this information when we were planning to get pregnant, we know we would have done that genetic carrier test. Not everyone would, which is okay: some won't agree with it, some won't truly understand it, and some won't be able to afford it. Life is full of decisions we must make based on our own beliefs, ethics and values, and we all have the right to make decisions we believe are best for us and our families. But to make decisions you need to have all the information and, most importantly, to know what your options are. It is about choice. This is where we saw a huge gap between how Australia and the rest of world deals with genetics, a gap we were determined to close, in order to stop others feeling our pain. We wanted to change people's understanding of genetics, to increase the uptake of genetic carrier testing and, most importantly, to make access to it free and equitable.

Learning all this information after Mackenzie's diagnosis, it was hard not to hate the world and what was happening. We had begun by asking 'Why us?', but after discovering the statistics on genetics we started to think 'Why not us?' Genetic disorders are common and can happen to anyone. And without any change in the process surrounding genetic testing it would continue to happen to people for no reason other than DNA and bad luck.

None of this means we would change our time with Mackenzie in any way. Ever. Some people have asked us this question, which floors us. Of course not—we love our daughter. For us, we would live our time with Mackenzie a thousand times over, even the pain, but I would never choose for her to go through that again. I love her that much.

And despite everything we learned, nothing could change either Mackenzie's diagnosis or her future. Every day felt like an emotional balancing act as we lived on a knife's edge, worried that one wrong move would send us slipping deeper into the darkness of depression. But we knew we had to make a change or at least try to do something, even if our impact was small.

Our campaign

'You never know how strong you are, until being strong is your only choice.'

Bob Marley

In the first few weeks after Mackenzie's diagnosis, we spent hours sitting around when Mackenzie was asleep discussing SMA, genetics, genetic testing and how we felt the system had failed us. As we learned more, the discussion evolved and matured. Initially we were talking about how to stop SMA from devastating other lives, but then we realised it was so much bigger than this: SMA was just a symptom of the wider issue of genetic disorders.

We thought about how many children were suffering in hospital because of genetic disorders. The Jeans for Genes website revealed that one in twenty Australian children will be born with a genetic disorder or birth defect. I can't even fathom that. Of course, those genetic disorders vary in severity, but there is nothing more incomprehensible and confronting than to see a beautiful, innocent child who is affected by a condition that severely impacts their life.

Through genetic carrier testing, we realised people could be provided with information and choices. They could learn about the gene mutations they carry and what a child's chance is of being affected by a genetic condition. They could learn what, if any, treatments were available, or whether the condition was incompatible with life. Families deserve this knowledge and the choice of whether an existence that involves serious and life-threatening illness is something they are willing to risk, depending on their values and beliefs.

Some GPs, obstetricians and IVF clinics know about these tests and offer them, but the majority don't know about the tests at all. Some pathology labs are even in the dark—I remember when Jonny and I went to get our genetic carrier testing done, the pathologist had to call up their boss to ask what the test was.

Following Mackenzie's diagnosis, some of our friends and family tried to have these tests done but were turned away by doctors and labs. They were given a variety of reasons why the tests were unnecessary, from 'You have no family history', to 'Those tests don't exist in Australia' and 'You should be fine—it is rare and it will just cause you stress'. This made our blood boil. This has to change.

In some situations, genetic carrier screening may lead to a decision to end a pregnancy if the genetic condition is severe or incompatible with life, and I am aware that this may make some people uncomfortable. But it is also important to note that screening can mean affected children will get earlier treatment to help with their condition, perhaps saving them a lot of pain and heartache. I remember being told about one little girl who was born with a condition the doctors could not diagnose.

For years they did tests until she was close to passing away. In a last-ditch test, the doctors checked for a rare genetic condition. It came up positive and it was a condition that had a treatment—not a cure, but at least a treatment. The little girl is now at home, healthy and happy, and luckily there wasn't any irreparable damage. But if genetic carrier testing had been done on the parents, they may have known there was a risk of the child being affected by that condition and a test and treatment could have been given at birth. Often, the earlier a treatment is given, the better the outcome.

While I know the topics of genetic testing can be confronting, I want to cut off the inevitable discussions about designer babies or eugenics. Please understand that we are not talking about eye colour, gender or even missing limbs and blindness, we are talking about severe or lethal genetic conditions. I implore you to research what these conditions look like in real life, to see the experiences in Children's Hospitals and palliative care, to gain understanding on the matter. It still won't be for everyone and that is okay. Genetic testing is about choice.

Knowing the pain and heartache that could have been spared by a simple blood or saliva test made us angry—and determined. Knowing that a test that has long been around in the medical community, that could help save lives, stop pain and give people choice, isn't done routinely—that really hurt us. But the fact that this test is barely known about in the wider medical community was incomprehensible. What the fuck? Yes, we got angry. It was soul-shattering that something so simple could have prevented our baby from suffering a slow and potentially painful death. Why wasn't something being done about this?

Then there's the financial cost of genetic conditions on the healthcare system. For each family of a child with a genetic disorder there are specialist medical appointments, physiotherapy appointments, occupational therapists, psychologists, palliative care, medications, research and Centrelink carer payments, not to mention the severe emotional cost on the families. By offering routine free genetic testing, Australia could become a world leader in genetics, reduce the suffering of affected children, stop the emotional pain of families, save money, give treatments early and, most importantly, save lives. From every angle, routine genetic testing just seemed to make so much sense.

We often wondered *why us?* This is a question most people ask when tragedy strikes their family. Sometimes we wished this would happen to someone famous—not because we would ever wish this pain on anyone else, but because they would at least have the power and influence to help make a change. We are just normal people, what on earth could we do? We didn't know but we had to try.

After a while we decided to tell our story to those in power and make them aware of what is happening every day to normal families like ours. I decided to write to the federal health minister, Greg Hunt, the then prime minister, Malcom Turnbull, and our member of parliament, Scott Morrison. In the letter I described Mackenzie, how we had planned for the pregnancy, what it felt like to hear her diagnosis, explained her condition and what life now held for her, and what could have been different. My parents, with their years of public service experience, suggested we instead send our letter with a photograph of Mackenzie to every member of the Australian parliament, all 275 of them.

So that is what we did. I wrote the letter and my parents hand-addressed 275 envelopes and personally delivered them to Parliament House in June 2017.

Over the next couple of months, responses to our 'Mackenzie letter' trickled back to us. Some members of parliament didn't bother to respond at all or, worse, someone on their staff told us we had got the 'wrong' department, not realising we had written to every member as a representative of their constituents and asking them to personally make it their mission. In two cases anonymous government employees returned the photograph of Mackenzie along with a blank 'With compliments' slip, an act of disregard for our daughter that left us seething. Once my dad wrote a withering letter back as Mackenzie's grandad, explaining their mistake, but they never wrote back. We had to hold our anger and think of the long game.

Eventually, the majority of members replied, expressing their sorrow on hearing of Mackenzie's diagnosis, and some took it further by stating they would personally write to the federal health minister, Greg Hunt, urging him to meet with us and outlining their support for routine genetic carrier testing. Minister Hunt would have received dozens of letters from his parliament counterparts.

However, the people who amazed me are the ones who took it even further. Then deputy leader of the Opposition, Tanya Plibersek, personally called us to convey her sorrow and support, while then shadow health minister Catherine King offered full bipartisan support on anything the government actioned relating to SMA and genetic testing. Barry O'Sullivan rose in the Senate and delivered a five-minute speech on Mackenzie and SMA (which can be found on YouTube). David Coleman personally organised a meeting for us with the New South Wales health minister and came to Mackenzie's farewell party and sent us flowers when he learned of our loss. Ross Vasta, Terri Butler, Natasha Griggs and Karen McNamara all offered our family support. Most of these people knew Jonny's dad personally through his work at Parliament House and provided him a shoulder to lean on.

In addition, the responses we received from Malcolm Turnbull, Greg Hunt and the then treasurer Scott Morrison were also quite exceptional, but more on that later.

As the letters came in and things began to progress, we had another family meeting to discuss what to do next. Before we started meeting with any members of parliament, it was important to be clear about what we were actually asking for. So I wrote a ministerial brief, an extract of which follows (the full brief is in the appendix).

Recommendations
SMA specific
- That the Commonwealth Department of Health create and distribute SMA information packs to registered GPs, IVF clinics, obstetricians and midwives advising about the disease, its symptoms and prevalence and available testing.

Genetic carrier testing
- The federal government should make carrier screening for a large number of severe childhood disorders freely available to all couples who are considering a pregnancy or are early in a pregnancy;

- In order to implement such a program, a large-scale pilot project should be conducted as soon as possible to determine the operational requirements to offer pre-conception screening on a population-wide basis;
- Information on genetic carrier testing be sent to all relevant medical professionals;
- Genetic carrier testing be routinely recommended as part of care of pregnant families at all levels by GPs, IVF clinics, obstetricians and midwives;
- Accurate and unbiased information about genetic carrier screening be provided to every couple considering having a family and testing encouraged, bearing in mind that a patient may decline any or all screening;
- Carrier screening should be done, and genetic counselling provided, ideally before pregnancy, however, it should be made available to any woman once she is pregnant;
- If an individual is found to be a carrier for a specific genetic disorder, their reproductive partner should be offered testing and genetic counselling about potential reproductive outcomes. Concurrent screening of the patient and her partner is suggested if the testing is undertaken during pregnancy;
- If both partners are found to be carriers of a genetic condition, genetic counselling should be offered to discuss options (i.e. prenatal genetic testing, termination or no further action);
- When an individual is found to be a carrier for a genetic disorder, they should be encouraged to inform their relatives, who are also possible carriers of the same mutation, of the risk and the availability of carrier screening;

- Carrier screening for a particular condition generally could be performed once in a person's lifetime, and the results could be documented and available in the patient's health record; and
- Both prenatal carrier screening and newborn screening be undertaken for genetic disorders as both have benefits.

Genetic carrier testing cost
- The cost of genetic carrier screening be covered/subsidised by the government.

Preimplantation genetic diagnosis cost
- The cost of PGD to be covered/subsidised by the government for those identified as being carriers of genetic disorders.

Obviously, during our campaigning our priority was always Mackenzie, so when she was awake our full attention was on her, but when she slept I spent time reaching out to people who I thought could help by using their voice or their platform. I was a woman on a mission: I wanted to make others aware of this hidden reality, this earth-shattering thing that no one was speaking about. I wanted to shout Mackenzie's name from the rooftops. Despite this passion, I was very scared of putting myself out there; I was a private person who didn't like attention. I knew this was going to be hard and exposing, but the idea of doing nothing was scarier to me.

I started slowly, at first just using Instagram @mylifeof_love to talk about Mackenzie. I started with no followers but at the time I didn't care. All I wanted to do was talk about my daughter and share photos of her, just like any other proud parent. After a while people started following me, then more and more people wanted to hear about Mackenzie. I developed a strong Instagram family who seemed to always have my back and I cannot adequately express what that safe space and friendship gave me.

Eventually I wanted to take the next step. I needed to swallow my pride and reach out to influential people for help in spreading our story. I was a nobody with no voice—I needed people who had a platform.

The first person I wrote to was a hugely popular mummy blogger in Australia. At the time she had just one little girl not much older than Mackenzie, so I thought she might be sympathetic. In an email I explained Mackenzie's story and asked if she would help me spread the message about SMA and genetic testing. A month went by with no response, which seemed odd because she was prolific online and responded quickly to posts on her Instagram. So a month later I emailed again. This time I received a response within hours, but it was not quite the one I had been hoping for.

In her reply she berated me for having the 'gall' to ask her not once but twice to use her platform to talk about my daughter— apparently not even friends facing their own struggles had had the nerve to do such a thing. She made it clear that her platform was solely for her daughter, to show life's 'pretty things' and to make money. She suggested I go hassle a 'real celebrity' rather than making her feel like a bad person. I felt devastated, angry and ashamed at her reaction, questioning whether I been wrong in contacting her. Even if she didn't want to do it, even if what I had asked her was out of place, could she not have been kinder to me? To try to comprehend even for a second the pain I was feeling or put herself in my position?

Within the next few days the blogger launched a campaign to encourage people to be kinder to each other on social media; it was intended as some kind of kindness project in response to some hurtful emails she had received recently. I was flabbergasted. Did she see my email to her as hurtful? Did she not see how her own email would impact a grieving mother? Her hypocrisy left me reeling and I instantly stopped following her on Instagram. Maybe she is a lovely person—lots of people seem to think so—but that wasn't what I saw. This was the first of many shocking reactions to our story. It put me back in my box for a long time.

Asking for help is hard for me; it makes me feel vulnerable and exposed. But I learned early on that change doesn't happen unless you nudge it along, so I had to push myself outside my comfort zone, expose my heart and ask for help. It didn't come naturally, and this episode left me nervous about approaching anyone else for a long time.

Unfortunately, this wasn't my only negative interaction. Over the next two years I would sometimes meet celebrities at events or around Sydney, some of Australia's sweethearts, and if we got to talking or I felt strong enough, I would talk to them about Mackenzie. Some were moved and promised to help us raise awareness by posting about Mackenzie but never followed through. Others flat out refused to assist us. The rational part of me knew that they are perfectly within their rights to say no: in most cases they didn't know us and they must have people asking things of them all the time. But another part of me took it personally, like they were slapping Mackenzie. I have cried many times over feeling like people don't care about the death of my child or of future children from SMA, and it hurt even more when I read their next Instagram post on something mundane like a pair of shoes. I wondered how they would behave if this was happening to them.

These days I mostly wait for people to offer to help or for media outlets to approach me to write about Mackenzie. Luckily, I've found that I rarely need to ask people to assist because once others started telling our story, media offers began coming in on their own. One after the other, people wanted to tell Mackenzie's story and help to raise awareness. We were blown away by the response. Media is certainly not something we are comfortable with, especially as police officers—we like our privacy and don't want attention for safety reasons. We also knew putting ourselves out there would expose us to online personal attacks. However, we quickly learned that no one was going to listen to our message without hearing our personal story.

The people in media with whom we had contact were beautiful souls. I know there must be some bad ones out there but I haven't met them. Nearly every single journalist who has written about us has stayed in contact and continues to follow me on Instagram. For us these were people who have wanted to use their voice for good, to help make a change and to help a family struck down by a situation over which they had no control. The ripple effect of their actions just keeps going.

Despite my initially brutal Instagram experience, what happened from there was beautiful. The kindest people began reaching out to us to help, like the beautiful Australian actress Teresa Palmer. She and her team at Your Zen Mama, which

Teresa runs with Sarah Wright Olsen, published our story on their website and have also published other pieces I have written.

And then came my best and kindest supporter, Marcia Leone, otherwise known as @NotSoMumsy. I cannot express the love and compassion she has shown my family when she really didn't know us at all. To look at Marcia, a long-limbed and glamorous model with the picture-perfect family and house, most wouldn't know that she has suffered her own losses. She lost two sisters when she was younger and then struggled with secondary infertility after the birth of her first baby. She created her business around being a mum but is also someone who gives back to others. Marcia not only published our story, raising a huge level of awareness for Mackenzie and genetic testing, but she did a charity fundraiser for Mackenzie's neurologist Dr Michelle Farrar's research into SMA. She also messages me from time to time just to see how I am, which is perhaps a small thing but has a huge impact on my life. I know she has my back.

Later, television sports presenter Erin Molan reached out to us also, one of the kindest and most beautiful women I have ever met. She got behind us, despite already being involved with so many charities. Erin is one of the main reasons this book came about. I have so much time for that woman.

As our story got out, I heard from people who wanted to get genetic testing—sadly, this usually ended with them contacting me saying they weren't successful. We were raising awareness among the public but still not reaching the medical professionals. People just couldn't get the testing they wanted.

This is when I started my blog, www.mylifeoflove.com. I had been using my Instagram account to spread our message but it is so restrictive in the number of words you can write, so a blog seemed to a be a way in which I could explain what a genetic test was and how to get one.

While I was preaching from the small platform I had, we had a couple of strong members of parliament working behind the scenes. David Coleman was working hard to organise a meeting for us with the New South Wales health minister, Brad Hazzard. And Senator Barry O'Sullivan arranged a meeting for us with the assistant federal health minister, Dr David Gillespie.

In August 2017, we met with Dr Gillespie at Parliament House. We were already travelling to Canberra for an event organised by SMA Australia, a support and education organisation for SMA, to raise awareness and campaign for the addition of nusinersen onto the PBS. Jonny, Mackenzie and I attended the event flanked by both sets of our parents, David, Wendy, Ross and Linda. We sat at a table with Mackenzie in our arms as families spoke to politicians about their children's lives, followed by professionals like Dr Michelle Farrar explaining what could be done in the treatment space. This was a very difficult meeting for us because it was primarily focused on getting nusinersen on the PBS, and while this was an important step for all of the SMA community, it was not what our focus had become. We cared about the broader issue of genetic testing.

Following the SMA event, Jonny, Mackenzie, myself and Dr Farrar met with Dr Gillespie. I had talking points, pamphlets and research papers and we went in feeling excited, nervous and prepared. Sadly, this meeting was not at all what we had hoped for. I am not sure what background information Dr Gillespie had received but he didn't seem to know why we were there, nor did he seem to think he could change anything we were talking about. After fifteen minutes we were ushered out feeling deflated and not at all heard.

But we dusted ourselves off and one week later were back in Sydney to meet with the state health minister, Brad Hazzard. This meeting was everything we could have hoped for. Minister Hazzard was responsive, personable and professional. Also present were his assistant, a genetics counsellor he had invited, David Coleman, Dr Farrar, Jonny and me; my parents looked after Mackenzie while we met. In the meeting I described our lives, Mackenzie's diagnosis and what we hoped to achieve. Minister Hazzard asked a few questions of the doctors in the room and at the end announced that he would help us. He promised to personally write to every GP in New South Wales introducing them to genetic testing and encouraging them to offer genetic carrier testing to all potential parents. And he actually did.

Our family and Dr Farrar left the meeting in tears. The change was coming.

Making memories
with Mackenzie

'The best and most beautiful things in this world cannot be seen or even heard, but must be felt with the heart.'

Helen Keller

When we found out we would lose Mackenzie, Jonny had only been back at work for two weeks. He instantly stopped work. We were lucky that we had both been in the public service for around twelve years each, which meant we had some personal and annual leave that allowed us to stay home and focus on our baby. We used up every minute of leave we had to give us time to dedicate our lives to her.

We were also so lucky to have the support of friends and family around us, including those who recognised that we would need financial help. A GoFundMe campaign was set up, and that money gave us the time and the resources to make precious memories with our daughter. Without it we would have had to go back to work or take out a debilitating loan. That GoFundMe threw us a lifeline.

We sat down and wrote a list of the things we wanted Mackenzie to experience in the time we had left with her, a baby bucket list. Number one on that list was travel. We scrambled to organise a passport for Kenzie, paying extra for the rush job. During her naps I studied locations that would have good medical resources if she got sick. But in the end we realised taking her overseas wasn't an option. Travel insurance for a terminally ill baby was possible but very expensive, and ultimately it wouldn't be the best choice for her wellbeing. It was a blow initially but we soon came up with an alternative. What better than to show her the country she was born in?

Our first holiday with Mackenzie was organised by our hospital social worker, who had put in an application to the Starlight Children's Foundation charity on our behalf. These sorts of organisations don't tend to do holidays for babies, being of the belief that babies cannot gain enjoyment from travelling. But Starlight could see that as a family we needed this trip and we needed the memories. We were lucky enough to be offered a trip to Broome for a week and within two days of finalising the arrangements, we were off! We honestly didn't know how long we would have her for so we felt like we had to rush.

The memories of that holiday are some of our best. We were, and remain, so grateful. We spent the time pretending to be a normal family on their first holiday. We flew to Perth on the way to Broome, and just the simple act of walking along the Swan River as a family was bliss. When a dolphin popped up out of the water, it felt like a memory that would last.

In Broome, we decided to move south for a few days to the Eco Beach Resort. Glamping on a private beach dotted with hammocks was amazing. We named the little gecko and green tree frog that stayed in our tent, always checking they weren't going to surprise us before going to the toilet or the shower. We have so many photos of us lying with Mackenzie in the hammocks on the private beach or in our glamping tent. We always undressed her if it was warm enough—it had been a cold winter in Sydney, so this was her first chance to enjoy warm air on her skin.

Mackenzie would often sleep cradled between Jonny's legs as they swayed in a hammock while I went to arrange drinks and sandwiches for lunch. One day I noticed a sign in the office area advertising helicopter rides along the red cliffs that afternoon, a fifteen-minute trip for $100. On a whim, I booked us in. It wasn't what Jonny expected me to come back with! But an hour later we climbed into the helicopter with Mackenzie strapped to my chest in a wrap. As the helicopter took off I looked down to see a wide eye peering up at me, but by the time we landed she was fast asleep. An experience perhaps more for us, but a memory we treasure.

The owners of the resort knew our story, so on our last evening they set up a table under fairy lights on the cliff edge to watch the sunset. I remember Mackenzie looking up at those lights with awe as they sparkled back at me in her eyes.

Back in Broome, we went to a microbrewery with Mackenzie and it was here that we started our tradition of dipping her dummy in anything she could taste. On this trip we learned she loved mango beer and aioli. As far as we were concerned, she could experience everything we could give her.

One night we drove our car across the red dirt out into the middle of nowhere. There were no lights around and the stars spattered the sky like a thousand strings of fairy lights. It was magical. I remember the look of wonder and awe in Kenzie's eyes as Jonny and I hugged her in silence, looking up. It was there, in that magical place, that we thought Mackenzie was like a shooting star—she would shine fast but bright.

Another day we took Kenzie to a pearl farm. During the presentation about how pearls were made Mackenzie was a little cranky, so I swayed her in my arms away from the group so we didn't bother them. The next part of the tour was by boat on the crystal-clear water alongside white sand. It looked gorgeous but I didn't want to disturb the group if Mackenzie grizzled, but the whole group convinced me to jump on board with them. It was so kind of them and a lovely memory, and she did really well. Back at the shop, we picked a pearl to take home—my Mackenzie pearl.

Finally, the day before we left, we organised a ride on one of the only hovercrafts in Australia. It felt so odd as it took off, gliding along the mudflats. The tour included a walk to view dinosaur footprints preserved in rock. As we were walking Mackenzie needed to be fed, so the group moved on to see more footprints while I stayed. Mackenzie was nestled in her wrap latched onto my breast as I stood in the ancient footprints, with no one else in sight. It was just us in that moment, and I was happy. Later, the hovercraft took us out on the mudflats to watch the sun set, accompanied by champagne and cheese. The people on that tour never knew that they were involved in creating such wonderful memories with our little girl.

On that first family holiday we did everything we could that might allow Mackenzie to feel, touch, see, hear, smell or experience something new. Those memories will last us a lifetime and we can never thank the Starlight Foundation enough for the chance to make them. If ever there was a worthy cause for people to donate to it is that.

Back to Sydney and reality, there were more appointments to check that Mackenzie was still okay. We came to do these in three-week blocks. We would spend a week doing all her appointments—neurologist, physiotherapist, hydrotherapy and nutritionist—to check she wasn't deteriorating and didn't need anything different. Then as soon as we were given the all clear we were off for a week or two on our next adventure. Sometimes our families were also able to join us.

On one trip we had a getaway with my side of the family in Kangaroo Valley on the south coast. We went to the local pub, watched movies, played board games and had a bonfire. It was magical to have this time as a family, and my precious niece and nephew got to know their baby cousin.

Another time, Jonny and I took Mackenzie to Cairns to see Jonny's extended family, which was so special. We had family catch-ups, dipped Mackenzie's toes in the water at Cape Tribulation and took her on the train up to Kuranda where Jonny's Aunty Angela works. In Kuranda, we took Mackenzie into the butterfly sanctuary and the bird aviary; the look on Kenzie's face when a butterfly landed on her nose was priceless. We stayed at the family's holiday house at Palm Cove where we swam with her in the pool and let her sleep in our arms as we read. One night we showed her the super moon as we walked along the jetty.

Then there was our road trip from Sydney to Byron Bay, stopping at the Big Banana at Coffs Harbour on the way. I'm not sure what we were thinking when we organised such a long drive but she took it like a champ! We stayed at the Byron at Byron rainforest resort, which was magic and where we made some of our favourite videos of Mackenzie. Jonny gave her an Australian citizenship test, which basically meant we let her taste Vegemite for the first time. She was a bit unsure at first, mouthing it with a grimace, but then opened her mouth for more. I think she passed! One morning after she'd woken early, Jonny rugged Mackenzie up and they went to watch the sun rise near Tallow Beach. This has become a very special spot for us all and one we have returned to many times. Naturally, we also took her stargazing at the lighthouse, the most easterly point in Australia.

We also went to the snow because we wanted Mackenzie to experience all types of weather sensations. Most of our family were able to make a daytrip from Canberra up to Mount Selwyn. While the cousins, aunt, uncle and grandparents tobogganed, we had our cute little snow bunny snuggled in our arms.

One of her other trips was to Tasmania to visit the property my parents own down there. We fished, went platypus spotting, went to apple orchards and wineries, visited the art museum Mona and took her sailing.

Jonathan: I think some people wonder why we travelled so much with Mackenzie after she was diagnosed. After all, wouldn't travel only cause her unnecessary stress? She's only a baby—how could she possibly care where she is?

Obviously, there were selfish reasons for wanting to travel with Mackenzie. With the help of the Starlight Foundation, we chose the remote town of Broome for two main reasons. Firstly, we wanted Mackenzie to feel sun and saltwater on her skin, and secondly, as neither of us had ever been there before, all our memories of Broome would involve Mackenzie.

I can tell you with complete certainty that Mackenzie loved her travels. I could tell you many stories about the pleasure our travels brought her but I'll give you one example that brings tears to my eyes to this day. During the winter we had Mackenzie, Rachael and I arranged a daytrip to the snow. Both sets of grandparents came along, as did Rachael's brother and his family.

While we were all taking turns on the toboggan and generally having fun together, it started to snow. These big flakes were falling heavily around us, which felt magical. I became concerned that Mackenzie may get cold, but when I got to Rachael I found a happy little girl in her arms, looking wide-eyed at the sky and sticking her tongue out to catch snowflakes on it.

Now that might seem like a simple thing to you, but let me help you understand why it was such a magnificent moment for me. As Mackenzie got older, the effects of the SMA obviously worsened. I saw my daughter's increasing curiosity about the world around her, but her body failed her a little more each day, so she couldn't play with toys, pick up simple objects or generally explore like other children her age. Mackenzie catching snowflakes on her tongue was the one and only time I saw her do something fun in the same way any other child her age would. She had that experience the same as any other child, and for a moment she didn't have SMA.

We cherish the fact that Mackenzie travelled by boat, car, taxi, Uber, train, plane, hovercraft, yacht, golf buggy, helicopter and ferry.

She saw snow, rainforests, sand, the sea and deserts.

She saw sunsets and sunrises, beaches and rivers.

She saw fireworks, sparklers, stars, fairy lights and light shows.

We went to the zoo, where she saw lions, tigers, giraffes and elephants, as well as gazing at fish and dugongs at the aquarium. She went to the Archibald awards, the Museum of Old and New Art in Tasmania, Parliament House, the Vivid festival of light, and she even participated in the City2Surf.

Just to name a few.

As we travelled, we found different flavours to offer to her to taste. In Palm Cove we discovered she was a huge fan of balsamic reduction!

On the eleventh day of every month we celebrated her month-day, knowing she would most likely never live to see her first birthday. We would sing happy birthday and get her a cake, one that had icing, custard or something else nice that she could taste. We were never concerned about her sugar intake as we decided from the beginning that our little girl could have anything she wanted!

When we were with Mackenzie we felt like the luckiest people in the world. As her parents we were given the honour of showing this precious little soul the world we live in. We got to watch her reactions as she experienced new sights, sounds and sensations. Despite the tragedy of our situation, we didn't want to be anywhere else.

Happy normality

'In some ways, suffering ceases to be suffering at the moment it finds a meaning.'

Viktor Frankl

Although we went on many trips to make sure Mackenzie experienced the world, some of our best memories are of just being at home with our baby girl. Watching her coo and smile in some normal activity, sometimes, for just a minute, we could forget we would lose her.

At home we enjoyed a simple life. Kenzie wasn't the greatest of sleepers, which we think is partly because she wasn't moving much to work off energy. She tended to wake up every two to three hours—it could have been SMA or just being a normal baby. As well as dealing with SMA, ultimately, we were still just new parents trying to find our way.

At night, I would wake up every two hours to feed her, which of course could be tiring, but I never felt the need to complain, I enjoyed every second. And boy oh boy, could my baby feed!

She was breastfed almost exclusively up until we lost her, and each feeding session took no longer than five minutes. She fed on one side and was done, often falling into a blissful milk-drunk sleep with her mouth open. This was quite unheard of for an SMA baby; most couldn't be exclusively breastfed due to issues swallowing and ended up having a feeding tube.

She was so in love with the breast that she would coo as it was approaching. It was, and remains, my favourite sound in the world. During these moments only the two of us existed. She would sometimes look up at me with love in her eyes, but more often than not she was serious and determined, concentrating on the job.

Kenzie usually woke each morning between four and five o'clock. Because I had spent a lot of the night up with her, Jonny would look after her for the first two hours while I slept. He describes his mornings like this:

Jonathan: It would happen the same way almost every morning: any time between 4.30 and 5.30 a.m. a poke in the ribs and a two-word sentence would signal my shift had started. Two words that would drag me from my slumber, wearily to my feet and to Mackenzie's side.

'She's awake.'

With a groan, I would take Mackenzie to her bouncer in the lounge room and orient her towards *Sesame Street* playing on ABC iview. This would usually give me time to make a coffee and gulp down breakfast to help me wake up and find the energy to entertain her long enough for Rachael to get some much-needed sleep.

After a little while, Mackenzie would tire of *Sesame Street* and begin to grumble. Now it was time for The Wiggles to shine. I've heard many parents complain about having to listen to The Wiggles, but let me tell you, they are angels from heaven. Mackenzie and I would watch, listen, dance and obviously sing along to our favourite songs for ages. She loved the colours, the characters and the music.

Eventually, if I was lucky, I would see her eyelids grow heavy, and I would play either 'The Lion Sleeps Tonight', or '. . . Baby One More Time' on repeat while I bounced her rhythmically. I would do this for five minutes, making sure not to make eye contact for fear I would distract her.

If I couldn't get her to sleep it would inevitably end with me handing a crying Mackenzie to a sleepy Rachael with another two-word sentence: 'Feed this.'

At the time I was aware that these mornings wouldn't last forever, but I don't think I could have imagined how fondly I'd look back on them.

Once Jonny had done his two hours, I would wake up and he would go back to bed for a couple of hours. Usually Kenzie was ready for a nap by the time I had woken up so after a quick feed she would lie on my chest and sleep while I watched *Offspring* or some other show. I loved those hours. I never tried to put her down in a cot or a bassinet to sleep—I wanted her in my arms. I had nowhere else to be.

Around 8.30 a.m., Kenzie would be up from her nap, which meant it was dress-up time! I got so much pleasure in dressing her. Honestly, if baby stylist was a job, I would change careers in a second. (Is it?) So we would sing, dance, I would dress her in outfits, and we would do a photo shoot. Kenzie seemed to love it and the girl sure knew where the camera was!

Mackenzie's favourite song of all time was Britney Spears' '. . . Baby One More Time'. It was ridiculous how much she loved it. If she was crying we would play it and she would instantly stop and fall asleep. We had it on repeat constantly. I wish I could put videos in this book but if you want to see Britney working her magic on Kenzie, just have a look at my Instagram.

By nine or ten the whole household was up. Jonny and I would take turns to get ready. Every morning, without fail, as I stood in the shower I would look up to see Kenzie's head popping around the corner of the bathroom door. Jonny would hold her there (with him out of sight) as 'she' sang Britney. I still look up now as I shower, hoping to see her.

Once we were dressed we were ready for an adventure. We made sure she did something new every single day and it was documented in a diary with a photograph. It could be anything from walking around Centennial Park (a very special place for us) and having lunch, to seeing a new friend, going to the zoo or aquarium or just reading a new book. During our regular walks around Centennial Park, Kenzie would sleep, watch the trees overhead or listen to The Wiggles. Sometimes we would take her to the gym for a session with a personal trainer, taking turns to play with her as the other did squats.

By late afternoon we were often home and ready for our night-time routine.

From 5 to 6 p.m. Mackenzie went into her sensorium! Jonny had set up our bedroom for Kenzie's evening entertainment with dozens of different lights, anything to give her senses a treat. We projected YouTube sensory baby clips on the ceiling, had an octopus that shone stars on the walls and another projector that shone planets, and a set of speakers which emitted music and lights. She would absorb all the lights, colour, movement and sound with wonder and delight. Often when her grandparents were visiting, we left them in the sensorium with her, giving them some alone time with her and special memories.

By six o'clock she was usually done with the sensorium and it was shower time, which she loved! Jonny would hold her in the shower while I washed her, both of us singing her favourite songs as the water ran over her. Her shower favourites were 'Friend Like Me' and 'Prince Ali' from *Aladdin*, the *Muppet Show* opener where the guest star that 'Kermit' introduces is 'Miss Mackenzie Casella', and 'Old MacDonald'. In each song I was allowed to jump in at certain times to provide backup singing, but the main attraction was Jonny. 'Old MacDonald' was a favourite because I would pick the animals and Jonny would act them out. I loved picking the most obscure ones I could think of to try to trip him up, but the man has skills—you should hear his unicorn! She looked at him with wonder, like he had hung the moon.

Jonny was without a doubt her favourite toy and her constant source of entertainment. That man was born to be a dad. Whereas I was comfort and love.

After the shower, drying and changing her was my thing. While Jonny finished in the shower, I would take Kenzie to her room. Most nights she got a baby massage and was straight into her pyjamas. When my parents were staying with us, they got the job of drying and changing. Mum would always do a long relaxing baby massage with essential oils and Dad was responsible for entertainment.

Next up in the routine was food and her night-time songs. She would have a feed while I played her our special song, a beautiful instrumental version of 'Sweet Child of Mine' as Jonny heated up dinner. During this time, we didn't care about cooking. That was just time away from her, so we often had food delivered or ate whatever various kind people had dropped off for us.

After her feed she wasn't quite ready for bed, so we would pop her in the bouncer while we ate and then she would lie on my chest to sleep as Jonny and I watched television. Yes, if she was a 'normal' baby she probably would have been in her cot at this time of night, with a monitor and a proper self-settling routine, but our limited time left with her meant I *never* wanted her in another room. She liked sleeping on me and I loved that.

Around 10 p.m. we'd head to bed. Jonny would get himself ready first while I stayed on the couch with Kenzie asleep on my chest. Then he would scoop her off my chest, loving the challenge of keeping her asleep to give me more time to get ready for bed before we woke her for her next feed. Sometimes she would stir and sometimes it was impossible to wake her. The cuteness was unreal.

While I rushed to get ready for bed, Jonny would change her nappy and get Kenzie into her sleep suit, which he called her 'flight suit'. Once she was in it they would go on a 'booby hunt' while I finished running around. Jonny would hit play on the song 'Danger Zone' by Kenny Loggins and fly Kenzie around the house searching for the booby until I was ready and in bed. At that time Kenzie would catch sight of the booby and with Jonny's assistance come in for 'landing'. There was never a dull moment with Jonny, and Kenzie loved every second!

After a feed we would give her a cuddle and then put her in her bassinet, which was next to our bed. With a few rocks she generally went straight to sleep. Another beautiful day.

As you can maybe tell, our time with Mackenzie was filled with songs and laughter. Jonny has a pretty good ability to turn anything into a song and I have developed a few skills myself, so she was constantly surrounded by music, laughter, light and love. Our style of parenting was to soothe with love, and anything she wanted she could have. We were given a unique situation and did what we could to bring light to her life.

I love that despite the longing and pain I feel whenever I miss Mackenzie, when I write about her in this way I am not crying. Instead I smile when writing about our days with her. These memories are everything to me. They fill my heart with joy.

Losing Mackenzie

'I will never forget the moment your heart stopped and mine kept going.'

Angela Miller

At the start of October 2017, we took Mackenzie to Tasmania for her seventh month-day, where my parents have some land and moor their boat. We rented a house in Huonville with Mum and Dad and had a beautiful holiday. Kenzie loved it—four of her favourite people all giving her different sensations and love. We hiked through forests, took her fishing and platypus spotting, and went down to Bruny Island, one of the southernmost points of Australia. We had almost reached all of the tips of Australia on our travels with her.

For Mackenzie's actual month-day we went sailing for the day on my parents' yacht down the Huon River. We brought along a few different cakes for her to try new flavours and sang happy birthday. For some of the sailing trip she and I lay below on the bed and watched *The Wiggles*, and then when she was napping

I popped back up with the others. Later I sat up on deck with her nestled asleep in my arms. It is such a beautiful and perfect memory for me.

At the end of our holiday, Mum, Jonny, Kenzie and I flew back to Sydney to pack up our house in south Sydney. We loved our house, but it was too far away from the hospital, and Kenzie didn't enjoy the time in the car. So we had found an apartment to rent closer to Sydney Children's Hospital. Dad was going to stay on in Tassie then fly up later to help us move.

A couple of days after we got back to Sydney, Kenzie had a bad night's sleep. She was unsettled and a little cranky. Bad sleeping wasn't unusual for Mackenzie, but she didn't often stay up all night crying. She also appeared to have a bit of congestion.

In the morning, Jonny and I were both exhausted. We discussed this unusual behaviour and around 7 a.m. decided to call her palliative care team, who said they would come around and check on her. However, for a variety of reasons they did not arrive until much later, and by then it was too late.

Around 11 a.m. I was on the couch with Kenzie while Mum packed up our kitchen and Jonny took a nap. As I sat smiling at Kenzie, I noticed she was turning a funny colour, becoming pale blue and white. I yelled out to Mum to come and check what I was seeing, hoping I was imagining it. But she saw it too.

Mum grabbed Mackenzie from me and slapped her on her back to try to loosen whatever was blocking her airways. I called an ambulance, explaining our situation, then ran to wake up Jonny. I don't even remember my call to the ambulance. I ran back to the living room where Mum was about to give Mackenzie CPR, but at that moment we noticed her colour coming back.

We sat and watched her breathing as we waited for help to arrive, vigorously rubbing her back to try to move whatever was stuck. We tried to talk calmly so Mackenzie would be calm too, but inside we were terrified.

The ambulance arrived. The paramedics were grim and worked quickly and quietly as they examined her. They put her on a breathing apparatus. It felt so surreal. We decided that I would get into the ambulance with Mackenzie, Jonny would follow the ambulance in our car and Mum would stay to contact people. Never again would I return to that home filled with all our belongings and memories.

Jonathan: I was fast asleep when Rachael came bursting into the bedroom yelling that Mackenzie had stopped breathing and the ambulance was on its way. I leaped out of bed, fumbling to get dressed. As panic set in, I very deliberately took a few deep breaths to slow myself down and switch to a work mindset. Very rarely will you see emergency service personnel run to the scene of an emergency; walking helps them keep their cool and assess the situation in a safer and more complete way. I dressed myself, took a few breaths and walked into the living room.

Before I knew it, the ambulance had arrived and the paramedics were in the house asking questions. One asked to see the Do Not Resuscitate order. Still in shock and denial, Rachael said, 'This isn't that.' The officer turned back towards Mackenzie. After hearing Rachael's reply, I looked at the situation in front of me and said to myself, 'Yes, it is.' Retrieving the DNR from the drawer, I handed it to the officer, who was grateful.

I got into the ambulance and lay on the stretcher with Kenzie on my chest. With lights and sirens the ambulance sped to Sydney

Children's Hospital. The paramedic asked me questions that I answered the best I could, but I could see from her face that she was worried. So I did the only thing I could do and sang quietly in Kenzie's ear, trying to calm us both.

At emergency there were around twenty people waiting for us, including Mackenzie's neurologist, Dr Michelle Farrar. I could see by everyone's faces that we were not in a good situation. Michelle later told me that as we came out of the ambulance, she didn't think Mackenzie would make it through the next hour.

A blur of tests and terror followed and eventually we were moved from emergency upstairs to the intensive care unit (ICU) where they covered her little face with a new and more permanent oxygen mask. I wish we had known at the time that we would never again see her for more than a few seconds at a time without that mask. I would have soaked in every single contour of her face and kissed her beautifully soft skin.

Initially Kenzie was awake, and we tried desperately to entertain her with The Wiggles and singing. I still remember her little eyes peering over the oxygen mask, pleading with me to pick her up and make it better. I felt useless. My heart was being squeezed in a vice; I could physically feel it happening, like my heart was actually breaking. I wanted to scream and be sick but I had a little girl relying on me.

Eventually the relaxation drugs they had given her kicked in and she lost consciousness. Part of me was thankful because it meant she wasn't in pain, but at the time I didn't know I would never see her awake again. To this day I hope against all hope that from that time onwards she couldn't feel anything.

For the next four days we watched her vitals get dangerously low, then dangerously high, then stabilise. Her heart rate was skyrocketing and so was her temperature, but her limbs slowly began to go cold. I wanted to wrap her up to keep her warm, but she needed the sheets off to help cool her body temperature down. I would put cold cloths on her warm head but her little fingertips felt like ice. The nurses and doctors would give her paracetamol or ibuprofen to bring her temperature down, and she would appear better for a little while before struggling again. We went from thinking we could take her home to fearing she wouldn't make it and then back again. It was a loop of highs and lows filled with desperation.

For the first twenty-four hours we didn't sleep or leave Mackenzie's side, and after that there was always one of us there. It was as if we felt that by being there constantly we could somehow protect her from harm and bring her back safely to health. We barely ate and had to be ripped away and sent upstairs to shower. Every fibre of our beings needed to be with her, but we noticed her vitals would sometimes get worse when we were around which we put down to her somehow knowing we were there, so at times I forced myself to move away and allow her rest.

Since the moment she had been taken off my chest when we arrived at the hospital, I had only been able to hold her once. She wasn't allowed to breastfeed and had a nasal tube inserted, so I sat beside her and pumped my milk in the hopes that I could give it to her when she got better. It all felt so wrong.

I kept showing photos and videos of Mackenzie to the nurses and doctors. She was covered by so much medical equipment and I wanted the people who were caring for her to know the little girl who was underneath it all. Our little girl.

Our parents were at the hospital much of the time but also unpacking at our new apartment, trying to keep busy and be helpful. Eventually the whole family was at the hospital to visit Kenzie and us but I was hardly aware of this, being so focused on Mackenzie.

When we first arrived in the ICU the two heads of the unit met with us in a small family room near her bed in case Kenzie needed us. I started to hate going into that room. They sat us down and explained the seriousness of what was happening to Mackenzie. Blood tests had revealed that Kenzie had the common cold—that was all. But it was enough to cause this emergency because SMA meant her little body could not fight it off. The mucus had filled her lungs and one of them had collapsed. They put in a feeding tube and were giving her morphine for any pain, but too much could slow her breathing and make it harder for her to recover. They gave paracetamol for her fever, but it was getting so high that it alone wasn't working so ibuprofen was added, although it could cause stomach issues since she wasn't feeding. It was a constant balancing act, back and forth.

In these meetings over the next few days, Jonny and I were asked to reiterate our priorities. We always said the same thing: we wanted more time with her but not at the expense of her quality of life. The most important thing was her comfort at all times. We made it clear we did not want her to suffer or to be put on life support.

We talked briefly to a couple of the parents of children in the ICU. One boy had a head injury after a fall; it was touch and go for a little while but eventually the mother was given the good news that he would be going home. When we congratulated her she said, 'Don't worry, your little one will be next.' We explained that Mackenzie had a terminal illness and would eventually pass away no matter what we did. This woman literally stopped speaking, backing away from us with fear on her face. Jonny and I looked at each other in disbelief at her reaction.

Every morning and afternoon Mackenzie would have chest x-rays. And then three times a day she would have suctioning to clear her chest. This began with a physiotherapist tapping her chest for about ten minutes to loosen up the mucus. Mackenzie liked this part and often fell asleep, at least at the start when she was conscious. But even afterwards, when she was unconscious all the time, we could tell what she liked and didn't like by her heart rate, and the tapping seemed to soothe her. After the tapping, though, they had to put a tube down her throat and into her lungs. A physiotherapist would push down hard on her chest while a nurse suctioned the mucus out. Jonny always left the room, unable to watch, but I stayed because I felt like I owed it to her. The suctioning was horrific and is burnt into my mind.

At one stage her vitals dropped and doctors and nurses ran in to revive her. My mum began having a panic attack and I remember telling her to leave—I had to focus on Kenzie. Mum ran out of the room as Jonny and I watched what we thought was our baby dying. At one stage I noticed that the nurse who was hand-pumping oxygen to Mackenzie was chewing gum; it was such an everyday moment for the staff, I guess, but for us it was our world ending. Finally, they got her back. When they did, I slid down the wall in the corner of the room and sat in a ball and cried.

Soon she turned a corner and it looked like her lungs were clearing. We became overconfident and thought perhaps she would be able to come home in a day or two. But somehow, either due to the nasal feeding tube or the ibuprofen, Mackenzie developed an internal bleed in her stomach. She was given blood transfusions in the hope that soon the cut in her stomach would clot, so then they also had to drain her stomach of blood. I remember changing blood-filled nappies.

We had told staff early on that we would not keep making her fight at the cost of her quality of life. We wanted her to feel no pain. She was struggling to breathe by this point and her limbs kept getting colder. She hadn't opened her eyes for a couple of days.

We met daily with the heads of the ICU in that little room. We were honest about our wishes and priorities and they were honest with us about what they believed was best for her. In each conversation we all agreed where the final line was, but we still had another couple of things we could try that meant she might come through. But this also meant that we had to watch our little princess go through procedure after procedure. There were tubes and needles coming out of everywhere.

Her haemoglobin levels were being checked to see whether they had stabilised with the transfusions, hoping the cut that was causing the internal bleeding would clot and heal itself. We agreed we would give her some more time and do one last haemoglobin test, but we knew it was unlikely to fix itself.

Finally, after four long days and nights in the ICU, the time came for our final conversation.

Our little girl had fought so hard. The time had come to let her go.

They moved us into the big double room at the end of the ICU, pushing two beds together to make one large bed for us all to be in. Gently we placed her down on the bed and lay on either side of her.

We were given what the staff called a memory box—I know these are a wonderful thing for families like ours, but they just shouldn't exist. Inside the box was a pair of scissors to cut off locks of hair and plastic keepsakes to put them in. There were nail polishes to paint her nails and books to read to her.

We filled the room with her favourite music, mostly The Wiggles, in the hope that she could hear it. We whispered everything we wanted her to know. At one stage I remember hearing the nurses outside our room laughing; it was a shocking reminder that for everyone else this was just a normal day.

I hated cutting off bits of her hair and cried as we did it, but we also desperately wanted to keep part of her, the little bits of wavy hair that grew so blonde. So I brushed her hair and clipped some little sections, being careful not to change how she looked.

We decided not to paint her toenails: she was perfect as she was, an almost-new human. So instead we painted one of our toenails each, the second on the left, the one we believe is most closely connected to the heart. We call this our Kenzie toe and to this day the whole family always has this toe painted.

We read books to her, some of her favourites like *Moo, Baa, La La La*. The most memorable was a book that my dad read to her through his tears called *The Invisible String*, about the love that connects us. We needed her to know that she would always be attached to us, no matter where she was.

Our family came in two at a time. They read to her, touched her and said goodbye. I cannot express the pain that was in that room. They then all moved outside, leaving me, Jonny and Mackenzie.

We lay with her between us, the tubes still coming out of her and a mask covering her beautiful sleeping face. At some stage we fell asleep, all three of us cuddled in bed.

The doctor came in and woke us. Her haemoglobin had dropped, meaning the bleed hadn't stopped. It was time to take off her mask when we were ready.

We asked for a couple more hours while we said our goodbyes. We cried, shedding our tears all over her. We eventually fell asleep again, all touching and hugging.

When we woke up, Jonny and I looked at each other. We were supposed to let them know when it was time. When would it ever be time? But eventually we knew that holding on was only for us, not what was best for her. I walked out of the room and told her nurse it was time. The hardest words ever.

The head of the ICU came in and he and the nurse slowly removed all the now unnecessary tubes until all that was left was one cannula and her oxygen mask. The head then administered pain relief into her cannula so she wouldn't feel anything. He advised us that when we took the mask off, she might last minutes or hours while she tried to breathe on her own.

He took the mask off her face gently as she lay between me and Jonny. We finally got to see the beautiful face that we hadn't seen for days, but it didn't look like her anymore. She was puffy and yellow, with little marks and grazes where the mask had sat. My baby.

She took two tiny little breaths. We watched her little chest go down, up, down and then stop. She was gone.

The doctor put his stethoscope to her chest trying to find a heartbeat. After a minute he turned to us and said, 'I am sorry—she is gone.'

I wailed. I wailed so loudly as I rocked her little body back and forth. She was limp and cold. My baby.

For an age we just held her and cuddled her, breathing in her scent and touching her hair. Eventually we undressed and bathed her, wiping away all the blood from her nappy. We dressed her in her own clothes and swaddled her in a hospital blanket. They told us someone would take her down to the morgue, but I refused. No one would carry her to the morgue but me.

So I picked her little body up and held her tightly, with Jonny standing right beside me. We tried to look like I was holding a normal little baby, but one look at us would have revealed that our whole world had just been shattered. Slowly we walked out of the ICU and through the hospital down to the morgue.

I saw the cold silver morgue table they wanted me to put her down on, laid out with one of the same blankets that they use for babies when they are born. The same type that she was wrapped in when I first touched her. I bent down and lay her gently on the blanket. We kissed her goodbye.

Jonny and I held each other, howling in pain, the sound of a bag zipping up around our baby beside us.

Walking away from her was the hardest thing I have ever had to do. As we left the morgue we realised we were lost and alone, with no one to guide us and no baby in our arms. I had just left her with strangers in a cold room. Eventually we found our way back to the ICU room we had been given, devastated and in shock. We were expected to leave the hospital without her.

Mackenzie didn't deserve this. She was innocent and beautiful. She deserved to grow up, to go to school, to love, to laugh, to learn, to walk, to live. I know she would have contributed to our world in the most amazing way; she was the kindest, most beautiful little soul.

My heart will never be the same. I am no longer scared of death, because I will be with her again.

Jonathan: A children's intensive care unit is a place of complicated emotions. In one section you have families who attend for a night because of something relatively minor and can leave happily the next day, in the next you find the darkest and deepest sadness you will ever encounter. Although the ICU at Sydney Children's Hospital is flooded with fluorescent lighting, I was so intensely sad while I was there that in my mind it is dark.

Mackenzie was admitted with a cold, the resulting complications of which took her life. We were brought in for meetings several times a day with the doctors who were frank but kind. In the hospital we had to forgo our role as her parents and act as her advocate, to make decisions in her best interest and not ours. I believe my experience as a police officer helped a little to separate my emotions from the situation and make objective decisions based on the information given by the staff. The doctors later told us that we'd made the same decisions along the way that they would have for their loved ones, which provided some comfort after Mackenzie passed away. Returning home after such a devastating experience, it's easy to second-guess the decisions you made so this small sentiment from the doctors helped me move forwards in a way I'm sure they'll never know.

Mackenzie passed away in a dimly lit corner of the hospital surrounded by love. Rachael carried her to the morgue with me walking beside them, occasionally touching the cooling hand of my daughter. We got to the morgue, placed her on the table, and had to walk away.

The following days were pure torture. I felt like I would never understand this world. How were we expected to keep breathing and living?

When we left the hospital it was the middle of the day and the sun was shining. How could the world still be turning? Didn't they know what had just happened? Couldn't they feel it?

Initially we went to an apartment on Bondi Beach, booked for us by my parents. We couldn't face going home to the apartment that our family had kindly moved us into while we were in hospital, a new place but filled with her clothes and toys. The apartment in North Bondi was directly above the famous café Speedos. There was a mix-up with the keys which meant we had to drive around Sydney getting the right ones after leaving the hospital. It felt unfair and surreal.

When we finally got in, I walked through the door, crawled into bed and pulled the doona over my head. I remember our parents coming in one by one to kiss my head, but I didn't say a word. I was broken and had withdrawn deep inside.

I was still breastfeeding Kenzie when we went to hospital, so I had to keep expressing small amounts at a time to gradually reduce my supply and try to avoid developing mastitis. Jonny said watching me express my milk in the days that followed was one of the saddest things he had seen. I couldn't bring myself to pour it down the sink—it was milk *my* body had made to sustain *her*—so I began taking it with me into the water at Bondi Beach. Letting it wash out with the waves as I spoke to her.

During those days we only allowed family and my friend Kath to visit us—any more was too much. One day Jonny and I were sitting staring out at the ocean, tears rolling down our cheeks, when suddenly whales appeared, breaching and playing in the water. We called our parents to tell them, knowing they were all out together somewhere. In fact, they were standing on the opposite headland watching the same whales at play. They were standing on Mackenzies Point in Bondi. She was still with us, we knew it.

Mackenzie's grandparents

Written on behalf of Mackenzie's grandparents by Wendy Banham, with contributions by David Banham, Linda Casella and Ross Casella.

We eagerly anticipated Mackenzie's birth as she was Rachael and Jonny's first child. On one side of the family we already had two grandchildren, Alara and Henry (Chris and Alison's children)— and on the other side Linda and Ross already had three—Ethan, Sienna and Sophia (Rachel and Michael's children). We were so very happy to see a new addition to our growing family.

Mackenzie Karen was born at 2.44 a.m. on Saturday, 11 March 2017, and shortly after her birth both sets of grandparents were at the hospital. The day before, David and I had been to see Rachael and Jonny, intending to make a quick hospital visit but in the end staying for nearly twenty-four hours. After we arrived, Rachael was induced and began true labour. She asked us to stay around to help and we did whatever we could, providing moral support and back rubs. After many hours of labour, medical staff realised that Mackenzie wasn't going to be born naturally and finally decided that a caesarean was necessary. We weren't in the room for the birth but were nearby, and Ross and Linda arrived soon afterwards, after zooming up from Canberra.

There we were, the four of us, in a little alcove near the delivery room of the Royal Hospital for Women, in the quiet early hours of that Saturday morning, waiting. At around 4 a.m., Jonny wheeled in a little trolley with a bassinet and presented us with the closely wrapped bundle of Mackenzie. We peered into the bassinet and she stared back at us, quiet and calm, with that thousand-year-old gaze that newborns have. It was quite a surprise to see just how much she looked like Jonny (and Ross). We talked to her softly and spent some peaceful moments admiring her before Jonny whisked her off to see her mother, as Rachael had still not had the opportunity to hold her post-caesarean.

Later that day, when the other members of both families arrived, we returned to the hospital and everyone else became acquainted with their new niece and cousin. It was a lovely moment as we jointly celebrated Mackenzie, as she had been named. We loved the name, Mackenzie, and were particularly pleased with her middle name, Karen, which is also Rachael's and my middle name. Of course, Mackenzie was soon shortened to Kenzie.

So, life with Kenzie began and everything was normal.

It continued to be normal until the day, ten weeks later, when we got a call from Rachael and Jonny and learned that Kenzie was not developing as expected, that she could not physically do what came naturally to most ten-week-old babies. They told us that she had a disorder called spinal muscular atrophy (SMA), passed on from both sides of the family as a terrible inheritance—and it was terminal. We were in shock. None of us had ever heard of SMA or had any idea why it had shown up in little Kenzie or what it meant. It took a long while for the reality to sink in and for us to understand SMA, and Kenzie's prognosis. It wasn't good, two years at best, but it was more likely, we were told, that she wouldn't see her first birthday.

I remember being on the phone with Linda, talking, talking, both of us bewildered and disbelieving, trying to understand and accept. But there was no real acceptance of the situation, and over time we developed a form of resigned amnesia.

After our initial shock and grief, remarkably we somehow adjusted to our new normal, as ordinary people so often do. Kenzie seemed healthy and happy, and we loved her. However, we were driven to understand and the four of us researched and compared notes and became amateur experts on SMA. Rachael and Jonny felt strongly that this was not the time to mourn. And they were right: Kenzie needed us, and we put all our efforts into making her life the best that we could. As well as this we did our best to support Rachael and Jonny, to show them our love in whatever way they needed, and this was constant, although changing over time.

As two separate families, we also came together in unexpected ways. Our tragedy drew us closer, and we worked cooperatively whenever the need arose. Essentially, we treated every day with Kenzie as special but also completely routine. Rachael and Jonny had to make some truly heartrending and difficult decisions about Kenzie's care and future, but they also quickly decided that they wanted her to experience as much of life as a young baby can. They planned trips away and as well as these big events made sure that each day she had something new to experience. A taste or a smell, or a sound or movement (like Daddy singing and dancing with her, or her own little nightly disco to Britney Spears), being read a story (her favourites were *Moo, Baa, La La La* by Sandra Boynton and *Where is the Green Sheep?* by Mem Fox) or watching The Wiggles (she liked Emma), and she loved the theme song from the animated series *Daniel Tiger's Neighbourhood* (watching with a little grin on her face). While we were not always there for the day to day, Rachael and Jonny kept in close touch and made sure that we knew about and shared in Kenzie's life.

Gradually Rachael and Jonny's initial grief and bewilderment became something more active. They asked themselves how this could have happened given how carefully they had prepared during the pregnancy, doing everything they were asked and then some, taking every test that was offered. One test that hadn't been offered was the test that would have identified early in Kenzie's life that she had SMA, or, even earlier, that both Jonny and Rachael were carriers. They asked questions, firstly of the medical specialists and then, once they realised that these types of recessive genetic disorders are not routinely tested for unless there is a family history, they approached politicians. The more they spoke about this the more they were heard, until eventually they wrote a letter to each and every federal politician, telling their story and asking for something to be done so that others would not have to go through this same thing. And the politicians listened.

As parents and grandparents, we did our best to support and

cheer them on. Collectively, we helped with practical matters where we could, such as advice with writing the letters and delivering these to Parliament House, monitoring the media and giving feedback on their interviews, maintaining personal contacts and telling our story to anyone who would listen (and a few who wouldn't). We were and remain so very proud of our children's strength, resilience, determination and, above all, compassion in working to make a difference. Elsewhere in this book Rachael has told this story, so I won't repeat it here. Suffice to say that we are their biggest fans.

Everyone on both sides of the family came together frequently to spend time with them and Kenzie. We have many wonderful memories, including a family day spent tobogganing at the snow, watching the snowflakes falling gently on her face. As grand-parents, it felt like we couldn't get enough of her and her bright eyes, her smiles, chuckles and gurgles. Early on she lost the ability to move her body and legs and had only limited movement in her arms and hands. Despite that, she was exceptionally good at communicating with a look. You could have a whole conversation with her, exchanging smiles and laughter and chatting. And she would talk back in her baby way. We did our best to make her life beautiful and full of love. Remarkably, she was well and didn't need to go to hospital, except for routine medical checks and regular hydrotherapy sessions.

When Kenzie was seven months old, David and I had a trip away with Rachael, Jonny and Kenzie to Tasmania. It was memorable and fun. She even got to sail on the Huon River. Rachael and Jonny had arranged to move to a new apartment when they returned, so I went back with them to Sydney to help pack.

A few days after our return, Kenzie developed a cold and was clearly not well. Her condition deteriorated rapidly overnight and by the next day she was rushed to hospital. Despite this, the move could not be postponed and so everyone arrived to help finish with packing up the old house. Serendipity, in an odd way, because it meant that we were all there, close by, often at the hospital, while Kenzie was fighting for her life. Nothing can erase the memory of those terrible four days of anguish, hope, heartache and despair.

We four grandparents were at Rachael and Jonny's new home, working to unpack and organise things. I remember seeing Linda coming up the steps to the flat, in tears, and then Ross, myself and David dissolving in grief after we read Jonny's text: 'Sorry to do this by message . . . Kenzie passed away about 10 a.m. She's no longer struggling, no longer in distress. It was peaceful, in our arms listening to 'The Lion Sleeps Tonight'. Love you all very much.'

Our message back was, 'What can we say . . . we are devastated. Our beautiful little girl is gone but never forgotten. She is forever in our hearts and we love you so very much.' Linda and Ross sent, 'You are truly an inspiration to us. You have both taught us so much. An absolute honour to have met your beautiful Mackenzie and we will miss her dearly. We love you and hold you three close in our hearts for all time.'

As grandparents we grieve over her loss, and as parents we grieve doubly for our children's loss. A death in a family sets people apart, whether we like it or not, but the death of a child, someone so young, forces us to question deeply and wonder about the meaning of life. This can't help but change who we are and has brought us closer together than ever. We've all learned more about ourselves and what we are capable of than we ever thought possible. We remember her every day, but more than that, Kenzie continues to inspire us to be better people, and to make her life have a deeper meaning.

What do we do now?

'You were unsure which pain is worse—the shock of what happened or the ache for what never will.'

Simon Van Booy

The days after we lost Mackenzie were a bad dream from which we could not wake. I wanted to sleep because it would give me some relief, but the catch was that every time I woke up I had to remember once more that she was gone. I started to use sleeping tablets in order to make sure I only woke up just that once in the morning rather than fifteen times a night. It would still hit me like a tonne of bricks, but at least this way I wasn't waking up multiple times remembering, just that one smashing realisation every morning.

Each time I remembered it was like being stabbed in the heart; I am surprised the world couldn't hear it cracking and bleeding. If how I felt was made physical then I would have been bloodied and bruised. I would have had broken bones poking through my skin, my muscles would have been shredded and exposed as blood flowed out of me. But my pain was not physical, it was all inside me where no one could see the complete and utter devastation.

We tried to tell ourselves that we were lucky in how Mackenzie died. She was not in and out of hospital for months on end, suffering constantly. We never needed the at-home palliative care teams. Mackenzie never needed any medical devices at home and to look at her, you would never have known she was ill. How can a world exist where you try to be thankful that your daughter's illness and death was not a worst-case scenario?

A few days after Mackenzie died, we left the place in Bondi and took the cautious steps into our new apartment. We didn't even get a reprieve from life to quietly grieve. There was so much expected of us. Adult responsibilities that felt far beyond our capabilities, impossible decisions that we couldn't avoid.

We had to find a funeral home—how do you pick a funeral home that you trust with your child?

We had to decide on her final outfit. Should she be in something comfortable? Something cute? Something new or something familiar?

Would we give her something to take with her? Her favourite doll or toy? Her favourite dummy on a clip, or do we keep that one for ourselves?

Would we cremate her? Where would we keep her ashes?

How would we say goodbye? Who would be there? What music would be played?

How would we want to remember her?

How is a parent supposed to decide these things? Yes, we could have sat back and asked others to do those tasks, but she was our daughter, our baby—I felt like these things had to be done right. We never wanted to regret something associated with closing the earthbound chapter of her life.

We chose one of the funeral homes recommended to us by the hospital. It was near us, a family-run place. At our appointment we met the lovely owner and we sat around a table in a back room to discuss the process. I remember being at the meeting, but my clearest memory was looking through a book to choose an urn we would put her in. We had decided she would be cremated and that she would stay with us, in our home. Jonny had suggested that Mackenzie's ashes would be put together with my own when it was time for me to go. It felt right and made me weep.

Looking through the book I saw an urn in the form of a little white baby bird. Instantly I knew that was the one.

I remember discussing the costs and it all felt so wrong; not only was our child dead but we had to pay everyone for everything associated with her death.

At our new home, I went through her clothes and picked out a beautiful little dress. It had been bought for her by my parents, chosen by my dad. I delicately laid it out on her change table along with one of her signature headbands, her favourite dummy and clip, and a little white unicorn toy (for which I kept the matching big one). The family took it in turns to come into her bedroom and look at her outfit laid out, ready for her final journey.

I spent hours making a playlist of her favourite songs and picking a series of photographs to be projected at her funeral.

We decided to have a private family funeral for Mackenzie where we all got to see, touch and kiss her one final time. In the days before I walked around the mall at Bondi Junction among families doing their everyday activities, while I was there to choose what to wear to my child's funeral. An assistant asked me curtly if I needed help. I wonder what she would have said if I told her what I was actually looking for rather than just saying, 'I'm okay, thank you, just browsing.'

The morning of her family farewell, I somehow got myself ready, one foot in front of the other. I can't believe we made it there. I remember looking in the mirror, this aged version of myself who looked broken and numb.

Jonny and I got to the funeral home early to sit with her. Walking in, our eyes automatically searched for her, and at the end of the room a tiny small white coffin sat surrounded by candles with the most perfect bunch of yellow tulips beside it. Seeing her, a pain so deep ripped through us, causing a disconnect between the half of us that felt numb and in disbelief and the half that needed to scream. I wanted to run and scoop her up and hold her in my arms in the way that only I knew how, but instead I took small purposeful steps, steeling myself for what I would see in her coffin.

She looked so small and perfect in so many ways, but at the same time she didn't look like herself. Her headband wasn't sitting right, her ears poking out of it rather than underneath as I always had it, her colour was pale, and when I touched her she felt different, cold and dewy. I hated imagining where she had been . . . without us. I felt like I knew too much about what they did to people when they died, before they were cremated or buried. I forced myself to not think of that.

When our family arrived, the adults came down to see her. No one knew how to act—how can you know when you can't believe what is happening? When it was time to start, we closed the coffin lid. That movement alone should have caused me to disintegrate if feelings can have physical repercussions.

We sat around her in a circle, wanting her to feel surrounded by love. We had brought a bag of her toys and each chose one to hold so we felt close to her. In our other hand we all had a glass of Mumm champagne—I was given it when I gave birth to her, when I became her mum, but we hadn't had a chance to drink it yet. This felt like the right time.

Jonny and I both gave a speech. I chose to write mine as I had difficult things I wanted to say, whereas Jonny just spoke from the heart. My parents read one of her favourite books each; it was devastating to watch their pain. Then we all took turns to speak about our happy memories of her and special moments. We watched home videos on a screen and looked at photos as her favourite songs played quietly.

We wanted her funeral to be real: no stranger talking about her despite never meeting her; no priest, given Jonny and I aren't religious. We wanted to be surrounded by her things and remember her, in every tiny detail.

Finally, we each took turns to say goodbye, her cousins, then her aunties and uncles, followed by her grandparents and then Jonny and I. We didn't want this moment to end, knowing it was the last time we'd ever see our baby. In that moment I broke down and sat next to her, howling.

Walking out of the funeral home and saying goodbye to the staff, who were also crying, I remember asking them to look after her. Then it was over. I would never touch the hand I had memorised ever again, never feel her fingers curl around mine. I would never kiss those perfect little lips I had created.

Our wedding day at The Grounds of Alexandria, 12 February 2016.

Pregnant with baby Mackenzie!

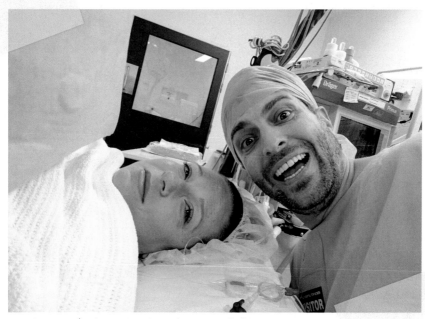

Mackenzie's birth—after forty hours, including two of pushing, she finally arrived by caesarean.

Jenny's parents, Linda and Ross, meeting Mackenzie.

My parents, David and Wendy, meeting their granddaughter.

Our beautiful newborn baby. All I can see in this photo is love.

The sweetest little face.

Mackenzie 'reading'
her favourite book
on one of our
adventures. She
travelled so well.

When we were
home, this was
our usual position.

We love this photo:
she knew where the
camera was.

Jonny was born to be a dad. He was Mackenzie's favourite toy.

I could never get over how beautiful she was.

This was taken on my surprise birthday picnic with Jonny and my parents. My only birthday with Mackenzie.

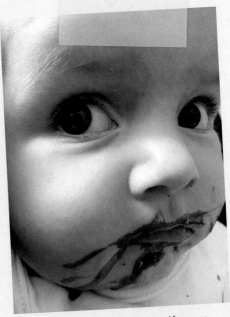

I was sure she was asleep, but when I looked into the pram this is what I saw.

Mackenzie loved trying new flavours.

On our own private beach in Broome. Mackenzie loved the warm air on her skin and the rock of the hammock.

Watching Mackenzie catch snowflakes on her tongue is one of our favourite memories.

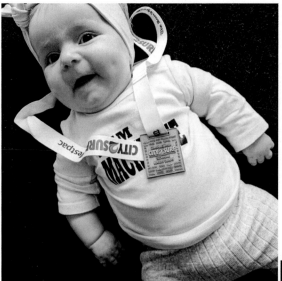

Mackenzie successfully completed the City2Surf.

Oh my gosh, that face! This was taken while celebrating her 'monthday'. She was pretty happy to get her cake.

A sneaky photo Jonny took of me in my happy place with Mackenzie.

Our family.

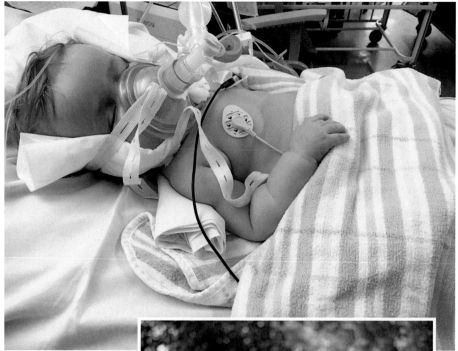

Above: Mackenzie in hospital, just three days before she died.

Right: Jonny and me at Mackenzie's farewell party. An impossible day.

The first time we met the Minister for Health, Greg Hunt. What an incredible man.

Jonny and me with the leads of Mackenzie's Mission, the day Minister Greg Hunt announced the research project to us.

Jonny and me during one of our rounds of IVF. This was taken just before an egg collection.

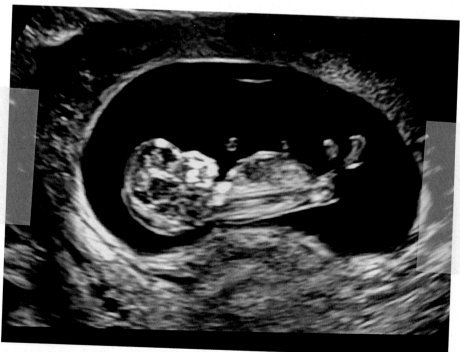

One of the few photos we have of our baby Bella.

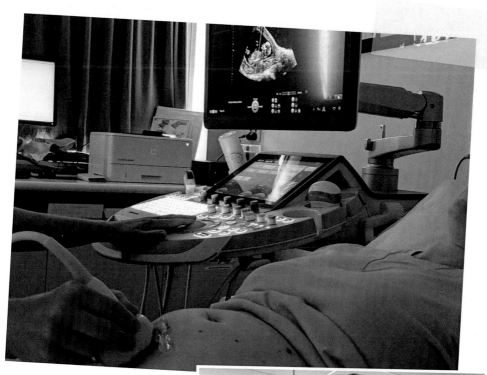

Having an ultrasound and
CVS for Bella.

Our termination for
medical reasons with
Bella. Broken.

Left: During an interview with Erin Molan on 2GB.

Receiving our surprise gift of IVF with Genea from Kyle and Jackie O on KIIS.

Above: The celebration step we bought in Mackenzie's name at Centennial Park.

Right: A television interview for ABC's 7.30 Report.

Renewing our vows with Elvis in Las Vegas.

Another round of IVF, so hopeful but so scared.

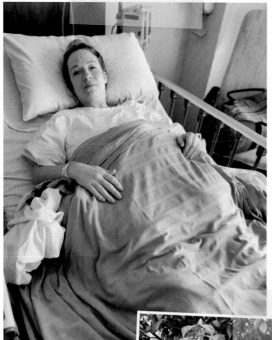

Just out of surgery from
my laparoscopy and
hysteroscopy.

Ten weeks pregnant
with baby Leo.

Two days later we held a large party in Centennial Park for her, a chance for our friends and loved ones to say goodbye. I wanted it to be the first birthday she would never have.

We chose a spot next to a little lake with geese and ducks. In the trees we hung decorations, a unicorn piñata and pastel balloons, with matching picnic rugs spread on the ground. Scattered around the tables and on the picnic rugs were photos of Mackenzie's smiling face, reminding us of how beautiful she was. There were platters of food, drinks galore and a huge dessert table with cupcakes, cake pops and everything else that should be at a kid's birthday party. Finally, we had almost a hundred pastel helium balloons gently anchored around the area.

Setting up, I was frantic. I needed everything to be perfect.

Hundreds of people showed up from near and far to show Mackenzie the love she deserved. I spoke to every single person who was there and thanked them with all my heart.

The official service part was carried out by the wonderful Nicky Surnicky, who had been our marriage celebrant less than two years earlier. We made sure Nicky had spent some time with Kenzie because we wanted the person talking about her to love her too. It felt right to have someone who married us at this next part of our lives. Nicky had never done anything like this before, but we were honoured when she said yes. She was perfect in the role and said some beautiful words.

Jonny and I both spoke. My whole life I have hated public speaking, to the point of almost passing out before doing it, but in this moment and at other times when my speeches are about my daughter, I get strength I have never known. In saying that, speaking those words was so hard. What if I said something wrong? What if I missed something I wanted to say? All I know is that I spoke from the heart. The only thing I remember was asking people to say her name, begging everyone to not let Mackenzie become a dream.

I got through my speech, though not without tears.

We ended the formal part of the party by asking everyone to stand up and as a group sing Mackenzie her favourite song, an idea my dad had. We passed out some beautifully printed lyrics made by my sister-in-law Ali and as a group belted out '. . . Baby One More Time' by Britney Spears. It was so perfect looking out at hundreds of people singing to her.

After this we released 99 balloons into the air for her to play with, keeping one for ourselves. The balloons floated in waves over the trees and up into the clouds and above. It was a beautiful party, as perfect as it could be.

For the remainder of the afternoon people mingled in groups talking quietly, eating and drinking, to a background of all of Mackenzie's favourite songs. I spent the day speaking to and hugging people as they offered me their sympathy. I drank champagne to fortify me as I tried to be a 'host', just wanting to get through the day but also not wanting it to be over, because I had no idea what the next day would bring. I probably drank more than I should have but it got me through somehow.

Over the next few days, we crashed. The farewells were done and we had nothing more to focus on, nothing more we could do for her. We had nothing and no one left to orbit around.

I sat in Kenzie's room looking at her clothes, touching everything she had ever touched. I tried to catch her scent on everything but she hadn't been here long enough for things to hold her smell.

Despite only being with us for seven months and eleven days, she had become the focus of our lives and without her we were lost. At a time when we wanted the days to pass by quickly, there seemed to be more minutes to fill than ever.

We decided we had to get away, and within four days of deciding to run away we were gone. But not before we got Mackenzie back.

I will never forget the day that Jonny and I sat in our living room waiting for the funeral home to bring us back our baby. The man gently handed over the tiny little urn; my baby was now ashes. It was such a surreal and impossible moment. The urn came with a certificate promising that the contents were our loved one and not someone else, a necessary thing but something I had never thought of. That moment was so heartbreaking.

Our trip away was so hard and something we kept very private. We flew to New York for a week. It was once a dream of ours, the one place we had wanted to go before settling down, but it felt like a sick joke that we were now going under these circumstances. It was the busiest place we could think of and we hoped it would distract us from our life for just a moment. But it didn't, Mackenzie was always there with us. We had brought her passport along, the one she never got to use. We decided that for our whole lives we would always travel overseas with her passport and we would choose special moments to put a sticker in it—that way she would always travel with us. Her New York sticker of the Big Apple happened at sunset on the Brooklyn Bridge, and she also got a Hawaii sticker of a dancer in a grass skirt on a stopover at Waikiki Beach on the way home.

Back in Sydney, in the weeks and months that followed it was like we had to mentally and physically relearn how to do some things. Ordinary events became landmines to navigate around. I didn't want to catch public transport or go grocery shopping, and the idea of going back to work terrified me. I didn't want any normality because that meant life was moving forwards without her.

I could move through sections of life, but they had to be associated with her. For instance, I could write about her, I could look at photos of her, I could campaign for change because it was about her. But 'normal' acts, things that I did before we had her, were just too hard. It wasn't a sustainable way of living and I knew that, but we had to be kind to ourselves. So we only did what could and tackled 'normal' things slowly, one by one, together.

I began having some bad flashbacks to our time in hospital and would panic whenever I heard an ambulance siren. I found a grief and trauma specialist to help me and saw her once a fortnight. I also found comfort in writing, which in a sense is how this book came about.

I also started to reassess myself and who I was. I felt like I couldn't be the same person I used to be. One of the things I was so determined about was for people to associate Mackenzie with love, growth and change, not with sickness, sadness or tragedy. I wanted to make a conscious effort that Mackenzie would add to our lives, not subtract from them.

Jonathan: What I remember most about getting home after Mackenzie passed away was the silence. After we unpacked and had a second to breathe, we sat in our spots on the couch and realised how quiet it was. Just one week earlier, we had sat here watching TV while trying to get Mackenzie to sleep, keeping her settled or feeding her. I felt like I'd been caught in a time warp, back to over a year before Rachael was even pregnant. It felt like we had started all over again.

I felt guilty about little things, like getting a full night's sleep or being able to leave the house on a whim. Basically, everything that gets taken away from you when you have a baby comes flooding back the moment they're gone, and with that the guilt.

In the month after we lost Mackenzie my mum was diagnosed with breast cancer. We couldn't believe it. I struggled to breathe when she told me, feeling that surely this couldn't be real, not another battle so soon. After two surgeries and radiotherapy she was eventually cleared, but it was a tough time. I know she and Dad protected us from their struggles and fears, which I hated but also appreciated. They handled themselves with such grace and I was so proud of them.

During this time of grief, I became even more determined to stop other people going through what we did. Our campaign with the government and to raise awareness for more widespread genetic testing became almost a full-time job.

We also agreed to assist the palliative care organisation and review its processes around caring for children. It was evident to both us and them that their palliative care systems and processes were very focused on adults, which is only natural as the majority of palliative care is for adults, thankfully. However, when the sad need for palliative care of children occurs, this specialist area needs to be well equipped and educated in how children and babies differ from adults. We were lucky that the palliative care organisation that looked after Mackenzie was willing to listen and open to change.

We attended events to lend our support in raising money for causes that were close to our hearts, such as the Royal Hospital for Women where Mackenzie was born. They were so supportive of us at all times and we wanted to give back to them, so we allowed them to tell Mackenzie's story at their Gala Ball. It was a beautiful night and wonderful to see money being raised for such an important cause, but I cried so much when I watched our story up on the screen, seeing her face ten metres high. Many others cried too.

The head of the hospital, Trish O'Brien, and the reporter who made our video, Ali Gripper, introduced us to ABC medical reporter Sophie Scott and her producer, Rebecca Armitage, who would turn out to be wonderful advocates and supporters of ours.

We also threw ourselves into media, doing interviews with whoever asked to raise awareness, talk about our daughter and make her proud. It was the only time I felt strong and like I was still able to be her mother.

In the months following her death we were determined to put Mackenzie's mark on this world, not just through campaigning but also through tangible acts. We donated money to the Royal Hospital for Women and had a 'Baby Star' with Mackenzie's name on it placed on a wall in the hospital. We also bought a paver engraved with her name for the Celebration Steps in Centennial Park. And to this day, whenever one of us travels we leave a little M somewhere, her mark on this world.

Four months after Mackenzie died would have been her first birthday. It was an impossible day to wake up to but no harder than other days we had faced. Our family drove up from Canberra and along with Kath and her family we celebrated Kenzie Day under a beautiful giant willow tree in Centennial Park, next to the stone paver we bought for her. We had decorations, balloons, cake, bubbles and games, and we celebrated as though she was still here. I wish I had been able to see her turn a year old, to pick her dress and give my new toddler cuddles.

Perspective

'When you change the way you look at things, the things you look at change.'

Dr Wayne Dyer

Since Mackenzie was diagnosed I have learned so much about life, more than I can express. I will try my best to share this now but sometimes I wonder if there are adequate words to express what we have experienced. It is like my eyes are open wider than ever before. I can see things that most others can't, which is both a joy and a burden. Mackenzie was a little person, here for a small amount of time, but her effect has been profound on the lives of others, not just mine.

Before Mackenzie was born I thought I had perspective on life, but looking back, I was so naïve.

Back then I genuinely liked who I was: I knew I had positives and negatives, but overall I was content with the person I was. I would have described myself as kind, caring, empathetic and emotionally intelligent. I felt like I was always willing to listen to people, to help them where I could, and to hear their story and their problems, although I could sometimes be a little too keen to give my thoughts or opinions.

I was mostly an introvert and quiet in group situations, although once you were in my circle I spoke freely and was fiercely loyal to my friends. I was also strong, dedicated, determined and had Type A personality tendencies, which meant that I put everything I had into my work and my friends, but also that my balance was totally off and my expectations of others high. I was stressed all the time, but I also knew that was just the level I ran on. Even now my mind goes a million miles an hour, bouncing all over the place and constantly making to-do lists, which is exhausting. Back then, this meant I would sometimes have a short fuse and snap at people when I got frustrated. Looking back, I honestly believe I had a form of anxiety and was heading towards a crash.

Then we had Mackenzie and I changed forever. These days when I think of myself it's 'me before' and 'me after'.

I like myself more now, the 'me after' Mackenzie is a better person. All the qualities I outlined above are still me, but because of our little girl I am softer, as if the edges have been rounded off. I can slow down, and I know what I should put my energy towards. I have balance. I can have moments of stillness.

It is all because of perspective, because of Mackenzie. She showed me another side of life. She showed me what matters.

I have seen babies lying in hospital struggling to breathe. I have seen children unable to move and I have seen families be stripped of the life of a loved one. Before Mackenzie, I knew bad things happened in the world, but now I have seen so much more of life's immense capacity for cruelty and tragedy but also the beauty of true love. I think this has made me so much more in tune with what matters. Everything I hear now, I hear differently. Everything I see now, I see differently. The world has changed colour, the blacks and greys more defined and the colours more vibrant. Mackenzie turned up the light in our lives.

Being touched by tragedy grants a new perspective. I now know what is important and where my priorities lie is different.

Life is important.

Family is important.

Happiness is important.

Love is important.

Kindness is important.

Surrounding yourself with good people is important.

Some things that I used to be overly passionate about just don't seem to matter so much anymore. This doesn't mean I don't have a passion for life, it's just different. It is focused where it should be.

Traffic is bad? It doesn't matter. Someone says something stupid? It doesn't matter. Having a bad day at work? It doesn't matter—at least, not as much as we make out.

While I know everyone has their issues and everyone is allowed to react to the dramas of life, when I hear people talk about them without comparing them to a serious event, I can't help but roll my eyes.

Mostly the changes in me have been positive, but it also makes it hard to be on the same level as other 'normal' people. Things they get excited or upset about I can't join in on. I fake it where I have to, but it does leave me feeling alone deep down.

I am now also acutely aware of the language people use in general conversation, particularly words like 'retarded'. These words are hurtful, and I don't think most people understand the ramifications their words have on others. My perspective has changed with my experiences, and I hope these conversations will change too.

I am not done growing; in fact, I have a lot of growing yet to do. But while I still have a lot to learn, I feel like I have been given a secret door, a shortcut to navigating the maze that is life.

I wish I had developed this perspective without having had to go through this but I choose to see this as a gift that Mackenzie gave me. She made me a better person, she changed my life. To forget my new perspective and not act on it would feel like I was dishonouring her life.

That doesn't mean I don't get upset about things or that I don't roll my eyes if others get upset, but it is about placing a situation in perspective and then moving forwards. It is also about having compassion, and understanding these deeper things in life.

I hope that as you read this book you can glimpse the perspective that Mackenzie gave me and perhaps better understand what is truly important in your own life, but without having to go through the pain.

Our grief

'Grief is like living two lives. One is where you pretend that everything is okay, and the other is where your heart silently screams in pain.'

Unknown

Until Mackenzie was diagnosed, we had lived a mostly normal life. Like most lucky people, we were largely ignorant of the pain that losing a loved one brings. We had lost some older relatives, mainly our grandparents, and as sad as it was to no longer have such wonderful souls in our world, we felt that they had each had a long and good life. It was, in a sense, the natural order of things. But after our normal world came crashing down, it seemed that in our innocent existence before Mackenzie's diagnosis we had been oblivious to the possibility of anything shattering our complacency and redefining everything in our lives.

Our immediate family had largely managed to avoid real harm or tragedy. However, Jonny's extended family had experienced the loss of someone young when his cousin Luke passed away in his early thirties from a brain tumour. I was relatively new to the family at that time but I had met Luke and instantly loved him for the joking, calming charm he exuded. We all deeply felt the sadness of his loss and the unfairness of someone so young being taken from this world before they had fully lived. It provided a reality check for Jonny and I, but it still did not in any way prepare us for losing our own daughter.

On reflection, I think it must have been so hard, so painful, for Luke. He was fully aware of his prognosis, of how his illness was progressing, where it might lead, and the probable outcome. I have no doubt that this awareness was with him in every waking moment. He was a truly courageous person. He dealt with his personal grief face to face, and with grace and even humour. No arguments. We miss him so dearly. Would our little Mackenzie have been as courageous if she had been aware of her illness? Because despite being so young, she too was brave and full of life. She was braver than me. She showed me how brave she was through her laughter, her smiles. By giggling when she played with her daddy. Yes, she was the bravest of the brave.

After we learned of Mackenzie's diagnosis, we were living the life that everyone fears. Everyone has a secret fear that one day their life will change in an instant, that they'll get that phone call or a knock on the door. Suddenly, that was us.

Initially I was in pure shock and almost denial. I could not begin to comprehend what had happened to us, to her. It was a grief that we thought would kill us.

The shock eventually mixed with a tremendous sense of the injustice of our situation that fed my overwhelming sadness. I thought, 'She is a baby. How can the universe give a baby a terminal illness? She is so perfect, small and innocent; she deserves to have her life, to see what she is capable of, to fulfil her potential. This is too cruel.' It was a nightmare from which we couldn't wake up.

When I wasn't blaming myself I had to blame somebody. I was incredibly angry at the world, the universe, the gods I didn't believe in, the medical professionals. Why did this happen? Why Mackenzie? Why us? Every day with her we had to live knowing that she was not going to, that we would watch her take her last breath, plan her funeral, see her in a casket.

I have read many definitions of the word 'grief'. Everybody grieves in their own way and there is no right or wrong. Grief is loss. Grief is sadness. I started to grieve from the moment I was made aware of my inevitable loss but long before we lost Mackenzie. My grief made me question life in ways I had not previously considered. What does life mean? What is its purpose? *Is* there a purpose? Does life just end—is this it? Are the promises made by religions of a life after death real? Where do we go? Will I get to see my baby again? As part of our grieving we were compelled to examine how the world works and adjust our beliefs based on our reality, not on what we would like to believe.

I have never been religious, and no one in my family is particularly so either. Our beliefs are generally science-based: we believe in the big bang, we believe in evolution. Not that science and religion are mutually exclusive; that depends on your religion (and probably also on your source of scientific evidence). My brother and I were never christened or baptised or in any other way committed to a nominated religion. My parents were both christened into the respective churches of their families, but my parents were of the view that children shouldn't be told what religion they are or what they should believe in. They thought that we could learn in our own way and in our own time about the different types of religion and then decide for ourselves what, if any, suited us. I really respected that and believed that my children would be brought up the same way.

As I got older I did dabble with religion. I occasionally attended church and went through a phase of learning about different religions, but in the end I realised that I didn't truly believe in any of them. I had good friends who were Christians and could, at times, see the comfort they drew from being part of their church's congregation. They gained a sense of belonging and shared belief. But that was not for me. I just couldn't accept that some divine being was adjusting people's life, dishing out pain and suffering under the pretence of a plan. Hardly a day goes by without somebody somewhere committing acts of evil in the name of their god, even against followers of the same god simply because of a different interpretation of a religious text or some slight from the past. How is that healthy? How is that sensible? And ultimately, no one can win that fight, so what is the point? All fighting about religion will lead to is pain, exclusion and ultimately actions that are contrary to a core belief such as 'thou shalt not kill'.

Religion, or more correctly 'religious doctrine', seems to be the cause of so much hate and anger, but I can understand why people want and need to believe in something. Surely even committed non-believers still need to believe in something, even if that something is nothing. Faith or conviction in someone or something helps to ground you on a path through life. Faith has the ability to provide you with comfort and guidance especially when it comes to death.

To provide solace in times of need. To provide moral leadership, something that is often lacking in our society and perhaps sadly even lacking in many religions. But can you have faith without the dogma and doctrine of religion? For many, religion is their faith, but I think it is possible.

I find it difficult to balance the pain and evil in this world with the concept of an all-loving god. For me they negate each other. But I can accept the concept of faith. On our journey, Jonny and I have met many good people who have shown us, and more particularly Mackenzie, love and kindness. This, perhaps, has become our faith.

I don't discuss religion to put anyone offside but because it is fundamental to understanding our mindset and our grief. I don't mean to hurt those in our wider family who are religious, but in all that we have been through as a family it is hard for me to understand their beliefs, and no doubt it is equally hard for them to understand our lack of belief. Luckily, we treat each other with respect. They know my views so neither of us tries to convince the other of our beliefs. What we do show each other is love.

Bad things happen in this world. There are childhood diseases and terminal illnesses, conditions that cause parents to give birth to babies who will soon die, or be trapped in their own bodies, or have severe malformations. Many clever people are working to find solutions to prevent or treat these conditions, and we are seeing progress little by little. But we live in a world of inequity. We live in a world where someone can spend millions on a new car but down the road lives a family that cannot afford basic medical treatment. A world where women are stoned to death for acts that men in that society can do without punishment.

A world where someone is so scared to tell their community they are gay that they would rather commit suicide. I could go on, but you get it. Don't get me wrong, I'm no socialist but I do believe there must be some constraint on the inequity and imbalance in our society. More needs to be done to close the gap between the haves and the have nots.

When tragedy strikes and a person loses someone who is an extension of their very soul, that person is often forced to evaluate their beliefs. Some grasp onto religion to get through it, and there were some people who told us that our daughter dying was part of a bigger picture, that she was in a better place and that we should take consolation in prayer. We understood that these people meant well, but for us it was not helpful; it was only hurtful and pushed us further down the path of non-belief.

My lack of religion didn't shake me in this time, but what did take a hit was my belief in karma and a sense of order in the universe. I have always believed in the idea that if you do good things then good things happen. I believed in trusting the universe for opportunities but that ultimately you have control over your own life and that if you put your mind to something you can do it. But in losing Mackenzie this belief was ripped away from me too. No matter what I did, I couldn't stop this from happening.

I have tried to explain what it feels like to have this faith in the universe or even faith in your own control taken away from you, but I can tell people don't really understand. Deep down, most people want to believe that everything happens for a reason, that there is a bigger plan that we just can't see. I can't tell you how scary it is to have your beliefs stripped away and be left shaken with nothing solid to hold onto.

Both after Kenzie's diagnosis and her death I shut down for a period of time, encased in my grief. My emotions made me feel walled in, like there was no escape, and my mind couldn't make sense of what was happening. I was, and am, so lucky to be surrounded by Jonny, our parents and families, and some truly stunning friends.

After Mackenzie died, I kept asking our psychologist whether I was grieving correctly. Such a bizarre question to ask but I just didn't know what grief should look like. Was I crying too little? Too much? Was I allowed to smile or laugh? Was I having a breakdown? Why did I feel guilty about everything I did? What is normal grief? Am I permanently broken?

I soon learned that there is no incorrect way to grieve, unless, of course, you are damaging yourself or doing something unsafe. Everyone has their own individual way of grieving and what is right for you might not work for others.

I also learned to never judge how someone else grieves. Don't question what someone needs to grieve and to heal, how they take time out from the pain, how much time they need or what support they ask of you—just be there for them. What has helped me personally is to be open and honest with my grief. I have shared our journey and been honest about it, no matter how raw the emotions, because I want and need to tell people about Mackenzie's life. But sadly, even speaking the truth can be seen by others as 'milking it'.

The other thing that helped me through my grief was campaigning for change in Mackenzie's name, to create a legacy for her. Some people wonder whether they would have had the strength to do what we did but for me it was cathartic to work for her. It gave me the strength I needed just to live and it would have been worse for me to not have that focus. But our way is not right for everyone and some people in our position might prefer to close the door and not speak about their loss for fear of reliving the pain. As I said, grieving is different for each individual, there is no right or wrong. You never know how you will react until you are put in that situation. I know that grief is the price of love and it is a price I would pay over and over again for having Mackenzie in my life.

When I look back at the months after losing her, I don't know how I survived. All I can say is that I didn't really have a choice. The days kept coming and time continued to move forwards, sometimes fast, sometimes slow.

In the weeks following her death, I hated being around people. It was exhausting. Seeing people meant I would have to talk about her because to not do so was wrong, but people were wary of me so I would have to put on a brave face as well. I was scared to laugh or smile in public for fear of being judged. Whenever Jonny made a joke about something else to lighten the mood, which is his nature, I would tell him to stop because I was worried people would judge us. But I was also scared to cry in front of people and make them uncomfortable. It was a no-win situation that left us drained.

My normal way to pass time was to sit on my phone but I was scared of that too. I didn't want to see people's lives ticking by like normal on social media or in the news. I didn't want to see trivial things happening in the world or, worse still, horrors. And what if people saw I was online and judged me? When does it become okay to post again? Though what on earth would I post about?

Work was hard to navigate too. The time when we had to go back came closer: we had no more leave and no more money. But I dreaded it. Jonny went back first and found work was useful for his brain, but for me the idea of work was like purposely taking a step towards life without her.

On my first day back, about six weeks following her death, I walked through the door holding Jonny's hand, terrified and feeling like a kid on their first day of school. As I headed up to my floor, I saw some people looking at me with pity, or perhaps to see whether I was cracking. A few people turned and walked away from us, and a couple even talked to us like we had been on holiday and that our daughter didn't die. But a few brave ones came up and said they were sorry. They said her name and yes, it caused tears, but those people meant so much. Acknowledgment.

Jonny chuckles when he remembers my first day back. Not to be mean but in that black humour way cops have to develop. I walked to my new desk to unpack the things I had in storage; it was the only thing I wanted to achieve that day. Half the floor were new people—new recruits, I guess—who didn't know us. All they saw was this blonde woman walk onto the floor looking like hell then sit at her desk and cry for four hours. Four hours was all I could take, and all others could take, it seems, because then the boss came around and told me to go home. I did, but I got up the next day and came back. Day after day.

Jonny and I were moved into new areas, which was really good for us both. The people in my new team turned out to be great and the bosses were understanding and kind, but at first this move meant meeting new people. I thought most would know our story through all the staff emails and fundraisers over the last months, but it was a joint taskforce so there were people from other agencies as well. After a week or two I noticed a few comments that indicated they didn't know about Mackenzie, so I wrote a group email explaining and sharing photos of her. It wasn't easy to write but I felt it had to be done.

Life was beginning to get back to normal. In some ways normal was nice, but I also clung to my life being different. As exhausted as I was by the pain, as much as pure normality would be a relief, I dreaded normal. If life was normal it would be like she wasn't ever here. Like she was a dream.

It felt like we were standing still in life. If we began to move forward we felt distant from her. If we stayed holding onto her it was like we were made of eggshells, ready to crack at the slightest nudge. Everything about my life was balanced on a knife's edge.

I avoided crowds and got tired easily. I dreaded seeing groups of people I knew because they still often didn't know what to say, so instead they said nothing. To me, saying nothing is worse than saying the wrong thing. Silence is pretending she didn't exist, that our pain doesn't exist.

And we still feel this way.

I dread meeting new people and being asked the standard questions: What do you do for work? Are you married? How many children do you have? I don't want to lie but telling the truth makes everything hard and uncomfortable. In an instant, a light conversation becomes awkward, hard and tiring. When I go and get a massage or a wax and they see my caesarean scar and ask about my kids, what do I say? I am trying to relax but I end up telling them because I feel the pressure of our newfound knowledge—what if they are about to have children? They should be told about genetic testing. But sometimes I am just too tired so I talk about Mackenzie as though she is still with us. I never want to say I don't have any children.

Despite feeling so much pain, we try hard to not let it take over our lives and to let a lot of light back into every day. We try to wake up each morning and think of what we are grateful for, to think about our love for Mackenzie. We attempt to strike a balance between living our lives and keeping her memory alive and honouring her.

Each day we have so many little rituals for Mackenzie. In the morning we wake up and say good morning to her and always have a candle burning next to her urn, and every week we buy her flowers. We have a digital photo frame which cycles through photos of her which we often talk to and smile at. We talk about her during the day, make up songs to sing to her and watch videos when we feel strong enough or want to see her mannerisms again. Jonny sings to her when he rides his motorbike to work and back and also in the shower. There's a bird that lives in a tree close to our home and when it sings we say it's Kenzie saying hi. We have never seen the bird, but its song feels familiar. And in the evening Jonny and I both have our goodnight rituals for her. She is involved in our every day in a positive way.

As far as crying goes, these days we can't tell what will set us off. Something you would expect to make me start might not, but something simple reduces me to tears. Sometimes I feel so numb and dead inside that crying, when it comes, is a relief.

In the early days every moment felt meaningful—the first time we went to her favourite park, the first month since she passed, her birthday, our first Christmas, her favourite food. These moments are beautiful, and we celebrate them all, but I am exhausted, there are too many meaningful moments. It is hard and can be too much.

Another question that sits with me often is if I will ever be whole again. I think the answer is no. We have started to laugh again, and in most moments I believe we will have a happy life in the future. I hope we will create more children, that we will be a family and our lives will involve Mackenzie's memory. But even if good things happen to us, sadness will always sit alongside joy. Happiness will always be complicated for us. It is not as simple as 'moving on'.

In my grief I have reached out to find people who feel the same, for words that can adequately describe our pain. Searching for answers, I once came across a beautiful description of grief written by a Reddit user called Gsnow. I think it will help those who haven't experienced grief to understand.

For grief, you'll find it comes in waves. When the ship is first wrecked, you're drowning, with wreckage all around you. Everything floating around you reminds you of the beauty and the magnificence of the ship that was and is no more. And all you can do is float. You find some piece of the wreckage and you hang on for a while. Maybe it's some physical thing. Maybe it's a happy memory or a photograph. Maybe it's a person who is also floating. For a while, all you can do is float. Stay alive.

In the beginning, the waves are 100 feet tall and crash over you without mercy. They come 10 seconds apart and don't even give you time to catch your breath. All you can do is hang on and float. After a while, maybe weeks, maybe months, you'll find the waves are still 100 feet tall, but they come further apart. When they come, they still crash all over you and wipe you out. But in between, you can breathe, you can function. You never know what's going to trigger the grief. It might be a song, a picture, a street intersection, the smell of a cup of coffee. It can be just about anything . . . and the wave comes crashing. But in between waves, there is life.

Somewhere down the line, and it's different for everybody, you find that the waves are only 80 feet tall. Or 50 feet tall. And while they still come, they come further apart. You can see them coming. An anniversary, a birthday, or Christmas. You can see it coming, for the most part, and prepare yourself. And when it washes over you, you know that somehow you will, again, come out the other side. Soaking wet, sputtering, still hanging on to some tiny piece of the wreckage, but you'll come out.

The waves never stop coming, and somehow you don't really want them to. My scars are a testament to the love that I have for that person. And if the scar is deep, so was the love.

Gsnow

I think that now my mind knows I won't see her again, I won't hold her again, but the mind still plays tricks. Some nights I go about my normal goodnight routine, smiling and talking to her, but every so often I am stopped in my tracks, like I have been stabbed in the chest and can't catch my breath, when I suddenly realise my baby died. This is my life now; I won't see her again.

I long to see her in my dreams but my mind seems to think I am not ready because instead I have stupid meaningless dreams. These days, more often than not, I have dreams of babies dying. As I write this, last night it was a terrorist attack where they killed all the babies. The night before I had a nightmare that I miscarried.

Grief and pain are now constants in our lives. I can go for minutes and sometimes hours without feeling it, but then I am hit with a profound sadness that sears through me. There are a hundred little reminders every day of how life will never be easy. Like handing over my Medicare card at the doctor with Mackenzie on it and knowing I need to take her off but I can't. Walking into the living room every morning and looking at her little urn in disbelief that my daughter is in there. Driving past the funeral home where we last saw and touched her. The moments when we fear that we may never hold her siblings or, if we do, they will never know her. Hearing an ambulance siren and having flashbacks and panic attacks. Going for appointments at the hospital where Mackenzie passed away.

Every single birthday, Christmas, Mother's Day, Father's Day, anniversary and holiday without her. The wariness in people's eyes when they look at us. Seeing the account we opened for Mackenzie when doing our internet banking, and knowing that we need to close it down but can't. The occasional troll comment. And hearing people complain about their lives.

All this is hard. Grief is now the sea in which we swim.

But while I realise that life will never be the same, we also don't want it to be the same. Mackenzie was born and there will never be anyone else like her; she brought her own special beauty to the world. So as the waves of grief get further apart, the breaks are now filled with intense happiness for our luck in getting to be her parents.

Reactions to grief

'Maybe I can't stop the downpour, but I will always join you for a walk in the rain.'

Dr Sukhraj Dhillon

When we lost Mackenzie, our world naturally became engulfed in grief. Grief becomes a constant presence in your life. It affects how you live but it also affects every single relationship or friendship from then onwards.

I was surprised by how many different reactions there were and on how many levels—society, work, friends and strangers. What surprised me more was how much those reactions affected us and how often we were expected to hold people's hands and help them handle our grief. This seemed so hard and draining at a time when we didn't have anything left to give.

Society

Overall, I would say our society doesn't really handle grief very well, especially over the loss of a child. In Western culture there is a funeral and then it is almost expected to be done. There are few ways that we as a society help people deal with grief or acknowledge those we have lost, so many people end up dealing alone with emotions that are frightening, painful, strange and even bizarre.

Spouses who have lost their partners are widows and widowers. Children who have lost their parents become orphans. But there is no term to describe a parent who has lost a child. More than any other loss, society does not know how to handle the death of a child. If we don't have a word for that loss, how do we begin to describe it and to grieve? People often don't know what to say to someone who has lost a loved one, but doubly so for a parent who has lost a child. Instead people usually don't say anything at all. The feeling around death is silence and the silence around child loss is deafening.

It was shocking how many people didn't even acknowledge Mackenzie's death, not even to ask the simple question 'How are you going?' Did they not care or did they feel inadequate and uncomfortable? It was probably the latter in most cases, but either way it felt awful.

Losing a child is sometimes called an 'out of order death'. We are born, we live, we love (if we are lucky), some have children, and then eventually we die. There is an accepted order to life, and when a child dies before their parents, that death seems against the accepted order of things. In general, people seem to be so overwhelmed by the death of a child that some just push it away, never taking the time to truly understand what the parents' grief must be like. They don't want to know. They prefer ignorance. I dream of ignorance. I miss ignorance.

Everyone will eventually encounter hardships. So treat others how you would like to be treated.

Friends

I have learned that tragedy often reveals true colours and provides a natural sorting of the people in your life. Luckily, I can say that most people in our lives were wonderful.

In the days, weeks and months following both Mackenzie's diagnosis and her death, people reached out with such incredible kindness. Most would not have known what to say or do—they didn't sign up for this pain and sadness in their friendship—but they did their best and showed their caring nature in whatever ways they could.

For some it was as simple as a message every week or even month. Others showed it through actions, like arranging a cleaner, sending food parcels, or creating gifts for Mackenzie when she was alive and in her memory after she left us. Some people planted trees, named stars or made donations in her name. Others have written her name in the sand and sent us photos of it. Some made pictures or paintings of her and others simply wrote her name on a leaf and let it drift down a river. We had special pieces of jewellery made for us, people donating blood in her name and gifts given to local hospitals for her. Some donated their children's excess birthday gifts to hospitals or asked for donations as birthday presents when they thought their own children had enough. Others simply wrote their feelings in a card or randomly messaged us to say they had seen a rainbow or heard Britney Spears playing on the radio and thought of her.

What to some people may have seemed like small things meant absolutely everything to us. People simply saying her name aloud meant the world. Through this experience and watching some of these extraordinary people, I now know how to act when people around me have lost someone. They were the best.

I have a particular strong spot for my girls, the team of women who are the strongest people I know. They have stepped up and wrapped their arms around me, letting me speak when I wanted to and allowing me to step back when it all got too much.

The worst thing anyone could do was be silent or back away from us, but this happened even among our good friends. This was sad, but others' reactions to our situation were out of our control.

One friend caused me more pain than I can convey in words. In essence, this friend walked away from us when we needed her the most, with no explanation or apology.

Our friendship began in our late teens and for a long time we were inseparable, travelling the world together, learning about ourselves and getting up to mischief. Most girls know this type of friendship—she was my best friend and confidant.

For years we were each other's support through the ups and downs of life. She had a tendency to run away from the world when things got too hard, and on many occasions I found myself being her 'saviour', fighting her battles with people and boyfriends whom she said were treating her badly. No matter how bad her life got, I stood by her staunchly, and I expected the same in return.

But not long after Mackenzie was diagnosed, she disappeared. After a few weeks of silence, I asked her if she wouldn't mind contacting me a little more, even just a text or a call once a week would do. I explained I was drowning and that I needed her, to which she replied that I was being needy and she was too busy. It appeared that my daughter's terminal diagnosis was an inconvenience to her. When we did speak, she reduced our conversations about Mackenzie's life to discussions around money and image, as Jonny and I campaigned for change and accepted assistance through GoFundMe. Her focus was not on us.

She was going through her own transitions in life: a new pregnancy, a new partner, a new home and a busy career. While our lives were both busy and both changing in different ways, I asked her not to pull away from me. Even though I was going through pain, I wanted to be there for her in this exciting time of her life, the way I would have been if things were 'normal'. I knew I still had it in me to support her, as I had other close friends who were also pregnant. But despite her reassurances that she would be there, she wasn't. She walked away.

In part, I understand that one person's tragedy is another person's imposition. The more distant your relationship with someone, the less engaged they will be, which is natural. But when it's the person with whom you shared all your secrets, it's confusing—especially when I think of the people who were further on the periphery of my life who stepped forwards to help and support us.

A few months after we lost Kenzie, having not heard from my friend for some time, I was unsure whether to attend her upcoming baby shower. A week before the shower, I packaged up the many gifts I had been collecting for her while my own child slowly died. I wrote a long letter begging her to explain why she had walked away and asking if she really wanted me at her baby shower. I offered explanations for her behaviour: maybe it was prenatal depression or stress? Was she fighting with her new partner? I sent the letter with high hopes of reconciling, but all I received in return was a short text message: 'Thanks for the gifts, hope you are okay.'

I have only seen her three times since Mackenzie died and we have not spoken now for two years. Early on, she would occasionally comment on my social media posts as if we were still close friends. When she had her child, she messaged me the news. I initially thought it might an olive branch, but when I offered to visit, I received no response. I stopped looking at her social media posts after a while and then muted her; seeing photos of her new family was too much for me after the way she had acted—particularly when her child was dressed in something that Kenzie had owned. Eventually I was made aware that she had unfriended both Jonny and I from social media.

A part of me hoped that once she gave birth she would reach out; that she would realise the deep pain her actions must have caused us. I then hoped that she would reach out when her child reached the same age Mackenzie had been when she died. Deep down, I knew she wouldn't. In the past, she had always had difficulty admitting she had done something wrong, instead becoming quiet and withdrawn. I no longer want her to reach out to me, as her actions now feel like a direct attack on Mackenzie, on her life and on her memory.

I still have nightmares about her, and I feel uncomfortable when I go somewhere where I might see her. No one has ever hurt me like she did—leaning on me in her own hard times but walking away when things got tough for me. Luckily, we didn't have many mutual friends.

Sometimes I wonder what she told herself to make it seem okay, or what she has told others about why we're no longer in touch. How friends respond in your time of grief is so important; they get you through each day. And sadly, most grieving parents I have met since losing Mackenzie have a similar story—people who pull away, people who step closer and at least one person who causes significant damage to the grieving parents. It's easy to become fixed on the negative people rather than the positive. A psychologist once explained it to me as similar to inviting ten people to a dinner party and only nine turning up—many of us would fixate on the one who didn't turn up, but I try hard now to focus on the nine who did, difficult as that may be.

I do understand why people feel uncomfortable around grief and loss—it's a hard topic for everyone. But try to imagine it for the grieving person: this is now their life all the time, and your two minutes of discomfort is nothing compared with the discomfort they are living 24/7. I know it sounds harsh, but some people need to get over themselves. It's natural to worry about saying the wrong thing or reminding someone of their loss, but the reality is that grieving parents don't ever forget, it is always there, and silence is much less welcome than possibly clumsy sympathy. There is no justification for the death of a baby and all any grieving parent wants to hear is recognition of their pain, and the sentiments that life is cruel and that we are not alone.

During this time, dealing with such an array of reactions was quite confronting. Some we could dismiss as due to a lack of understanding, but other reactions hurt us quite deeply. It was like we had to grieve some of our relationships while grieving Mackenzie. Something our psychologist at the time said helped and has stayed with me :

> Picture your life like a bus journey: you are the driver and your partner the front passenger. People in your life fill up the bus, with those closest to you sitting up the front. During your life some people swap seats and move around the bus. Occasionally the bus stops and someone gets off or someone gets on. You can't stop who wants to get off, but at the same time, you can kick people off if you need to. It is your bus.

All I can say is that kindness and compassion make the world go around. It is my new religion as it can truly make or break a person. I try hard to make sure I spread positivity and kindness to the world in Mackenzie's honour and because I know first-hand that an act of kindness at the right moment can save a person's life.

In the months after we lost Mackenzie, we decided that acts of kindness would be part of our coping mechanism and her legacy. So we came up with our kindness list. Every birthday, anniversary, Christmas or whenever we needed to, we would do one or all of our kind acts, which included:

• Creating a Red25 blood donor group called 'Mackenzie's Mission' and donating blood and plasma under it in order to save lives. We advertised the group's existence on Instagram and at time of writing, 549 lives have been saved in her name.

- Using money with which we would have bought gifts for Kenzie to donate food, gifts, essentials and toys to Ronald McDonald Houses.
- Cooking meals at a Ronald McDonald House.
- Donating to Starlight Children's Foundation, Make-A-Wish Australia or to SMA research.
- Donating to GoFundMe pages and promoting charities on my Instagram.
- Reminding people about registering to donate organs.

Our friends, family and social media followers sometimes jump in on these actions. Some of my Instagram followers even donated their children's birthday presents to needy and sick children. I mean, honestly, how is kindness not the best! Why wouldn't everyone do it?

Overall, we are ridiculously lucky and grateful for the people in our lives and the love and warmth we have been given by our friends.

Work

Each workplace is different in how it deals with employees who are sick, experiencing a tragedy or are grieving. I wish everyone was supported and allowed the time they need to deal with their experience, but in reality this is not always the case.

Smaller businesses may be better positioned to take a personal interest in an employee's welfare, but they also may not be in a financial position or have the flexibility to provide the time you need off work. Bigger businesses more generally have the resources and flexibility to allow employees more time off in times of grief and tragedy, but you may also just be a number on a page.

Jonny and I had worked in the Australian public service for more than twelve years when Mackenzie was diagnosed. I had worked in various Commonwealth government departments but had been with the AFP for five years, and Jonny had been a loyal employee of the AFP for twelve years.

Overall, I believe our organisation has a successful way to manage the health of its employees in the event of terminal diagnoses, however, when it came to supporting employees whose children who are sick, we felt it was foreign territory—to us, the rules seemed to be made up as they went.

The AFP is a Commonwealth government agency with its national headquarters based in Canberra and what are effectively branch offices based in each of the state capital cities. Jonny and I are based in the Sydney office. When it came to the day-to-day treatment of our situation and our return to work, our local (Sydney) managers and staff were kind, supportive and flexible— which was the opposite of the approach from our national head office in Canberra. The local AFP staff fundraised for us, sent gifts and turned up to Mackenzie's farewell party. When we returned to work, they made it the smoothest transition it could be. The Sydney senior management made sure we were as happy at work as possible, regularly caught up with us and took it upon themselves to look after our mental health at work. To this day the AFP in Sydney are still looking after us. They seem to know that grief over the loss of a child does not end quickly; there is no timeframe to be 'over it'. We owe all of them a debt of gratitude.

But at the organisational and national level, we felt very let down. We had to endure months of arguing with Canberra-based administrators and management to have time off work with Mackenzie to witness her life when she was still alive, while also making sure we could afford to live and support ourselves after she had gone. It was a battle that went on until Mackenzie's death. We had to jump through more hoops than I ever realised existed.

These decisions caused us extreme financial, mental and emotional stress. Looking into it, organisations like the AFP are quite good at dealing with adults who have a serious or terminal illnesses. For a government employee with a terminal illness, the process is relatively simple: you use up all your leave—annual leave, long service leave, sick leave—and once that's gone you will be given miscellaneous leave with pay (or a lower level of pay) until you die, depending on your prognosis and life expectancy. But when the person who is terminal is the child of an employee, most organisations are stumped—they have no rules to follow. While the death of a child isn't common, thank goodness, it does happen every day and so as a society and as organisations we can do better.

I will never forget the lessons I learned while having to fight an organisation for time off work as my daughter fought for her life. Our experience taught us that a human resources department can, as the title suggests, at times only be about the management of humans as resources (do we have the agreed number of people and are they paid the agreed amount of money?), rather than the care or wellbeing of humans as people. At times in our dealings with senior HR managers, Jonny and I felt we were just resources. We both appreciate that the role of HR professionals is an extremely difficult and complex task, often entailing equally difficult and complex decisions. But we feel that in our case, more often than not, people who could have made a difference did not.

People who could have made decisions did not. People appeared to be worried about setting precedents, so they covered unsympathetic decisions with layers of unnecessary administration and found reasons to justify their inaction.

Many organisations seem to be struggling with how to handle the issue of mental health and how to assist employees in dealing with personal trauma, which is especially problematic in an industry like ours that comes with so many risks and hazards. And in our case, we wish those HR professionals had made different decisions with a different focus. But our organisation is fundamentally a good one; we are extremely proud to be a part of it. Jonny and I hope that rather than being consumed by the bitterness of our experience we can, over time, use these lessons to help make positive changes. But first we must heal.

We are lucky in many ways—luckier than most: we had leave to use, we enjoy our jobs, we had family support, work members and management at a local level who supported us, as well as people who supported us financially, allowing us to look after our daughter. But the pressures of work and money troubles can push a grieving parent over the edge. After the death of a loved one, most organisations don't have provisions in place to allow time off to grieve. Legislation doesn't even acknowledge miscarriage under twelve weeks as a loss requiring time off work. As for having time off to care for a dying child, forget it. This needs to change.

Trolls

After Mackenzie's death we were still gathering strength when we could to do occasional media and keep campaigning on awareness of genetic testing. Luckily most of the comments on my Instagram account were positive, caring and compassionate, but comments on media articles could be ruthless. We had comments that ranged from 'These parents are using their dead child for attention' to 'This baby died of natural selection'. I will never understand what sort of people could say such things but I learned early on to not read the comments.

We also experienced a bad side of social media. In mid-2018 we learned that photos of Mackenzie and our family had been stolen by Russian Instagram scammers. On their Instagram account they called her Sophia and used her photos to collect money for her 'treatment'. We have had many people contact us telling us they were scammed by them. Some have even told us that the scammers are Russian prisoners who use our daughter to earn money from inside jails. I don't know who they are, but they are scum. Jonny and I often wonder why they bother to use Mackenzie's image. Why not use photos of their own family? Why our daughter?

Initially I fought back against them publicly. I posted about the abuse on Instagram and got others to put in complaints to Instagram using their complaints form, but this didn't work. For starters, the complaints page was limited and only allowed Jonny and I to complain as the account holders, but the scammers blocked us from their account so we couldn't get the necessary information to complete the complaint. Somehow they found out who else was notifying us of the new accounts and blocked them too, which meant that every time they created a new account using Mackenzie's photos we could not even see it to report it.

For months we tried to contact Instagram; I must have sent hundreds of those forms. But their complaints process is abysmal. Sometimes the form wouldn't even send, sometimes they wouldn't contact me, and sometimes they would reply saying that what the scammers were doing didn't breach their code. Instagram had no higher-level complaints system that I could contact, no email and no office to front up to. I was distraught. It was frustrating and laughable that Instagram wouldn't protect her image or protect others from scammers, yet if someone posts a nipple or a piece of copyrighted music (as I once unknowingly did with a Kenzie video) then those posts would be pounced on within hours. We were using Instagram as it was meant to be used—to create a community—and we weren't being protected.

Eventually I had to find official government avenues to stop these pests and joined forces with Australian Communications and Media Authority, but it shouldn't have come to that. A year on and those scammers are still going. Until recently, I still had to go through the process of contacting ACMA every time I was made aware of a new account, who would then contact Instagram, who would then shut it down. In recent months I have finally been contacted by Instagram, who have informed me of the steps they are taking to protect us and others like us, as well as providing us with a direct contact. We are so thankful to have had this contact from them as it provides us such relief, but it took a long time to get there.

And to top it all off, in an article a journalist wrote about the scammers, trolls commented that it was my fault for sharing photos of my daughter online. The victim was blamed. Sometimes I wonder about the world we live in . . .

Instagram

I never expected this but I found a family online in the midst of my pain: my Instagram family. I love them.

For me, Instagram was initially a space to talk about Mackenzie. I figured I would post photos and my memories as a form of journalling, and if people didn't want to see it they could unfollow me. But instead, slowly the number of followers grew. People cared. If I posted things other than photos of Mackenzie they still cared, but they craved photos of my beautiful girl. I felt heard and felt that she was loved, which was the biggest gift.

I wrote about my grief, my pain and my love. I could have happy days where I shared memories, or hard times when I broke down, and these new friends would cheer me on, begging me to stand up again and keep fighting.

These friends will never know what they did for me. Most have never met me, but they gave me strength when I had none. I would get personal messages all the time. Some told me their story about losing a child, some had been affected by a genetic disorder, and others connected with my writings about IVF. I had parents write to me in the middle of the night when their child would not sleep, but they had thought of us and simply hugged their child instead of getting frustrated because we gave them perspective. Some were just kind humans who wanted to share our journey and hope for our happiness.

Not only did we get kind messages, thousands of them, but we also got actions. People shared our message. They told their followers about Mackenzie and SMA. They wrote to their local members supporting genetic testing. And they cared. This was always the number-one thing anyone could ever do for us.

I would get photos of people donating blood for Mackenzie, or donating money on her birthday to a local charity. They would light a candle for her or plant a tree in her name.

These people made me feel like the luckiest mum in the world. I often felt guilty for all this attention and love; Mackenzie is not the only baby to pass away, and other babies gone from this world don't all get the fuss and love Kenzie got. But this support well and truly made up for any negativity we received from sharing our story.

My Instagram family are so important to me. They are the most unexpected gift I have ever received.

Kath

I have many beautiful friends who were with me through the hard times. Dimi, Nicole, Em, Liz, Amelia, Lia, Jodie and so many others. They all helped me in different ways, and I love them dearly, but one person who deserves a whole section (if not a chapter) is Kath. She has been my rock.

I met Kath in Year 11. We had similar interests and ended up taking a few classes together, including psychology and photography. Initially I think we were in a silent competition with each other, but while I am no dummy there was really no competition for grades as Kath is extremely intelligent, always has been. At school we became friends, but this friendship was truly solidified in university and beyond.

We both chose to study psychology at the Australian National University and then worked in the same cafe and solarium (when they were legal, and hence my malignant melanoma).

All through university we studied together and bonded over our love of coffee and baked goods, then after graduation we remained friends. Like most friendships it varied in intensity, but always remained close. When I fell pregnant with Mackenzie, Kath was a pillar of support. She was already a mum following her own IVF battle and became pregnant with her second baby towards the end of my pregnancy. Kath, along with my mum, was my oracle of parenting knowledge.

When Mackenzie was diagnosed, Kath stepped even closer. At the time Kath had a lot on her plate: she had a two-year-old, was battling a horrible pregnancy and was in a bad way with her health, but still she was there for me with no questions, no hesitation. After she heard the news she came around as soon as she could, asking questions others were afraid to. She already had a strong medical knowledge but she researched SMA so she could discuss it with me and she knew about the clinical trials. She listened to my fears and my love for my baby girl.

Whenever I was down or needed help, Kath was always there to listen. She gave honest and helpful advice and I always left her feeling better. I have no doubt she has not known what to do at times, but she knows she doesn't need to fix things. She is just there, always. She has given me love, hugs and has taken me on trips away, anything to love me and make me feel supported.

Two years ago, Kath told me that her signal that she was thinking of me was two red hearts. Since then I have received a text message every single day from her without fail. Most are conversations, but occasionally she will just send me two red hearts. My love for this woman knows no bounds. She is the pinnacle of compassion, a beautiful person and everything I could possibly want in a friend. I am extremely lucky to have her.

Family

I can't even begin to explain how our families reacted and supported us. They have been incredible.

From the start of our relationship, Jonny and I have been made to feel loved and part of the bigger circle of both our families. When Mackenzie was diagnosed, they rushed to our sides. They have sat with us in our pain and felt every kick and heartache along the way. At times when we have needed more support they have physically looked after us and provided us with financial support. When we needed space, they sat back, but made us aware that they would always be there when we were ready to come out of our cocoon.

They love Mackenzie and miss her. They have had to grieve her and also watch their own children suffer at the same time, which would have been impossible at times, but they did it with grace, love and kindness.

They have banded together to become one mega family filled with love, admiration and compassion. I am so proud of them and feel like the luckiest girl in the world when I think of them. We are so blessed to be cushioned by the love of our family. Every single time we leave a visit with our families, Jonny and I always turn to each other and say how lucky we are. We are even luckier that our families have become friends in their own right.

My words here seem unworthy. I am at a loss. I hope we can repay the love someday.

Mackenzie's Mission

'You are never too young to change the world.'

Unknown

Following our letter to parliamentarians in June 2017, we heard from federal health minister Greg Hunt numerous times, and his interest meant so much to us: he showed us that to the Australian government, Mackenzie's life mattered. I felt like maybe she represented all the babies who should have been here.

In his first letter, Minister Hunt outlined a personal pledge that he would make change in Mackenzie's name in some way. While cautiously keeping our expectations in check, those words became a life raft that we clung to.

In November 2017, following Mackenzie's death, we received a letter from Minister Hunt expressing his sorrow for our family and also offering us a meeting. This was it, an opportunity to meet with the minister and plead our case, to open our hearts to him and lay out all of our newfound information on genetic disorders and explain why genetic testing was so important to Australia.

Our meeting took place after the holidays on 28 February 2018. In preparation for the meeting and with the help of our family I wrote the ministerial briefing I mentioned earlier. We wanted to make sure everyone was on the same page before the meeting. If this was our one chance, we didn't want to waste it.

Once I had completed the draft, I sent it to the group of professionals we had accumulated around us. Our 'team' reviewed and endorsed the briefing before it was sent to the minister and we are so thankful for the support they provided. It gave us confidence in our mission and what felt like the backing of the medical community.

Our medical team at this time consisted primarily of four people, all investigators working on the Australian Reproductive Carrier Screening Project (ARCSP). The first person on the team I want to mention is of course Dr Michelle Farrer. As Mackenzie's neurologist and our first medical supporter, we have a strong connection with Michelle; she knew our daughter and was there for us from her diagnosis through to her death and beyond. When Mackenzie was taken to hospital Michelle was there; when we lost Mackenzie, Michelle was there shortly afterwards, rushing to the hospital to ensure she saw her one final time. She is a wonderfully kind woman who is making Australia better, one of our unsung heroes.

A consultant paediatric neurologist at Sydney Children's Hospital, Randwick, and clinical academic at the University of New South Wales, Michelle is a specialist in SMA. When we first met her she was strongly focused on a treatment for SMA, and still is. However, when we began asking questions about genetic carrier testing, she listened and started asking questions too.

Since then Michelle has supported our campaign and often says she was inspired by Mackenzie and our desire to be proactive in the elimination of SMA, which is how she came to be on the ARCSP. Also on the ARCSP are Professor Edwin Kirk, Professor Nigel Laing and Professor Martin Delatycki, as well as more than thirty other dedicated contributors.

Professor Nigel Laing AO is head of the Neurogenetic Diseases Group at the Centre for Medical Research, University of Western Australia, and the Harry Perkins Institute of Medical Research in Western Australia. He also leads Australian Genomics' neuromuscular disorders flagship and is joint leader of its national diagnostic and research network program.

Professor Edwin Kirk is a clinical geneticist at Sydney Children's Hospital and genetic pathologist at NSW Health Pathology, Randwick. He is a conjoint professor in the School of Women's and Children's Health, University of New South Wales. He is also medical director of the Community Genetics Program (NSW), which offers screening for conditions common in people of Ashkenazi Jewish descent. Professor Kirk has been instrumental in our campaign.

Professor Martin Delatycki studied medicine at the University of Melbourne before completing his paediatric training at The Royal Children's Hospital. He went on to train in clinical genetics at Victorian Clinical Genetics Services and completed a doctorate on the nervous system disease Friedreich ataxia at the Murdoch Children's Research Institute. He is currently the clinical director of Victorian Clinical Genetics Services and co-director of the Bruce Lefroy Centre at the Murdoch Children's Research Institute. Martin led the establishment of carrier screening programs for cystic fibrosis and conditions common in the Jewish community in Victoria and studied the outcome of these. He has worked extensively on screening for the preventable iron overload disorder haemochromatosis.

Following this meeting request by the minister, we were contacted by ABC journalist Sophie Scott and her producer Rebecca Armitage to film a story about us and our campaign. On Thursday, 22 February 2018, the ABC's *7.30* aired what would become part one of our story; it outlined Mackenzie's life, her diagnosis and our family's campaign. We were so appreciative of their interest, and Sophie and Rebecca did a wonderful job. This was not the first media we had done but we were still so nervous. As soon as we saw Mackenzie's face on our television we began crying.

In the weeks before our meeting in Canberra, Sophie and Rebecca arranged to film part two of our story, this time of us attending Parliament House. They also arranged to interview Minister Hunt. We felt like we now had the weight of the ABC behind us—surely the minister had something positive to say if he not only agreed to a meeting but also to the ABC attending? But was it going to be positive enough for us to feel successful?

Arriving in Canberra, we were excited but nervous. While we'd previously had a good feeling from the minister, we were concerned the meeting might not result in the outcomes we hoped for. We went in ready to fight for our campaign.

Driving to Parliament House that day, I remember looking up at the iconic building that we had driven past for most of our childhood and wondering how on earth we had got here. We were two people with no political background or power. Could our baby girl really change Australia?

We shot some footage outside for the ABC before it was time to meet the minister. Walking through the doors to his office, we could feel the cameras pointed at us and the lights in our eyes. But then we saw a smiling face and an outstretched hand. As we introduced ourselves, we saw the minister's tears. In that instant I knew two things: this was a kind man and this meeting clearly meant a lot for him too.

Once the cameras captured the greetings, they left us to talk. In the room was only me, Jonny, Minister Hunt, Professor Kirk, Dr Farrar, Minister Hunt's beautifully kind assistant at the time, Briony, and a representative from the always supportive David Coleman's office.

This was the moment we had waited for. I hoped we could make her proud.

Before anyone could say anything, I started speaking. I felt I needed to control this meeting so I launched into it. As I spoke, I placed photographs of Mackenzie on the table between us. I wanted Mackenzie to be there, looking at us all. I spoke of our love for Mackenzie and our hatred of the illness that took her from us. I spoke about genetic testing, what it could do and the cost benefits to Australia in the long run. They were the words I had thought about for months on end and they were finally coming out of my mouth.

I handed the minister a draft paper provided by researchers at Monash University on the health cost effectiveness of genetic testing. The minister listened but it soon became clear that my speech wasn't needed; he had made up his mind about what he would do.

Minister Hunt spoke of his experience meeting children in hospitals who would have benefited from genetic testing. They could have received treatments in time and could have avoided pain or irreparable damage. Then, leaning forwards, with tears again in his eyes, he promised he would create change for Mackenzie.

We went away with hope. He was such a wonderful man to meet, so genuine and kind. We didn't know what would eventuate, but we trusted Minister Hunt.

He had heard us.

In May 2018, once again we heard from the minister and this time were asked to come to Canberra for budget night. We contacted Edwin, Martin and Nigel to ask if they had heard anything; they hadn't but had been asked to come to budget night too. Surely this meant something.

Sophie Scott and Rebecca Armitage asked if they could again film us for *7.30*. We arrived at Parliament House with Nigel, Martin and Edwin while our parents waited in the cafe for us. In our meeting, Minister Hunt turned to us and I became aware that I was holding my breath. He told us that in a few hours Treasurer Scott Morrison would announce the budget, and within it would be the largest health initiative in Australia's history, a $500 million 'genomics mission' that would be funded by the Medical Research Future Fund. We were told that the first project would be a pilot program into genetic carrier testing.

I looked at Jonny in amazement, and he stared back at me in shock. Then I broke down. The minister and Briony cried with us, as did Edwin, Martin, Nigel, happy tears that what they had worked towards for years was finally happening.

The minister outlined that the genomics mission would be a four-pronged attack. Firstly, it would provide genetic carrier testing as routinely offered screening and subsidised for all. Secondly, it would raise awareness among medical professionals. Thirdly, it would focus on research and treatments. And finally, it would increase access to IVF and preimplantation genetic diagnosis (PGD) for people like Jonny and me.

Once I composed myself, I turned to Minister Hunt and said, 'You have the honour of heading one of the most influential, life-changing portfolios in government. You should be so proud for using your power to really change Australia.'

The minister smiled and said, 'This will be one of the greatest achievements of my career.'

We shook the minister's hand and he said he would see us soon then we walked out of the room, still in shock. In the media courtyard where we met Sophie to be interviewed, she told us that the first pilot program would cost $20 million.

Minister Hunt had named the program Mackenzie's Mission. We couldn't believe it.

Through Mackenzie's Mission, the minister and his team were giving us everything we asked for—everything. I cannot express what we felt in that moment. To know that the life of Mackenzie and all the other babies who should be here would be acknowledged, that she would have a legacy that would save thousands of babies from suffering, filled us with joy. While most would not know our baby, her name will live in Australian history. Some families who may have been headed down our painful path could be saved. We are so proud to be her parents.

For the next hour we were stunned, going through the motions of thanking people and being interviewed by Sophie. How can any words possibly express how we felt? We were at a loss.

Finally it was just me, Jonny, Edwin, Nigel and Martin left. We went upstairs to the cafe to find our parents and tell them about Mackenzie's Mission. All of Mackenzie's grandparents cried—tears of joy, of relief and of pain that she wasn't there. They were so proud.

The next night Mackenzie's Mission was announced on *7.30*. We were nervous. Until it was said aloud to a national audience it felt like it could all be taken back. It could be a mistake.

But it wasn't. It was happening.

Jonathan: 'You were right—I didn't think you could do it, but you did.' Those are words I've found myself saying many times during the course of my relationship with Rachael. An eternal pain in the arse, my wife will see some injustice—poor customer service or a lack of compassion—and take considerable action. Her being a pest has benefited me more than I can tell you. When she first decided to write a letter to every member of the Australian federal government, I didn't see the point. I've heard stories of people who have written letters and sought change from the people in power with little to no luck. We were just another family suffering a tragedy in our lives—why would they listen to us?

You cannot imagine my surprise when within a few hours of the letters being delivered she started receiving emails and phone calls from members of parliament, pledging their assistance to our cause. And incredibly, after meetings with several members and finally with the federal health minister, Greg Hunt, Mackenzie's Mission was born.

Mackenzie's Mission is beyond what we ever imagined when starting out on this journey, and it's all because of Rachael. After the diagnosis, I didn't have it in me to do anything but take care of Rachael and Mackenzie. I don't know where she found the energy to campaign the way she did, but I believe Australia owes her a debt of gratitude for her work around genetic carrier testing. I believe it will change the way Australia and eventually the rest of the developed world approaches planned pregnancy.

That night we went with Nigel, Martin and Edwin into the budget lock-up. This is where a group of people, primarily journalists, are given a briefing and documentation around what the new budget will be. They are allowed to study it so they can report on the details as soon as the treasurer announces it. Well, that's my dummy's guide version. We sat in the health lock-up where Minister Hunt outlined the genomics mission and its first project, Mackenzie's Mission. We sat in the front row, proud parents.

At the end of the lock-up, no one apart from the minister and his team are usually allowed to leave until the announcement, but Jonny and I were whisked away up to Parliament House to be seated within the chamber as the then treasurer Scott Morrison announced the budget for the next year. We sat there in awe of what was happening, pinching ourselves.

The next day we were asked to come back to Parliament House one last time to meet Scott Morrison and attend the Press Club lunch. As we waited outside in the great marble hall of parliament, Scott Morrison walked towards us and introduced himself. He said he was proud to meet Mackenzie's parents.

Inside the Press Club we sat at a table near Minister Hunt and watched Treasurer Morrison talk about the budget, and then all of a sudden we saw our daughter's face flash up on the screen. We suddenly felt all the cameras on us and looking at her up there, beautiful and big, we both started crying.

In the two years since that day I have sat on a number of the committees for Mackenzie's Mission: the steering committee, the education and engagement committee, the community advisory group and the gene selection committee. Often I attend these meetings in work hours, juggling the two commitments, but it is worth every second. It has been such an honour to be among the people who work every day on this important project, which so far is over one hundred people. The passion, commitment and intelligence Mackenzie's Mission has within it is extraordinary; I wish I had the space in this book to name every member. The joy it brings Jonny and I when we hear the name Mackenzie's Mission is immense. The purpose of Mackenzie's Mission is to offer reproductive carrier screening to couples, which provides information about their chances of having a baby affected by certain genetic conditions. The criteria for selected genes were that the conditions would be life-limiting or disabling, with onset in childhood—such that couples would be likely to take steps to avoid having an affected child, and/or for which early diagnosis and intervention would substantially change outcomes.

I want to particularly mention how proud we are of the steering committee members Martin, Nigel, Edwin, Kathryn North, Tiffany Boughtwood and Jade Caruana. I say this with a huge emphasis on the three leads of Mackenzie's Mission— Martin, Nigel and Edwin. They are a delight to be around and their intelligence and compassion are beyond belief. Each of them deserves to win Australian of the Year.

We wanted to stop the tears from falling for other people, and because of our baby, Minister Greg Hunt, Martin, Nigel and Edwin and every other extraordinary person who has contributed, our daughter has a legacy. Mackenzie's Mission.

Growth

'I am more vulnerable than I thought, but much stronger than
I ever imagined.'

Sheryl Sandberg

Knowing how to keep moving forwards after a tragedy is near
impossible, but what is harder is maintaining some remnants of
laughter, hope and happiness. Without these three elements, life
isn't worth living. Tragedy doesn't just attack our present—it
rips apart our hope for the future.

I felt when Mackenzie was diagnosed with a terminal illness
I would no longer function like a normal person, that those three
elements of my life would never exist again, and my life as I knew
it would essentially stop. I knew I would keep living, one breath
at a time, but happiness and love seemed beyond the realms of
possibility.

I had become a member of a club that I didn't want to be a part
of. I didn't even really know it existed before Mackenzie.

About nine months after Mackenzie died, I found that I was able to laugh at times. I could muster happiness and still had hope for the future. While this was a comforting realisation, I felt guilty. But I knew that Mackenzie wouldn't have wanted her death to end my life too, so I tried to push that guilt to the side. I began researching happiness after grief to see if others felt the way I did. Two books hit home with me. The first book is called *Option B* by Sheryl Sandberg and Adam Grant. Sheryl is chief operating officer at Facebook and she writes about resilience and grief following the unexpected loss of her husband, and with Adam she writes about post-traumatic growth. They outline three main ways people handle grief:

- You can struggle and develop depression or post-traumatic stress disorder, which is a legitimate response to extreme tragedy;
- You can be resilient and bounce back to where you were before the trauma, almost as though it didn't happen; or
- You can bounce forwards. You can find strength and meaning, using the tragedy to propel you into a stronger place in life.

The second book is *Any Ordinary Day* by Leigh Sales, and explores how life can change in an instant, again discussing the idea of post-traumatic growth. The takeaway for me was that those who have experienced tragedy have a remarkable way of becoming happier people than those who have had an 'easy life'.

A traumatic experience is a life-changing event. It robs us of our belief that life is just and fair. It takes away our belief that we can have any control over our lives. But it is important to know that it is possible for tragedy to have positive ripples. It is possible to have post-traumatic growth rather than post-traumatic stress.

I can't say it is easy to see the possibility of post-traumatic growth early after a tragedy or a life-changing event. It is too soon, and the pain is too raw to deal with that idea, but eventually we knew we had to adapt to our new life.

With this in mind I knew that I had this new life and I had to live it. I would never have chosen this life for myself, but it is hard to feel completely sorry for ourselves when we had been given the gift of Mackenzie.

It is difficult to look at tragedy as a possibility, but I tried hard to reframe our loss, to remember that this was our opportunity to be different people, better people, than we were before.

I was and remain determined that Mackenzie will always be a positive in my life. She taught me about life and love. She gave me a superpower. To lose my life when she took her last breath would be disrespectful to her. She didn't get a chance to live, but I do. This is the reason why I didn't start smoking again after she died. I had been a smoker in my youth but I was determined to not turn to smoking, alcohol or drug use because I knew I had a healthy body, which is something she didn't get. I was deter-mined to make something of her life and weave it into mine.

I suppose if I tried to name what my post-traumatic growth looks like it would be resilience, perspective, tenderness and less stress, and I am now more reasonable, I think. Previously I would be sent into a tailspin of anxiety in certain situations but now I take those on and overcome them.

I knew from reading as many books on overcoming adversity as I could that people who have gone through these tough times feel more grateful in life than those who haven't. Ironic, isn't it? People who have never had tragedy or immense pain are generally grumpier or feel more hard done by than those who have.

With this knowledge I decided not only to campaign for Mackenzie's Mission but to also share our story. This was partly for me, because I found the act of writing and sharing cathartic, but mainly because I knew of so many families struggling with similar issues, whether it be the death of a child, genetic conditions, miscarriages or IVF. Once I began talking about our story so many people reached out with their own. I became a lightning rod for people's sad stories, which is hard at times, but I want to hear them. People need to be heard.

I believe it is important to challenge our feelings in a tragedy in order to make change. I know I have created change and learned my lessons from Mackenzie. She is the biggest gift to my life.

Tips on grieving

'Let us be grateful to people who make us happy; they are the charming gardeners who make our souls blossom.'

Marcel Proust

I am by no means an expert on grieving (honestly, who wants to be an expert on grieving?) but I have certainly learned something about helping others through it. In some cases, the level of support you provide will depend on your relationship before the loss, however, I know firsthand that sometimes the support of a stranger or someone who was on your life's periphery can help even more than someone close to you. People far away can move closer and those close by can disappear. But no matter who you are, please know you can help someone who is grieving. Here are my tips.

1. Just be there. Don't avoid people or be scared—they need you now more than ever.
2. You don't have to talk to be there; sitting in silence just holding them works or sometimes even providing a distraction.

3. If you are unsure what to do for them then just ask what they need. Provide a list of what you could do and let them pick what they need or want.

4. Leave little care packages—food, massage vouchers, anything that would make them feel cared for.

5. Remember big dates: anniversaries, Mother's Day, Christmas. Set calendar reminders to send a little message or note.

6. You don't always have to be there. You have your own life, but a quick little message each day, week or month is enough to show you are thinking of them.

7. Let them share what they feel. Ask questions, even awkward ones. Most of the time people do want to speak and share, even about uncomfortable topics, so listen to them.

8. It is okay to be awkward. You don't have to know what to say, so don't let that get in the way of being there.

9. Don't disappear. Be around when others fall away. Chances are that when a tragedy first happens lots of people will be around to help, which is definitely needed. But as time passes, people forget as their lives move on. They don't realise that the pain of loss doesn't go away so quickly for the person grieving. So be there even months on.

10. Don't ever impose your timeline on someone else's grief. People are all different. Some people need more time than others and no one person's time frame is correct. And if you are in a family that is grieving, don't feel guilty if you are mending while someone else is still deep in grief. That is okay too.

11. Don't judge their grief. Everyone deals with grief differently. Just because someone isn't behaving the way you think you would doesn't mean it is wrong.

12. Just because they have one good day, don't expect the next to be good as well. Grief comes in waves, good and bad.

13. Do something kind. Little gestures of kindness create huge ripples. The acts of kindness we received did more for our mental health than people will ever know.

14. Don't be afraid to say the person's name. I am terrified Mackenzie will become a dream. When people say her name, my heart sings. I heard somewhere that when a deceased person's name isn't remembered, they die again. So if there is no cultural taboo associated for the person grieving, *say their name.*

15. Say something. Anything is better than nothing. Yes, it might come out wrong, but most people will understand that you are not an expert. Silence is so loud, and I can guarantee that someone going through a hard time will remember those who were silent as opposed to those who tried. One of the best things you can say is: 'I hear you, I see you, I acknowledge your pain. I'm here, keep speaking.'

16. Continue to share your life with them. Make them feel included in normal events, turn to them for help too. Kath was there for me every day but also let me be there for her. It gave me purpose and kept our friendship close. Conversely, people who were once good friends of mine didn't tell me they were pregnant because they were afraid to share their happiness with me. Continue to let people in and don't assume they won't want to be bothered by your life.

17. Don't minimise their pain or sugar-coat it. There is no need for you to explain their grief with quotes or clichés; it doesn't help and it trivialises their loss.

18. Don't say 'Let me know if I can do anything'. While it's a lovely sentiment, most people won't let you know, so think of something nice and just do it.

19. Don't be afraid of them. They are essentially the same person they were before.

20. Don't be afraid to cry in front of them, even if the person themselves is not crying in that instant. Your tears mean you care and you have empathy.

As I mentioned above, kind gestures are one of the main things that pulled Jonny and I through our pain. In some cases they were things that made our life easier and others just made us feel loved and like Mackenzie mattered to them. So here is a list of gifts and kind gestures that helped us and might help a grieving person in your life.

1. Organise a cleaner (as a group, if expensive).

2. Drop off food or order a food delivery.

3. For the artistic, create a drawing or painting from photographs.

4. Give a massage, acupuncture or meditation voucher, anything that will relax them and maybe take their mind off life for a minute.

5. Write the name of the person who has gone in the sand and send a picture to the person grieving, or write their name on a leaf and take a video of it being sent down a stream. (We received both of these and it was so beautiful; they came out of nowhere.)

6. Plant a tree in the person's name.

7. Make a donation in their name.

8. Name a star after the person, buy a plaque for a bench.

9. Light a candle for the person and send a photo to the grieving person.
10. If the grieving person has children, offer to look after them so they can have some alone time.
11. Donate blood in the person's name.
12. Give a memory gift. There are so many out there, such as teddy bears made to be the same weight as a baby, or lockets engraved with names.

These are just a few of the gifts we received and every single one of them made our heart sing. I have also had many people ask me how they should grieve. While every person's way of grieving will be different to another and no one way is 'correct', I do have a few tips.

1. Don't be afraid of antidepressants. They have been a lifesaver for me and Jonny, never clouding our grief but helping us put it into manageable chunks. It is not a failure or a permanent thing and it is not scary. Find a supportive doctor and have an honest discussion.
2. See a grief counsellor or a psychologist who specialises in grief. I found a wonderful specialist and our sessions are very helpful. In Australia, you can arrange a mental health plan with your doctor and access Medicare rebates on sessions.
3. It is okay to tell people what you need. Don't be afraid to ask for help, whether that is space, tangible assistance like food or just someone to sit with you. People generally want to help.
4. Be kind to others around you who are also grieving. Don't expect them to grieve like you.
5. Buy a motorbike. (That one is from Jonny!)

IVF

'It's not whether you get knocked down, it's whether you get up.'

Vince Lombardi

At the same appointment in which we learned about Mackenzie's diagnosis we were also dealt the blow of hearing that any future kids we had may also have SMA, given it is a genetic condition.

In order to avoid this we had two main choices. First, we could get pregnant naturally, test the foetus at three months and endure an excruciating wait to hear if the baby was healthy. Then there would be hard decisions to make if the baby was affected.

The second option would be to undergo in-vitro fertilisation (IVF). With IVF we would create embryos in a lab like 'regular' IVF, but then we would be able to test the embryos for SMA. Any affected embryos would not be transferred, meaning none of our future children would have to go through what Mackenzie did.

Hearing this information, I was hit by a thousand conflicting feelings. Talking about having more children in the same hour of learning Mackenzie would die was more than my brain could handle. I didn't want to think about more children, all I wanted was for my baby to stay safe in my arms. Despite this overwhelming feeling, once future children had been mentioned I needed to know the answer.

On a normal day, hearing our future would involve either IVF or an agonising pregnancy would be devastating news, but I remember feeling relief. There was at least a choice and our future had some sliver of hope. When you pick apart that moment, it is beyond belief. Life can put you in a situation where you can be happy about something that would normally be devastating because you have been told something a billion times worse.

So here we are: IVF. I never thought I would end up at this point but I suppose no one thinks that they will need assistance to have children at first. It seems like such a fundamental right for everyone, but as we learned and many others know, that just isn't the case.

Three months after learning of Mackenzie's diagnosis we sat in Dr Alison Gee's office, who worked for Genea. She was recommended to us by Kath and John; she had helped them conceive their two little ones. We did our research and found that the clinic had an excellent reputation, with experience in genetic testing. We wanted to start the process as soon as we could because we hoped that Mackenzie would be there when her sibling was born. I wanted to have memories of them together. Plus, at thirty-three I knew my age would soon become a factor.

Mackenzie slept through the whole appointment in her pram and was the perfect baby, as always. I can't even describe what a weird and painful appointment it was as we sat there, stunned, still trying to absorb the information that had been given to us. Weird and painful would describe much of our life from that point on.

Meeting Dr Gee was an important moment for us but at the time we didn't realise what a huge part she would end up playing in our lives. Dr Gee is a very matter-of-fact woman, straightforward but also kind and compassionate. Over time we would come to feel very close to her, but right then we just felt reliant on her for our future.

Dr Gee explained that before we could start IVF we would need a genetic test to be designed specifically for us. They would use our blood, Mackenzie's blood, some markers sent from America and some amazing science that I don't completely understand to create a test. The test would take three months to develop, but once completed it would be used to test any embryos we created through IVF. It would show where on our DNA the SMA gene was so when testing genetic material from our embryos they would know where to look for defective DNA. Called preimplantation genetic diagnosis (PGD), it is an incredible but expensive technology. I strongly believe PGD should be subsidised by the government as in the long run it would save Australia money and heartache, not to mention helping families that need it. It's a battle Genea have been fighting for quite some time.

Looking at each other nervously, Jonny and I agreed to proceed. We provided our blood samples to Genea but luckily they could use the blood that Sydney Children's Hospital already had from Mackenzie, as we really didn't want her to go through any pain or discomfort for the test. We signed the forms, paid the couple of thousand dollars the test cost and went back to focusing on Mackenzie. All thoughts of IVF left our minds.

Less than two months later, Mackenzie passed away.

In early December, just over a month after losing her and in the depths of our grief, we were contacted by Genea to say the test was ready. Jonny and I were torn. We felt utterly and completely destroyed without Mackenzie and couldn't see anything positive ahead of us. Our loss was so fresh. We were parents without our child in our arms.

But even though it was so raw, we also felt like time was getting away. When Kenzie was born we had found ourselves at a wonderful place in life—we were married, had bought our first tiny property and had a baby. Then she was taken away and we weren't where we thought we were. I wanted to feel a baby in my arms once more, my baby. So when the test was ready, we decided to start IVF. Once again, Jonny and I were given a choice that could have caused waves in our relationship but luckily, as with everything, we were on the same page. We both wanted siblings for Mackenzie despite the fact that she was no longer with us, or perhaps even more so because she wasn't.

As part of our treatment preparation, I had my egg levels checked. The first test showed that my levels were low, which worried me. The second test was an ultrasound that counts the follicles, and it showed my levels were average to high. The contradictory results no doubt made it harder for Dr Gee to decide how to proceed. I also had a range of blood tests and Jonny had his sperm checked again; luckily, everything looked good.

The reality of IVF is a lot more complicated than many people think. For starters, there are different levels of IVF and different 'add-ons'. When a couple is struggling with fertility, initially specialists will attempt to identify what the problem is. It could be polycystic ovarian syndrome, endometriosis, hormone imbalances, low egg quality, anti-sperm antibodies, sperm DNA fragmentation, problems with sperm count, morphology or motility, or it could be the frustratingly unexplained. The solution will depend on the problem.

If you are 'lucky', a fertility specialist will have a solution that does not include full-blown IVF, such as supplements, ovulation tracking, surgery (to deal with issues such as endometriosis) or artificial insemination, but sometimes, and in our case, IVF is needed.

With mental, physical, emotional and financial effects, IVF can be absolutely brutal. If you haven't been through it, understanding the true impacts can be difficult.

We have been incredibly lucky on the financial front. Telling our story to the world has often been hard and has come with some negativity, but there have also been many positives. One was the financial assistance we received, without which we would never have been able to do IVF, though it still hurt our bank balance over time. Just after receiving the call to say our genetic test was ready we were doing media interviews, telling our story in order to push our campaign forwards. During this period we received a call from the Kyle and Jackie O Show, a hugely popular Sydney morning radio program. They said they had heard our story and wanted to give us a platform to raise awareness about SMA and genetic testing. It was a surreal moment walking into the studio to see Kyle and Jackie. I had listened to them for years and was incredibly nervous, but they were so nice.

As I sat there and laid out our pain for thousands of people to hear, it turned out we were there for another reason as well. During our segment, Kyle and Jackie admitted to us that they actually had us in the studio for a 'Give Back'. 'Give Back' is a semi-regular segment where an unsuspecting person who has been through a tough time receives an incredible gift of kindness. I never for a second thought we would ever be on the receiving end of this but I am so incredibly thankful for it. They surprised us with a gift of $30,000 worth of IVF through Genea. We were beyond blown away. If you Google 'Kyle and Jackie O Give Back Mackenzie' you can see the video and the absolute shock on my face as I burst into tears. In our eyes they were effectively giving us our children—we were so lucky to receive this gift and I knew it.

Sadly, we worked our way through that $30,000 and a GoFundMe to assist us very quickly, but people's generosity blew us away on a daily basis, often reducing us to tears. We received some help and kindness from Genea and silent assistance for our last two rounds and without this we would never have been able to continue; every single person who contributed to our dream quite literally changed our lives. Despite everyone's generosity, we still had to dig significantly into our own finances to fund some of our IVF, not to mention all the side treatments that can assist such as vitamins, acupuncture, psychologists and massage for stress. It gives you an idea of how unattainable IVF is for many people in Australia, something that I hope changes in the near future.

To give you an idea, an average cost of an IVF round is $12,000, and Medicare gives you approximately $5000 back. Then any additional service can cost $500 to $1000 per embryo and couples can create 10 to 15 embryos per round on average. These are rough calculations, and not all IVF rounds are the same, varying in the hormones used and how long you take the hormones for. In fact, not all of my cycles were the same. I will go through one of my average cycles to give a glimpse of the process, including the discomfort, the pain and the mental torture.

A normal IVF round began on day one of my cycle. I would call the nurses at Genea and they would figure out when day 21 of my cycle would be and arrange for me to come in for a blood test then, to check that I had successfully ovulated. Once that was established I would start on my first hormone, usually a nasal spray taken morning and night called Synarel. It is designed to decrease the amount of oestrogen produced by the ovaries and allows for a more controlled environment for the specialists to stimulate egg production. It also meant that I didn't ovulate until they wanted me to.

The spray was easy to administer but left a bad taste in my mouth. It also irritated my nose but I had to make sure I didn't sneeze for five minutes as this would remove the drug. The hormonal effects were more difficult as it left me feeling sad, on edge and impatient—basically, I was a ball of rage. It would have been better to be alone during that time but unfortunately I still needed to work. I would try hard to not speak to people or snap too quickly, but I wasn't always successful. I tended to warn people, so they knew there was a reason. It was painful to feel so much tension in my body and I would get headaches and backaches. Plus, I knew I was supposed to be relaxing as stress is not good for IVF but it was impossible. It's like when someone tells you to smile and all it does is piss you off.

Once I started my period, I would usually be asked to get a blood test again to check the hormone levels. When they were happy with these I would start the stimulation drug. For me, this was usually a drug called Pergoveris, which I would have to self-administer as an injection. At first we had to mix it ourselves and draw up the solution in a needle, and this was usually Jonny's contribution if he was there. Later it came in an EpiPen style where all we had to do was dial the dose on the pen and place a needle on the end.

Jonny and I did the first injection together; in fact, for the first few rounds we did every injection together. We would sit in Mackenzie's bedroom so we felt close to her, like she was with us. We wanted her to be a part of it. I would sit in her nursing chair, Jonny would do the antiseptic wipe and I would do the injection. We would usually send love and energy into the universe and pray to any higher beings we thought might be listening (when you get desperate you will do anything). Finally we would sing a little song we liked to call 'Grow, Follicles, Grow'.

The first time I injected myself felt very strange. It goes against instinct to pierce your own skin with a sharp object, but after that I was fine. Luckily, needles don't bother me. They bother Jonny, though, so he would often make gagging noises—thanks, Jonny, that didn't put me off at all . . .

Over time we stopped doing the injections together. It just wasn't always possible with our different shifts, but also because we learned that our routine of wishing and praying did nothing. There was no point in our routine as the universe wasn't listening.

Pergoveris was supposed to stimulate the follicles. Each month in a normal non-IVF cycle, numerous follicles attempt to create eggs, however, the energy is then placed into one of those eggs and the rest drop off. Stimulation makes each of the follicles try to make mature eggs rather than just one.

The side effects for me from these injections were usually the same. They included headaches, a foggy brain and an aching body. I would become extremely tired but my sleep was restless, and of course my stomach would be bloated because a number of follicles were trying to grow.

From around seven days after the injections began the specialists would start monitoring my body closely. I would get almost daily blood tests and internal ultrasounds.

While I can write about all of this fairly clinically, the process is actually very stressful. Every test day I would wake up early to head to Genea, feeling nervous and quite sick about what today's results would show. The scan is an internal one, or as Kath coined it, the 'dildo cam' (I think you can guess why). The scan itself doesn't hurt but it is uncomfortable. They scan each ovary then count and measure the follicles. The ideal is for multiple follicles to be growing together in a group at the same rate, not some small and some large. At around 18 millimetres the follicles are more likely to hold a mature egg; the smaller follicles are unlikely to yield eggs or yield immature eggs that are not able to be fertilised. Every single time I had a scan I held my breath, feeling scared about how many follicles we would see and what size they would be.

In the afternoon, the nurses would call me with Dr Gee's instructions based on the ultrasound and blood test. If they wanted the follicles to grow more, they would ask me to keep taking the medication and tell me when to come in for my next scan. When as many follicles as possible were at 18 millimetres or above, but usually smaller than 25 millimetres, I would get the call to say it was time to take the trigger injection. This is a one-time injection in each cycle that tells your body to ovulate. The eggs go through a final stage of maturation before they are released.

The trigger injection always feels like a big deal. It was the one injection that Jonny and I always did together in Mackenzie's room. We'd usually kiss, and Jonny would sing the follicle song. The timing of the trigger injection must be very precise. It is normally at night and more often than not ours was at midnight. This is because the eggs must be collected exactly 36 hours after the trigger injection, otherwise the body will ovulate and the eggs will be released and unable to be collected at all.

After the trigger injection, no more medication is taken until the egg collection 36 hours later.

On the day of collection we would go into Genea early in the morning, Jonny always trying to lighten the mood by playing something like Salt-N-Pepa's 'Let's Talk About Sex' in the car. For the surgery, I wasn't allowed to eat or drink and couldn't use moisturisers, perfumes or nail polish. I always took a photograph of Kenzie or carried one of her toys with me. We would check in to the day surgery rooms and fill out paperwork until it was time to change into the robe. Then we would wait until Dr Gee, the embryologist and the anaesthetist visited to explain the procedure and what their role in it was. It was a process we would become very well versed in.

The egg collection is usually done under a light anaesthetic, where you are awake, or a twilight, where you are knocked out.

The first time I went in I asked for a light anaesthetic so I could know what they were doing. They obliged but, apparently, I kept talking about Mackenzie, crying and wanting to hug everyone, so the decision was made to always knock me out. Every single time Jonny made a crack to the anaesthetist about wanting a stash of his medication at home to administer to me when I annoyed him.

When it was time, they would wheel me into the theatre in my recovery chair and I would move onto the theatre bed, legs in stirrups with all my parts exposed for all the room to see. After confirming my details for the millionth time, the anaesthetist would put the oxygen mask on me and insert the cold liquid through the cannula into my hand. Then I would be gone.

Jonny always opted to come into the room for the egg collection, which can't be a fun or romantic sight to see. He was gentle and caring to me afterwards, so I am assuming it is rough to watch.

The eggs are collected vaginally using a needle and ultra-sound to find the follicles and withdraw the fluid, including the eggs, from each follicle into a test tube. Each tube is handed to the embryologist, who identifies if they contain eggs. Afterwards, while I was wheeled into recovery, Jonny would go to do his part.

I felt for Jonny: he had just watched the unsexiest thing of his life and then was expected to go and 'provide his sample'. Poor guy! It doesn't help when your wife, who is still out of it on medication, yells across the recovery ward, 'Good luck, baby—think sexy thoughts, like me two years ago, not me now.' Yep, that happened—I don't remember it but Jonny and the staff sure do.

Jonathan: I hate IVF—there, I said it. After months of watching your wife inject needles into her stomach, seven egg collections—or was it eight?—disappointment after disappointment when you either don't get as many eggs as you hoped or watch the numbers slowly deteriorate over the week before the best ones can be tested, I can honestly say I hate IVF. The doctors have been incredible, the staff, the scientists and nurses have all done everything they can to help us along our way, but ultimately, Rachael is injecting hundreds of needles over a two-year period with nothing but sadness to show for it. All the while, I sit next to her, trying to understand, trying to help, but as the guy, my duties start and end with me providing a sample each time we have a round. I can never understand exactly what Rachael has had to endure, I can never know the emotional rollercoaster of month after month of hormone stimulations, all I can do is be there and try to be her strength each time the bad news comes in and she falls apart.

I believe it's important to find the funny in situations wherever you can. I remember once I had to give a sperm sample to be tested for morphology, count and whatever else they test for. At Genea, the test would have cost around $300, so Rachael booked me into the public hospital to do it for free. I had already provided several 'samples' at Genea, where they provide a comfortable reclining chair, fantastic privacy, and everything else you might need for situations like this—first class all the way. At the public hospital, I was greeted by a staff member who was clearly angry that I was five minutes late. She escorted me to a small room that had a school chair and small desk with a 'sexy' magazine from about 2004 on top. She threw me a sample cup saying, 'Be quick, and clean up after yourself if you make a mess.' I could hear her keyboard clacking through the wall about two feet from where I was standing.

The sample nearly didn't happen!

For us, once the eggs are collected and Jonny has provided his sample, the embryologist injects one single sperm into each egg, which is called intracytoplasmic sperm injection (ICSI). This procedure is usually used when the problem is male fertility, that is, sperm can't successfully get to the egg on its own. For us it was different because we were using it to be certain about the genetic material. You see, in 'normal' IVF, numerous sperm are placed in a dish with an egg and left do their own thing to fertilise—a battle of the fittest. But for us it was important to be sure that what is tested is the embryo itself and not the genetic material of any unsuccessful sperm left around the fertilised egg. That's why just one sperm was injected directly into one egg, making the genetic test more accurate.

The average number of eggs collected in IVF procedures is twelve to fifteen, from my research. I would usually get between nine and eleven—not bad, but not great. Most people who undertake IVF will tell you it's all about quality, not quantity, which is mostly true. Yes, you could have fifteen eggs, but if they are poor quality, they won't survive; with five good eggs you have a chance. However, for us, because we were also doing genetic testing, we felt like we needed quality *and* quantity.

After the egg collection you go home feeling sore, very bloated and worse for wear, not to mention worried and hopeful all at once. This is where the excruciating mental torture starts. Yep, we haven't even got to the bad part yet.

The next day the clinic will call to report how many of the collected eggs were mature and how many fertilised; any immature eggs will not fertilise. Very quickly you begin to see your numbers dropping off. It is heartbreaking. Over the next few days the embryos should develop and increase in cell numbers, and we would receive regular updates on these stages. On day one they want to see that the eggs have fertilised and created two cells. On day three the embryo should contain between six and ten cells. On day five they want to see the embryo form into a blastocyst. For 'normal' IVF, most clinics will transfer embryos on either day three or five, but usually the latter. But we had to wait an extra day for another stage.

For us the process needs to go to day six, where they hope that the blastocyst will turn into a hatching blastocyst, which means it breaks out of its 'shell' in preparation for implanting on the uterus wall. We want this hatching to occur because this is when the cells are exposed enough for the embryologist to carefully extract a couple of cells of what will eventually become the placenta and test them with our PGD.

In addition to preimplantation genetic diagnosis for our SMA, we were also having preimplantation genetic screening (PGS) where embryos are checked for chromosomal issues like Down syndrome. It doesn't take any more cells to do and it means we reduce our risk of miscarriage due to chromosomal problems.

It is an excruciating process to wait for calls at some time during days one, three, five and six and be told how many embryos have dropped off. You spend each day on edge, jumping every time the phone rings. I cannot tell you the stress this part of the process causes me.

Some embryos won't progress fast enough or will just stop developing, perhaps due to a biological issue. Either way it is heartbreaking.

One thing you realise with IVF is that you have no control. I hated that feeling of uncertainty. I needed something to focus on, something to keep my mind busy and my fears at bay, so

I researched like crazy—literally, sometimes it made me crazy. But I needed to do something positive to help us be successful, to contribute to my family's journey. It was a strong desire to pull back control over my own life.

Initially we thought that, given we had no fertility issues, getting embryos would be easy. We thought our main difficulty was SMA. In hindsight, I'd say we went into this process feeling too sure we would be lucky on the first go. We thought that IVF would be a simple matter of going through a process, and that surely the universe couldn't keep hitting us. Once you lose a child the universe eases up on you, right?

We should have started with lower and more realistic expectations. People say that the first round is like a trial run and they are kind of right, but some people also only need one round. Our situation was confusing because technically we had no issues— maybe my body was rejecting the process because it didn't need it? But really, we didn't know why it was failing. It was heartbreaking.

This is a summary of each of the rounds we had in our first block.

Round one: we collected eleven eggs. On day one they called to say only seven were mature and of those three fertilised. We were shocked; it was our first round and we certainly didn't expect that. On day three they called to say that those three embryos were all looking okay but not great. On day five we were in Canberra visiting our families for Christmas. Genea called to tell us that two hadn't developed past day three and only one had made it to a blastocyst stage, but it wasn't strong enough to test or be frozen. Our first round failed—we didn't even get any to testing. Merry Christmas—no Mackenzie in our arms and no hope in the freezer.

Round two: we collected eleven eggs. On day one Genea called to tell us that six of the eggs were mature and four fertilised. On day three we were told that two were good and developing well (eight cells), the third was okay (six cells) and the fourth had fallen behind (four cells). At day five they told us that two were good and a third was in the race but still a bit behind, while the fourth was gone. They needed to give the embryos another day though because they hadn't hatched enough to take the edge cells for genetic testing. On day six Genea called again to tell us that two had hatched (broken out of the egg membrane) allowing then to be tested and frozen. The third couldn't be tested but we asked for it to be frozen, just in case. Two made it to testing—we couldn't believe it. We were over the moon until we remembered that we still needed them to test healthy. The wait was excruciating. Two weeks and two days later I received the call standing in a post office, and my heart began racing so fast I thought I would have a heart attack. The embryologist said one was viable and had only tested as being a carrier of SMA (like we were) but the other had tested as being clear of SMA but it had a chromosomal abnormality. I didn't know how to feel. Was this a success? Two rounds of IVF and one healthy embryo? I went home to tell Jonny and his positivity rubbed off on me. One was wonderful—we would take what we could get.

Despite getting this one healthy embryo we decided not to transfer it yet. Firstly, we had decided that, ideally, we would like to aim for two more children. If we transferred that one embryo and it stuck then we would not be able to try for our third child until I was around 38; we were worried that by then I wouldn't have many eggs left or they wouldn't be good quality. In addition, I was nervous about how I would handle it mentally if we transferred that embryo and it didn't stick. There is only around a 50 per cent chance of an embryo implanting successfully so if it didn't, would I be strong enough to take it yet? Plus we still had some of the donated money from Kyle and Jackie O, which stipulated that it was $30,000 or until a pregnancy. If we transferred that embryo and it stuck, the rest of the money would not be ours to use for future children. So we decided to continue with IVF and collect more embryos.

Round three: in this round we began adding medications and supplements to improve the results. On egg collection day we got ten. On day one, eight were mature and six fertilised. On day three they called to say four embryos were doing very well while the other two were still dividing and looking good but were slightly behind. So six were still in play—this was our best yet. On day five the update was that all six were still progressing; we couldn't believe it. The embryologist said that three of the embryos were beginning to hatch but needed a few more hours to develop cells that could be tested. But we had three! And the other three still looked okay, apparently at early blastocyst stage. Maybe would we get more than three!

On day six, Jonny and I knew we would be getting our call in the afternoon, so we took a walk down near the water, nervous but for once excited. The embryologist called and said, 'Well, I have some good news—two embryos have got to testing.' Two? Yesterday it looked like we would be getting at least three, plus potentially three more.

Apparently the third embryo had started to hatch but had then run out of energy and begun disintegrating. The other three had made it to blastocysts but were not showing any signs of hatching so they would never be able to be tested.

We felt absolutely devastated. We had now made around twenty embryos that for a 'normal' couple might have produced a healthy baby. But for us, because the embryos needed to be strong enough to be tested, we had a total of only four embryos that could be tested, two from round two and now two from round three.

I crashed emotionally. After finishing the call, I burst into tears on the side of the road. The whole way home I was wailing, the kind of ugly cry that takes over your whole body. Jonny walked beside me, doing his best to hold and comfort me. Once we got home, I curled into a ball on the couch. Jonny got me a Valium, a hot water bottle and covered me with a blanket. I cried uncontrollably. I cried for Mackenzie, I cried for the babies that I would now never meet and never know if they were healthy and could have been in my arms, I cried for the time added without a baby in our lives, I cried that it would be longer before I could hold Mackenzie's sibling. I was devastated. Jonny was too, but he holds more hope in his heart. Maybe it is because he doesn't have the hormones coursing through his body. But I think he remains more hopeful even in the dark.

The next few days we dragged ourselves around, knowing we had a two-week wait until we got the test results for our two remaining embryos. Jonny sits back and tries not to think about the test results, but I google. I google statistics and people who have been through similar experiences, but it doesn't actually help because every case is different. I knew there was a 25 per cent chance of the embryos having SMA, and also a 25 per cent chance of the embryos having a chromosomal issue, based on my age.

Finally, the two weeks were up. I was in the middle of a 12-hour work shift by myself with no one around who could take over from me when I received the call. When I answered the phone, I could tell it wasn't good news. They told me that, sadly, neither embryo was healthy. One had SMA and one had a chromosome disorder. I felt numb. I thanked the embryologist and hung up.

On automatic pilot I called Jonny and told him. I felt sorry for him, standing in uniform in a crowd. He was on a new team and it was one of his first shifts with them. Jonny asked if I was okay and if I needed him to come and get me. I said I would be alright and got off the phone, then stood staring for five minutes until I broke down. Eventually I realised I could not sit there alone for the next five hours feeling heartbroken. I called my boss who came and took over from me and then called Jonny to come and pick me up.

Jonny was 40 minutes away, so I waited in a nearby park, openly weeping. I looked around and saw I was sharing the park with some homeless people with mental health issues, but that night I was the person they were scared of.

Jonny and I now have a routine for when we get this type of bad news. Jonny puts me on the couch with a blanket and a wine or gin and tonic then orders us pizza and some Messina ice-cream for himself. It doesn't ease the pain, but what more can we do? Comfort eating helps.

I spent the night crying (again), watching Mackenzie videos and just trying to let myself feel all the emotions. The next day when I woke up, I looked like I had been beaten up, with eyes red and swollen from crying. While I looked awful from the outside, I was busy trying to rebuild myself on the inside. I knew that I needed to gather my hope and courage to begin again. We needed to dust ourselves off and keep going.

Rounds four and five: we continued to add and subtract supplements for these two rounds, hoping something would help my egg quality, which we suspected was the issue. Dr Gee and her counterparts were all confused by our results. They weren't consistent with our ease of pregnancy and our test results. For these two rounds I was so broken that I didn't even document what happened. From memory, both times we collected around seven or eight eggs, and of those only one made it to day six. That one little embryo didn't hatch so couldn't be tested, but we asked for it to be frozen anyway.

Over the time I did IVF I tried a range of things that might help our results, from high-protein/low-carb diets to the inclusion of vitamin D, coenzyme Q10, prenatal vitamins, fish oil, royal jelly tablets, dehydroepiandrosterone (DHEA), Chinese herbs, bee pollen, melatonin, raspberry leaf tea and human growth hormone (HGH). I tried acupuncture, keeping my feet warm, castor oil packs, positive thinking, negative thinking, praying, begging, meditation, yoga and even having the colour orange near me during stimulation (either an old Chinese tradition or someone on Google stitching me up, but I was willing to try anything).

I explained to my psychologist that sometimes I felt like my thoughts and actions could influence the outcome of our lives, of IVF. Maybe I didn't take the right photograph into IVF. Maybe I wore different socks to the egg collection. Maybe I wasn't thinking the right thoughts or maybe I hadn't found the right combination of rituals. She explained that this was common and called 'magical thinking'. It is something people tend to do when they are lacking control in their lives.

In our first 'block' of IVF I did five rounds in ten months. In those five rounds we got only four embryos to day six and to testing. Of those four, one was healthy (only a carrier like Jonny and I), one was affected by SMA, one had a chromosomal issue and the final one had both SMA and a chromosomal issue. So all up from five rounds we only had one embryo that we could transfer into me. We also had two blastocysts frozen that hadn't been tested because they didn't hatch in time, which meant that if we transferred them and they implanted we would have to treat them like a natural pregnancy and have the baby's placenta tested at twelve weeks.

We were devastated.

I felt stupid for thinking one round would work. We started our IVF path completely naïve about it all. We thought no fertility issues meant lots of embryos. Yes, a few would be affected with SMA, but the rest would be fine. We were so sure of getting embryos we had even agreed to find a way to donate any 'spare' healthy embryos to those who needed them.

I felt stupid because after losing Mackenzie, a part of me secretly clung to the concept of karma and there being a balance in the universe. Surely, I reasoned, if you lose a child then the universe would balance things out and cut you some slack. Life wouldn't be so cruel to rip your child from you and then make you battle to have her siblings, right?

Stupid, stupid me. There is no order to the universe, no god, no karma.

After our IVF journey, I feel a great admiration for, and connection with, others who have gone through it, especially those who endure years of treatments. The money spent, the tears wept—it shouldn't be this way for anyone. But the determination and amazing fortitude of these women and their partners who have such a strong desire to be parents deserves our admiration. I also believe they deserve more financial assistance to help them. We know we were lucky on that front.

But what was next for us? We decided to take a break from IVF for a few months and try naturally.

Bella

'We didn't get to meet you, we never got to see you but we will always hold you in our heart.'

Rachael Casella

I still struggled to understand how we had ended up here. I was now 34 years old and Jonny was 39. We had spent almost a year trying to get pregnant with Mackenzie's siblings and, despite being fertile, we still didn't have a baby in our arms. Five rounds of IVF and only one healthy embryo to show for it, and we didn't even know if this embryo would become a baby for us given there was only a 50 per cent chance of successful implantation. We felt lost and disheartened.

After the fifth round we decided to take a break to give my body and mind a chance to rest. We had also well and truly run out of the funds we had been gifted by Genea through Kyle and Jackie O as well as the GoFundMe campaign. Taking a break from IVF was a hard decision, especially as I saw my thirty-fifth birthday looming ahead, but the clinic thought my stress levels were affecting my response to IVF, so Jonny and I made the difficult decision to try naturally. We figured with no fertility issues getting pregnant should be easy—the hard part would be waiting to see if the baby had SMA.

With a natural pregnancy the process would involve a different kind of stress. First we would have to make it through three months, the dreaded miscarriage risk zone which is stressful for any couple, but for us we could be going through this stress only to find that our baby wasn't healthy. Having already had a miscarriage we knew what the risks were and could no longer be naïve about the possibility. Once we had got to twelve weeks, we would undertake the recommended test, a chorionic villus sampling (CVS), where an ultrasound guides a needle through my stomach to take a sample of the baby's placenta. This would be tested to see if the baby was affected by SMA or had chromosomal issues. There was a low risk that the test would cause miscarriage but we knew it had to be done.

Then it would be an anxious two-week wait to find out if our baby was healthy or not. There would be a 25 per cent chance they would have SMA and a normal couple's chance of having a chromosomal disorder.

Jonny and I had already made the decision that if a baby tested positive for SMA we would medically interrupt the pregnancy. I can assure you this decision and knowing that it might be our reality one day both terrified and upset us. We knew it would be the second worst thing to happen to us. However, before you judge us too harshly, please understand that we had first-hand experience of what the life of an SMA baby would be like;

that we would knowingly be giving birth to a child who would potentially suffer chronic illness throughout their short life and definitely pass away within a few short years. It was a decision we knew was the right one for us, but we hoped that this would never become a reality.

With all this knowledge, we decided to spend four or five months trying naturally before starting IVF again.

The first month we were unsuccessful, although in fairness we only decided to start trying just as my fertility window was closing. The next month we went back to Genea's free ovulation tracking as it had worked for us before. Initially the pregnancy test had an extremely faint positive line, however two days later the line disappeared and was now negative. At this stage I was starting to worry; while two months of trying isn't long, we had always felt like we had natural pregnancy in our 'back pocket'. It had always been our backup plan. If this didn't work, I didn't know how I would feel mentally.

We tried again the next month with tracking and we got a positive! I tested for the next seven days and each day we got positive lines, but they weren't getting darker. I had also tried a couple of digital tests as they have a higher threshold for the pregnancy hormone HCG and these were saying negative. Deep down I knew something wasn't right but Jonny was trying to be positive. We had a blood test to check and, sadly, it came back showing that I had been pregnant but wasn't anymore. It was a very early miscarriage or a chemical pregnancy.

We tried to see this as a positive: we had got pregnant so maybe we could again. But I still felt so deflated. Worse was the timing: the blood test results came three days before the anniversary of

Mackenzie's death. We had thought that maybe this pregnancy was meant to be, that it would be poetic that we were having a positive test result. So to discover we had lost the baby felt like a kick to the heart in an already impossible time.

It felt like our IVF experience all over again. Just as we had assumed we would have no problems getting embryos, that our issue would be testing them, we had also assumed we would get pregnant naturally and the only struggle would be waiting to be tested.

But like every other month, we got up, brushed ourselves off and tried again the next month.

Any couple who has had fertility problems will know that the least romantic sex is the 'trying to conceive sex'. Having to have sex around about five times in one week might sound fun but it is exhausting! Jonny now says that the definition of love is when two people don't want to have sex but they do it anyway.

In our fourth month of trying we knew we were using our last free ovulation tracking with Genea as Medicare only pays for three. The timing worked out well: the tracking and the trying to conceive would be all done before we headed away on a trip. It was a full schedule: first to Brisbane for a couple of days, then to Toowoomba for our friend Liz's wedding and down to Byron Bay for some couple time and to recreate some memories we had there with Mackenzie. Then we would fly back to Sydney for one night before driving to Echuca to spend a few nights on a houseboat on the Murray River for Jonny's friend Kim's fortieth birthday.

On our last day in Byron as we drove back to Brisbane airport, we decided that if we weren't pregnant this month, we would try for one more month as Genea usually closed down over Christmas, but we would start IVF again in January. Desperate to have a plan in place, we called our fertility specialist as we drove. Dr Gee looked at my cycle and noticed that I would be ovulating over new year when they were closed. So we had a choice: we could start the next cycle in November, which actually meant starting the medications the very next day, or we would have to wait until February. Jonny and I looked at each other and nodded in agreement. Dr Gee asked us to come into the clinic for a blood test the next day to check my levels and confirm I wasn't pregnant and to collect the medication.

Next morning we woke up early and headed into Genea before we started the long drive down to Victoria. It was all very rushed, but as always we were willing to do whatever we had to. As we crossed the state border we got the call from Genea to say that my HCG level was 4.7; over five was considered pregnant, so I was officially not pregnant. Again. My heart hurt but a plan was made that from that night I would begin taking the first hormone.

When we arrived in Echuca, our dear friends Kim and Jacs shared the exciting news that they were nine weeks pregnant. We were so delighted for them; they had been trying and were truly wonderful friends and humans. They had also been incredibly supportive when it came to Mackenzie. Despite being happy for them, I was pretty on edge and am ashamed to say that I broke down. I excused myself and went to our little room on the houseboat. I felt so ashamed to be crying—it wasn't at all to do with their happiness but more to do with my pain. We are so lucky that they are such kind and understanding people and understood my reaction, but I still felt like a horrible human.

After sobbing for hours, I eventually pulled myself together enough to take my first IVF hormone for that round. Each round usually began with hope for a future where we held Mackenzie's siblings, but this round just started with a lot of emotional pain and anxiety.

The next morning I woke up in a serenely picturesque place, floating gently as the birds chirped and cicadas buzzed outside. But I felt like I had been hit in the head, eyes swollen and red from crying, nose blocked. In the bathroom I noticed one last pregnancy test in my toiletry bag and decided to take it, I have no idea why. Maybe I had just become a sucker for punishment.

I went and made myself a coffee, and coming back a few minutes later I glanced at the pregnancy test. It had two lines.

No, that couldn't be right.

I looked again.

Two lines.

My immediate reaction was anger—enough playing with my emotions. I spun on my heel and went to get Jonny. Once in the safety of our room I thrust the test at Jonny.

He looked down and said, 'I knew it.'

'How could you have known it?' I demanded. 'We got a definitive blood test yesterday saying we weren't pregnant.'

Jonny said he had just assumed it had been too early. But I was not convinced—a blood test is a thousand times more accurate than a home pregnancy test. I had been down this road before and got my hopes up, but not this time.

My head was spinning.

After apologising to Jacs, I showed her the test, and she was as confused as me.

I called Dr Gee's office, who said that they wanted us to come in for another blood test, but we weren't going to be back for four days. They advised us that the hormone we were taking for IVF would not have a negative effect on a baby if taken for a few days so to continue with it in case we still needed to do an IVF cycle.

That afternoon we went into town and bought a digital test; if the last couple of months had taught me anything it was that digital tests were more reliable. The next morning the digital test popped up another positive result.

We stopped taking the IVF medication and the next few days were a confusing blur. Could I have champagne to celebrate Kim's birthday? Was I actually pregnant?

A few days later we were back in Sydney and another blood test came back positive. They kept doing blood tests every few days to check that my HCG levels were rising, which they were, so next we contacted the Royal Hospital for Women in Randwick. The RHW midwives, especially a wonder woman named Kate, gathered around us with compassion, understanding and a plan.

We had to wait four more agonising weeks until we were eight weeks and four days to have our first ultrasound. I was scared every time I woke up and every time I went to the toilet, expecting to see blood, but it didn't happen. The initial ultrasound showed a healthy little baby, although there is not too much they can tell at that stage. Bubs was measuring correctly for the gestational age and had a strong heartbeat. We got photos from the hospital like any doting parents, but we were acutely aware that it may be one of the only times we got to see this baby and the only photograph we would ever hold. We tried to soak it up but also keep an emotional distance. Once again, we were living on a knife's edge.

There was nothing else to do but go home and wait for another month to have the CVS, which would happen at around twelve and a half weeks.

Those few weeks were torture. I had the normal symptoms for a first trimester pregnancy: nausea, weight gain and extreme fatigue. I was struggling to get through each day without falling asleep and was dragging myself around. But, of course, I had to try to act normally because we decided to only tell our family.

At eleven weeks I couldn't wait anymore: I needed to see the baby again. What if our baby had passed away but here I was, falling more in love every day? I contacted RHW, who kindly arranged a quick ultrasound to give me some relief. I rushed to the hospital and held my breath as the ultrasound probe hit my skin, but straight away there was baby, and there was his or her heart beating at a perfect pace. I was so relieved.

Finally, twelve weeks and four days arrived. I went to bed early the night before; I had been sleeping more regularly, partly because I was tired and partly because sleeping gave me a break from waiting and from my mind circling. In the morning we went to a local cafe for breakfast and mostly sat in silence, in our own heads and unsure how to feel. We arrived at RHW an hour early but we didn't know what else to do.

First there was a meeting with the geneticists to go through the plan. They would find out when the results would be ready and make an appointment for us to come in, that way we wouldn't get the results over the phone when we could be anywhere, doing anything. We also met the rest of the genetics team, the people who would be delivering our child's fate to us.

The ultrasound room was busy: there was the head midwife, the head of the department who would do the CVS, the sonographer, a midwife who hadn't seen a CVS before and a medical student. We didn't mind who was there; if it was for training it was fine with us.

The sonographer started by taking a look at bubs, and straight away he or she was up bouncing about on the screen. The heartbeat was perfect and all the measurements looked good. I felt some relief.

Once they found the position of the placenta they decided they could do the CVS through my abdomen instead of vaginally. I was again relieved, as getting the local anaesthetic on my stomach would hurt less than getting it inside my uterus, plus it was a bit easier for the doctors. They disinfected and put some local anaesthetic on the area before, using the ultrasound, the doctor inserted a large needle into my stomach. She had warned me that the local would help relieve the pain on the skin but I would feel the needle push through my muscle to my placenta. I felt the pressure as the needle moved through me but, luckily, I am not scared of needles—all I cared about was staying still. The doctor had also advised me that they would have to make a push and pull motion to suck up a good sample of the placenta. It was an odd feeling, but not too painful.

And just like that, it was done.

I was so proud of Jonny for not passing out and continuing to hold my hand. He usually didn't like anything medical, but I guess over the last two years he had had to become more desensitised.

They said the sample was good, not overly big but with good-sized roots. They showed us and it really did look like little white roots sitting at the bottom of the sample tube, surrounded by a liquid that looked like watered-down blood. Those little roots would tell us our future.

A little band-aid was placed over the tiny wound and we waited to see if I would faint after the adrenalin wore off. As we sat, we were given the aftercare instructions. Within 24 hours we would get a call telling us the results of the standard non-invasive prenatal test (NIPT) test which would include the gender (if we wanted to know it) and more importantly the diagnostic chromosome result of trisomy 13, 18 and 21. We would have to wait ten days to find out the result for SMA and the full chromosome scan.

How were we supposed to get through ten days?

We left the hospital full of hope but beyond terrified. We knew we had a 75 per cent chance that this baby would be healthy. There was a 75 per cent chance that we were starting down a path of happiness in life; maybe we would be able to really smile again.

The following Friday at 2 p.m. I received a call from the genetics department at Sydney Children's Hospital telling us to be there in three hours to receive the results. Instantly my stomach began swirling, almost throwing up its contents. Jonny and I sat in Mackenzie's room holding her stuffed toys, wishing to the universe or any higher power willing to listen that this baby be healthy and that we would come home happy and ready to yell our news from the rooftops.

We showered and dressed before lying down in bed holding each other for a minute. So much was riding on this meeting and we had no control over it whatsoever.

We drove to the RHW in silence, both working through our emotions. Most of the lights were off in the foetal medicine unit and no patients or staff were around. I put my head in my hands on the desk while we waited, struggling to not throw up. When the head midwife, Kate, arrived saying the doctor was on the way I burst into tears, the pressure building up in me uncontrollable.

The midwife returned shortly afterwards with a doctor by her side. Jonny said he knew the results before the doctor opened his mouth, it was written on his face. Whereas I sat there searching his face for any hope.

He said he wasn't really sure how to tell us the results.

Jonny said, 'Just like a band-aid, be honest and rip it off.'

'It isn't a good result—your baby has SMA.'

I instantly went numb, all my desperate hope for happiness drained out of my body. I would not be able to keep this baby that I had been nurturing. I instinctively held my bump, feeling like I had failed our baby.

Jonny kept repeating the word 'No'; I could see the news jolting through him like an electric shock.

We asked the doctor our baby's gender and were told it was another beautiful baby girl. A baby girl ... Apparently, every other part of her was healthy. A full chromosome screen came back with nothing but a perfect baby. That news somehow made it worse.

The doctor and Kate clearly hated giving this news, and we knew this was not the first time for them. Such a horrible part of their job.

The doctor left the room after asking if we had any questions, but there really was nothing we needed to know. We knew the possible treatments and outlook for SMA even better than him— we knew what the future looked like and had already decided that it wasn't a life for our child.

As the numbness receded and realisation kicked in, the crying began. Kate held my hand as Jonny rubbed my back. We sat there looking at each other with pain and shock in our eyes. What more could we do? Nothing we could say would change the outcome; we knew from experience that we had to sit in our pain. We had to ride this initial shock, hold each other and come to terms with what had been handed to us. Fighting would do nothing, begging and praying would do nothing, it never did.

Before we left, Kate went to her office and returned with a bottle of champagne. Kate explained that this was something of a tradition, a 'pay it forward'. Each couple who had to receive the same news as us recently have been given a bottle of champagne. Once they had a healthy baby, they returned to the hospital with the bottle of champagne, paying it forward. We were now the owners of the champagne and were determined to return it as soon as we could.

After making another appointment for 8 a.m. on Monday, we made the now familiar walk to the car. Driving home in silence and tears, we walked through our front door feeling like we were once again being dragged through hell.

The weekend went slowly. We had now become experienced in handling heartache. It wasn't a perfect routine, but it was what we knew: couch, blanket, gin, pizza. For hours we did not move from the couch, just holding each other, crying and looking at each other's pain, unable to take it away. Jonny went into protection mode, fussing around and making sure I was okay.

That night we both took a sleeping tablet to try to knock us out. It's probably not the healthiest way to manage intense emotions but sometimes you just need to switch off, to pull away and protect your soul.

Over the weekend we had to tell the people we loved what we were going through. The hardest part was telling our families: they knew we were pregnant and had shared the anxious wait with us. Then we had to tell friends who didn't even know we were pregnant, including my Instagram family. To some it might seem odd to share this news with a group of people whom I mainly don't know, but for me it was an extremely important step. They were my friends and my support system.

Once again, our tribe gathered around, with family, friends, workmates and Instagram followers jumping up and surrounding us with love. Their thoughts and kindnesses meant so much to us—every message, every comment, every gift helped to lift us up. Once again it highlighted that those who were empathic and mature enough to handle our situation, our pain, were often not who you would think.

On Monday morning we got up early and dragged ourselves to the hospital. We weren't nervous, we had already had our dreams ripped away, we just knew we had to go through the motions. Kate took us to meet with one of the hospital specialists in foetal medicine, a lovely doctor who asked us how we wished to proceed. She made it clear that they were here to support any decisions we made.

Jonny and I advised that we would be having a medical interruption. Every medical professional we spoke to understood and, as much as they are allowed to indicate, agreed with our decision. The doctor explained that the procedure was a dilation and curettage, pretty much the same process as if we had miscarried, where they dilate your cervix and carefully remove the baby along with the placenta and other pregnancy 'products'. There are no words to describe what that sounded like to me.

I asked what would happen to our beautiful baby. They said that as I was having a general anaesthetic, the baby would as well and would only know warmth and love. She would fall into a deep sleep and then would be gone. Her precious little body would be treated with love, respect and care before being cremated by the hospital.

I listened through tears and heartbreak as they explained the procedures and the risks. How could we once again be being asked to make such decisions? Whether our child died now, knowing no pain and only love but we would never hold them or kiss them, or later, when they were in your arms, but they may have spent months or years suffering? Of course, I wanted to hold my child, of course I wanted to hug her, but I had to put my own needs and wants aside. Making hard decisions is part and parcel of the responsibilities of a parent and I knew that Jonny and I would take on all the pain and grief for our child instead of asking her to.

After signing the relevant forms and booking in on Thursday for the procedure, we left knowing we only had three days left with her, three days left to feel her inside me.

That afternoon all we could do was sit at home and cry. But the next day, once again we pulled ourselves up and realised that our daughter deserved more. At Centennial Park in Sydney, the place that housed all of those precious moments with Mackenzie, I took my bump, our littlest girl, on the same walk around Centennial Park that I had taken Mackenzie on so many times. We stopped by Mackenzie's celebration step and took photos. We walked past the spot where as a family we had celebrated Mackenzie's first birthday without her and then finally to the area where we had celebrated Mackenzie's life at her farewell party. Eating lunch in the park,

I cradled my bump before we went home. It was so special and important to do that walk together, just us girls.

On the final day we had our little girl, Jonny and I took a drive down to the Kangaroo Valley and Berry, the same drive we did when I was 36 weeks pregnant with Mackenzie.

That night we held my bump, took photos and told her tomorrow she would be with her sister. We also decided on a name for her, Bella. Italian for 'beautiful'.

The next day we were up early to be at the hospital before 7 a.m. We drove in silence once again before checking in to day surgery. The nurse who admitted me looked familiar and we sat trying to figure it out; it turned out she was the nurse who began Mackenzie's induction.

Less than an hour later I was in my hospital bed, a tablet inserted into my cervix to soften it and help make the procedure easier and safer for me. After about half an hour my uterus was cramping and I asked Jonny to get the doctor; I didn't care about my pain but I wanted to know that this process was not being felt by the baby at all. They said it wasn't, all the baby would feel was gentle rocking.

As I lay there waiting, surprise visitors started to arrive. First up was Dr Giselle Crawford, who delivered Mackenzie via caesarean. Oh my gosh, we were so happy to see her. She had sent a beautiful message after Mackenzie died that meant the world to us. Along our journey we have met some medical professionals who said they were unsure whether to contact families after tragedies; I think they were concerned about maintaining a professional distance. But for any medical professional reading this, we assure you that for a family to know that their loved one was thought of by people was the biggest gift you could give. Seeing Giselle was incredible. She spoke about Mackenzie and also Mackenzie's Mission with tears in her eyes, showing compassion and kindness. While medical professionals need to protect themselves, they don't have to be robots.

Next was Gemma, the midwife who looked after us for Mackenzie's birth. Jonny and I had always loved Gemma. She was a part of our journey and, along with our other midwife Cat, had visited Mackenzie just before she died. She had also been booked in to be the midwife for Bella. It was so nice to see her smile. Gemma told us that before she came up to the room she and the other midwives were downstairs singing a rendition of Britney Spears for Kenzie. We felt so much love.

Then came Ali Gripper, the lovely woman who had made a video of our story for the RHW Gala Ball and had become a part of the media start-up for Mackenzie's Mission; she is such a divine woman. While Ali sat with us in came Kate, the midwife, and Rebecca, the genetic counsellor we had been seeing for this pregnancy. We felt so supported and hoped Bella felt the love radiating through to her.

It was suddenly clear how connected we were to this medical complex. We had spent so much of our lives here in recent years.

Around 11 a.m. they came around to say the theatre was ready for me. Jonny and I instantly locked eyes. This was it.

Jonny walked beside my bed as it was pushed along the corridor, down one level and through the doors. I instantly recognised the theatre as where I had the D&C after our miscarriage. I think it was also the area where Mackenzie was born. A wall of emotion hit me.

Jonny kissed my stomach and whispered to Bella before kissing me. I watched the electronic doors close with Jonny peeking through until the very last minute. My rock, my soulmate, my everything.

As they wheeled me further into the theatre area, I heard a newborn crying; it must have just been born via caesarean. One life starts while another life was about to end. How can this world be so cruel? For the millionth time I asked, why us?

Nurses and doctors surrounded the bed, one asking me to confirm my name while checking my hospital admission bands. They asked me to say in my own words what I was there for. I whispered, 'I am here to medically interrupt my pregnancy with a D&C.' With those words spoken aloud I began crying hard and desperately for my baby. One of the nurses held my hand under the sheet while another got me tissues.

Still crying in the anaesthetic prep room, a box of tissues on my chest, I could hear the theatre staff preparing in the next room. When a young woman in scrubs came in and appeared to be looking for someone, I smiled at her between the tears, trying to make the situation less awkward, but she slipped out again. A couple of minutes later she was back, again pretending to look around while obviously gathering the courage to speak to me. Eventually she turned and asked if she could sit in on my procedure. I nodded yes as I continued to cry. She smiled and slunk out of the room, an awkward encounter for us both, I am sure.

The anaesthetist eventually arrived and inserted a cannula. As he told me I was going to start to feel a little tired, I remember begging him through tears to tell everyone to be as gentle as they could with both me and my baby, that she was very loved. He assured me he would pass it on. I laid my hand on my belly and said goodbye to Bella as my eyelids were dragged down.

When I woke up in recovery, the nurse beside me asked about pain. In reply, I asked groggily if they had been gentle with Bella, but she didn't seem to know what I was talking about and told me she was giving me some fentanyl. After that I was asleep again.

Around 2 p.m. I was wheeled upstairs and saw Jonny, who was waiting in the closest area to me that he could. He walked alongside the bed to the next recovery room where, over the next couple of hours, I slowly came to. They gave me some more pain-killers which helped but they also made me sweaty and dizzy. There were pads underneath me to absorb any bleeding. Around 6.30 p.m. I was finally discharged. The nurses and doctors were amazing and I am so thankful to them for their care, but I was missing my baby.

Over the next few days I tried to rest and let my body recover. It was so hard because my body still felt and looked pregnant but there was no baby in me. My Bella was gone. All that I could hope was that she was now with her big sister, that they had each other. Mackenzie wasn't by herself.

Not long after losing Bella I happened across comments about abortions made by someone I followed on Instagram. New York had just changed its laws so women could now medically inter-rupt pregnancies that were nonviable or threatened the health or life of the mother right up until birth. This person was saying it was wrong to terminate a baby under any circumstances, even if the baby had a terminal illness. She said that she would love a child no matter what and went on to post inaccurate information about how the procedures were performed.

I was struck by the ignorance of this. No one will ever know the immense love I have for my daughters, but with that love comes a responsibility to make hard decisions. To not say yes to a life of pain and force a child to go through that. We know in our hearts that this was the right decision for Bella and for our family. As a parent, you love your child more than anything, no matter what.

While this woman was entitled to her own opinion, as the mother of two healthy children she had never had to care for anyone who was terminally ill or seriously sick. She had no experience of what others have endured and could not possibly know what she would actually do in such a situation.

I have discussed medical interruptions with hundreds of people, most importantly with all of the families I had met through losing Mackenzie, parents who had also lost their own children. In nearly every single case the parents said they would not choose to let another child suffer what their sick child had gone through, and the one or two who would choose to have another child with SMA were at least making the decision armed with knowledge. There is nothing more frustrating to me than judgements made by people who have no experience on which to base their views.

Jonathan: I've found it very difficult to write anything of substance about Bella. This obviously isn't because I didn't care but simply because during the whole ordeal I was numb, in a way.

After the death of Mackenzie, then two years of IVF and countless negative pregnancy tests, being told our latest baby was another SMA sufferer didn't shock me. I was certainly devastated, but my priority once again turned to Rachael, her welfare and her mental health. I can barely recall the feelings through the numbness.

When the doctor entered the room to tell us the bad news, I knew immediately what he was going to say from his body language and tone of voice. I've found doctors usually get an air of nervousness when telling patients tragic news.

On the day of the interruption, I stayed with Rachael until she went through the surgery doors, then walked into Randwick for a coffee before returning to wait it out. After the surgery I took Rachael home, and once again I went through the motions of our disappointment and pain dance of pizza and gin.

I sometimes worry about the long-term effects this period of our lives is going to have on us.

No end in sight

'She is brave and strong and broken all at once.'

Anna Funder

I feel as though I am rapidly approaching the wall, the end of my rope, the spot where the cliff drops off, the place where my head will slip under the water. I don't want to be approaching it, I am doing everything I can to extend my capacity, but I am starting to struggle under the weight of it all.

After we said goodbye to Bella, we took the month of February to let my body recover while we planned what was next on our path to having a baby. For the past year we had been focusing on either IVF or natural pregnancy, one at a time. Instead of becoming gun-shy after all our struggles we went the other way and decided that we would throw everything at it. We would try to get pregnant every single month, and if we weren't on an IVF cycle we would try naturally. Whichever way worked. We would keep going through all the pain and suffering until we had a baby. This decision reflected our desperation.

People often asked me why we didn't just give up or have a break, but for us this was not an option. It isn't the same for everyone but a break would have hurt us more: we needed to keep moving forwards. Others asked why we didn't adopt or use a donor egg. These were all options we would look at in the future, but we just weren't there yet. For us, we had seen Mackenzie. We had seen her little button nose, her big blue eyes and her white blonde hair. We wanted to see her genetic sibling, a chance to see glimpses of her growing up. While genetics scared us, they were also something we craved because of her.

In March/April, I was lucky enough to get a coveted place in a detective training course. There were three stages and a final workbook in this process and over the past six months, while dealing with IVF and Bella, I had done the first two, and now I was being offered the third. It was something I had wanted to do for a long time and hoped to complete before having more children. This third stage of the course involved living at the Australian Federal Police College in Canberra for a month. I knew it would be an intense month: long days in class, late nights studying and some weekend work.

In October the year before, Jonny and I had also booked a holiday away to the United States for May. We had done so knowing we needed something good to look forward to. Because of this holiday we knew the only way we could fit in another round of IVF would be if I did it during my course, otherwise we would have to wait two months, which was not an option for us mentally. So we decided I would do a round of IVF while I did stage three of the detective course.

Before leaving Sydney in March I collected all my IVF medications. The plan was to have Genea in Canberra monitor me but

I would head back to Sydney for one day for the egg collection before returning to the detective course. Simple, right?

The day I got to the college I decided to check whether I was pregnant before starting IVF. Standing in my college room, I looked down at the test—it was positive. I didn't let myself get excited but instead tested each day to see if the line got darker. It didn't. Another chemical pregnancy designed to hurt my heart. I'd now had four chemical pregnancies over the past year.

So we kept going with our IVF plan. Each morning I would inject myself in my room before running down to breakfast. The cleaners must have wondered what was going on with all the medications and yellow sharps containers around my room. Every couple of days I would wake up early and drive to Genea's Canberra clinic for a blood test and a scan.

The cycle looked to be going okay, only around nine or ten eggs but they seemed strong, we thought. On the day I knew I would most likely have the trigger injection for the egg collection I went in for a final scan. The scan was uneventful, but a few hours later, while sitting in the classroom, I had a call from Dr Gee. She advised me that the sonographer had located a blood clot in my pelvis, deep vein thrombosis, and I had to go straight to emergency; she would send the hospital a referral.

After telling the instructor, I gathered my bag and went straight out to the car. I was shaking and crying as I drove to the hospital while talking to Jonny. He begged me to calm down so I could get to the hospital safely. Why was this happening?

At the emergency reception desk I had a sudden flashback to being in hospital with Mackenzie when she died. Through my panic and tears I tried to explain to the staff why I was there, that I had lost my daughter and was having flashbacks. They were quite lovely and after a short wait I was taken through to a private side room to wait and cry in private.

The doctor I spoke to was lovely but clearly relatively new. I had questions about what was happening. Would this cancel my IVF cycle? What did a blood clot mean for my eggs? Would this have a permanent effect on my uterus? But he couldn't answer my questions, which caused me more concern. I needed to have another ultrasound so they could see what they were dealing with. All he could tell me was that we needed to get the blood clot under control otherwise it could travel to my lungs or my heart and cause a pulmonary embolism.

As I waited, I spoke to Jonny, my parents and Kath on the phone. Jonny wanted to drive down from Sydney, but he was having a mini panic attack too and I didn't want him driving in that state. Mum and Dad wanted to come as well, as they were only half an hour away, but until I knew what was happening I wanted to be alone. Having people there would have made things serious. Kath, as always, calmed me down with her medical knowledge and realistic approach.

I know Jonny called his parents because Ross messaged to say he was sitting in the hospital waiting room. He didn't want to bother me by coming into the room, but he needed me to know he was there if I needed someone. What a beautiful man and what a sweet gesture.

Eventually it was time for me to have a scan. Like most of my scans these days it was the 'dildo cam'; it doesn't hurt but I have learned to hate the stress its results represent. As a doctor and a sonographer started searching for the blood clot I stared at the wall, not wanting to look at the screen. I was numb and hoping that if I looked away they wouldn't find anything. Turned out they couldn't, so they called another doctor in and the three of them poked around for anything ominous. Finally, they called in the big guns, the head of the department. He directed the sonographer, and just when I thought they were going to give the all clear I heard the words, 'There it is.' Once again, I began crying.

I was directed back to my room and waited to hear what this meant. The doctor initially told me that I would be in hospital on an IV containing a heavy-duty blood thinner for two days, but he needed to get advice from the haematologist. As I lay there Dr Gee called and I sobbed down the phone, trying to ask what would happen to my uterus. Once Dr Gee could decipher the question she reassured me that my uterus would be fine, there would be no long-term damage. However, this cycle of IVF would have to be cancelled and I may not be able to do another round for a couple of months while we got rid of the blood clot. I was relieved and began to calm down, but I wondered how we would clear this new hurdle in our path.

In the end, I was released from hospital with a script for anti-coagulants to self-inject twice a day for three months. I would also need to see a haematologist to find out what caused this issue.

I drove back to the college and started on an assessment that was due the next day. All I could do was keep moving forwards to the one goal I had control over.

Jonathan: To be honest, when Rachael called to confirm she had a blood clot and that round of IVF would have to be cancelled, I felt almost nothing. Of course she had a blood clot, and of course it would be cancelled. Why wouldn't it happen? The chances of it happening were so remote, but once again the dice was rolled and it didn't go our way. After the last few years, whenever a doctor tells us a risk is minute and hardly worth worrying about, we immediately have the feeling of impending doom and demand the test be done.

For the next two weeks at college, I pushed everything to one side and just worked hard. I felt myself disconnect from Jonny, from Mackenzie and from the idea of having a baby. I put my head down and did what I had to do to survive and to achieve the goal I had wanted for most of my life, to become a detective. In hindsight, I probably even let myself become someone else for a short time and pretended not to have the life I did. I am ashamed to say that those moments felt like sweet relief, but I also knew that to give myself a break was my only way to survive.

It was like my life was a battlefield and every so often I found an island, a refuge, where I could ignore reality for a while and breath before heading back to the battle.

This was the first time I had felt like running away from what was in front of me. That feeling scared me but I learned to just sit in those moments and enjoy the temporary release. It wouldn't last long because I knew deep down, no matter what happened, my life was mine, Jonny was my everything and I would never run away. But that didn't mean I didn't enjoy moments of my mind wandering to a place where life was different.

After four long weeks I completed the course and was handed my certificate. Back home, I was still feeling lost and disconnected from my life. I was honest with Jonny and even told him there were moments I felt like running away—not from him, never from him, but from my problems and my guilt. Mentally and emotionally I had pulled away from Mackenzie to get through the past four weeks and I felt so guilty for it, like I had let her down by not thinking about her as much or doing my daily routines and chats with her.

Jonny's response was perfection. He said, 'I'm surprised it has taken you this long to feel that way. Let's go on our holiday, reconnect, and if you still feel that way when we get back, we can address it.'

Isn't he beautiful?

Jonathan: As the months passed, we had failures with IVF and victories with Mackenzie's Mission. Our cat, Kaylee, began using Mackenzie's change table as a bed, which I didn't mind as I was sure it would only be temporary. We released a balloon into the sky for the month anniversary of her death, then six months, a year, and her second anniversary. We've added a second balloon to these celebrations for Bella and will do whatever we can to preserve the memory of our girls.

The time has passed quickly, but it feels like I haven't seen my girl in a decade. Her bassinet is still in our bedroom, and her car seat is still fixed to the back seat of the car. We're eternally optimistic we'll have another baby to use these things, but in two years of trying, we have almost nothing to show for it.

It was time to step back from our lives, but this time we would step back together and head overseas to celebrate Jonny's fortieth birthday. We couldn't really afford it, but we needed something to look forward to and make us smile. We used frequent flyer points to book flights to Los Angeles and ordered a new credit card to fund the day to day. Tomorrow would take care of itself, we thought.

In Los Angeles we met up with our friend and wedding photographer Kierstin, who showed us the sights of Los Angeles, including Pasadena, our first In-N-Out burger and Trader Jones, and most importantly, Disneyland, where we naturally took so many moments for Mackenzie. I bought her a pink Mickey Mouse balloon which we took to Snow White's house where Kierstin filmed us as we kissed and released it up for her to play with.

Next up we went to 'live' in New York for ten days. In the mornings we would stroll from our hotel to our favourite little family-run bagel place then wander around the city. We walked through Brooklyn, went to the Natural History Museum, and visited the classic *Friends*, *Seinfeld*, *Brooklyn 99* and *Sex and the City* locations. We went to the Plaza, Central Park, Rockefeller Center and hit golf balls at the driving range in Chelsea. We went to shows, ancient baths and walked the street. It was incredible in so many ways.

We flew back to LA for a night at Venice Beach before driving a red American muscle hire car out to Monument Valley on the Arizona–Utah border. It was somewhere Jonny had always wanted to go and was quite a spiritual experience. We went star-gazing at night and watched the sun rise over the valley in the morning.

From there we drove back through the Grand Canyon and on to Las Vegas. Vegas was an interesting experience and I'm glad we did it, but to see so much money wasted on sex, drugs and gambling was depressing. All I could think was what else that money could achieve. However, we did get to tick off a bucket list item by renewing our vows with Elvis. It was such a wonderful moment, watching my beautiful man cry as I walked down the aisle on Elvis's arm. But I don't think we would ever go back.

The holiday was everything we needed to reconnect with each other and also reconnect a little with Mackenzie. We continued our tradition of putting stickers in her passport as we travelled, making sure she was with us. Her Los Angeles stickers were put in at Disneyland and In-N-Out Burger, while in New York we put her sticker in while having champagne at the Rainbow Room. Her Monument Valley sticker was put in watching the sun rise and of course her Las Vegas sticker went in after Jonny and I renewed our vows with Elvis. We also put a little Mackenzie sticker on a sign in the middle of the desert. We felt she was with us.

But back in Australia, the weight of things slowly crept back onto me.

I knew I could get through this patch—I'd been through worse—but I had to work through things in a way that was safe for me. It felt like I was walking a wobbly tightrope, but rather than try a new direction and risk falling, I just kept going forwards the best way I could.

There was nothing I hadn't tried: I was still taking antidepressants, I spoke about my feelings, I was writing and trying to exercise. I was doing acupuncture, having massages and eating a 'fertility diet'. I let myself cry, I tried to be brave. I didn't know what more I could do. So I just kept going to work, writing this book, doing my daily chores, seeing the occasional friend; searching for those islands of relief to cling to when I could and waiting until my psychologist could see me again.

While we waited to be able to get back into IVF, I threw myself into work. Luckily, my team was very busy, so that provided a distraction for me. I was also really focused on completing my detective workbook. But at home, I felt lost. If Jonny was at work, I would go to the gym, cook my dinner and then I was stuck—what do I do? I felt lonely and all those nights did was give me time to reflect on where my life was, which was not something I wanted to do. On those nights I might take a sleeping tablet with a glass of wine and try to be asleep by 7.30 p.m. Sometimes the sleeping tablets worked and sometimes they didn't; when they didn't it was like being forced to watch a movie that haunted me.

I tried hard not to hit rock bottom because I knew that it would be that much harder to pull myself up from there, and in the process I could hurt the people who love me, not to mention tear apart the life I had spent so long building. So instead, I turned up to work and gave my all, attended Mackenzie's Mission committee meetings, kept working on my detective designation, paid the bills, went to the gym, took my antidepressants, wrote my blog, tried to eat well so my body could create other babies and kept taking whatever IVF medication I was told to take. I put one foot in front of the other.

So many people told me that I had taken on too much. They told me to slow down, but I knew that I couldn't. I've heard that for defence force personnel, the upper and lower thresholds of what they can handle are shifted by their experiences in war zones, so the point at which they hit stress is pushed higher but their ability to cope with quiet days is reduced. When they return home they struggle to exist in normal life as a result. I felt like that was me. I needed to keep busy and challenged because my threshold had moved and I needed to keep within its new boundaries.

The hard part is that as time goes on people almost forget that you have been through hell and that the hell is continuing. So you still have to deal with the everyday routine and people. On a few occasions I would start new friendships and give people a glimpse into my life, but mostly I learned to not really let people into my deepest thoughts. It didn't feel safe.

I was also becoming worried about the effect of my thoughts on Bella and Mackenzie. I know that might sound strange, but when you lose someone close to you, you imagine they are still around watching you and hearing your thoughts—well, I do, anyway. What would they think knowing their mum wasn't perfect? What if they were ashamed of my actions? So I would find myself apologising to the girls. Maybe more magical thinking but not an ideal way to live anyway.

During this time I had also pulled back from a lot of my family and friends. I felt bad pushing people away, especially my beautiful family, but I know they understood that I had to be selfish and only take on what I could handle. I needed to withdraw into myself for a time.

But in July 2019, my mum called to say they had found another lump, but this time it was in her ovaries, not her breast. Mum had called Jonny and told him first; knowing I wasn't in a great space, she wanted to know how to break it to me. I hated that she felt like she couldn't talk to me. Luckily the lump was benign, but they decided to remove her ovaries and fallopian tubes, just to be safe. It was something I was happy with—I am all for removing the issue.

Thankfully I can say that my mum is okay. She recovered nicely from her surgery and I am so proud of how she has handled both her breast cancer and her ovarian lump, as I am of all of our family members who have had their ups and downs over the past year. Mackenzie has taught them what is important. The 'panic' line in the sand used to be closer, but now things are in perspective and people like my mum handle themselves and these situations with such strength. I am in awe of them all.

Despite all this our family still smile and laugh every single day. Our hearts ache with pain but we are strong. We know that Mackenzie, Bella, Hope and all the other members of our family who have passed on would want us to smile. We know the strength of a laugh and the importance of keeping our minds healthy. During these darker times was when Jonny really shone. Even though I was struggling, instead of falling to pieces at home we would sing. Jonny likes to make up songs about Mackenzie, Bella, me and our cat Kaylee. We like the idea of the girls sitting and watching us, thinking we are silly but giggling along. The songs are infectious and I find myself singing back to him.

I want everyone to know that every day we think of our daughter and remember her with love. Sometimes there are tears but every day there are smiles. Through the darkness we know we are lucky.

We are the luckiest unlucky people.

IVF and the effects

'When we are no longer able to change a situation ... we are challenged to change ourselves.'

Viktor Frankl

I don't think we talk about IVF enough. Some people seem to be ashamed of going through it and don't tell anyone. Others don't say anything until they have had success. I have even heard of some women being told by male partners not to talk about IVF because the guy doesn't want people to know his sperm has any issues, leaving the woman to go through a hormonal emotional rollercoaster without the support of family and friends. Unfortunately, as you have read, it isn't always as simple as a few injections and you get a baby.

Of course, every couple is allowed to tell who they want, when they want, but I am shocked at how often this common feature of life is swept under the rug. At Genea I see dozens of women walk in the door every five minutes, and that is just one IVF clinic in Australia.

As I have said before, IVF can significantly impact every aspect of life: financial, emotional, physical and mental. It can impact on a couple's relationship, their friendships, their work and a woman's body.

What many people also don't understand is that IVF is expensive. We were exceptionally lucky to have significant financial help from places like Genea, the Kyle and Jackie O Show, silent donors and others who donated to us, but we were still out of pocket. It disturbs me to think of those who don't get assistance and I think that IVF, genetic testing and all the related surgeries, such as laparoscopies for endometriosis, should be subsidised by the government. And then there are all the other potential costs that you don't think about, like fortnightly psychologist appointments, doctors' appointments to get scripts for antidepressants and mental health care plans, or the cost of acupuncturists and nutritionists to improve egg quality and transfer.

I could write a book on IVF alone but one topic I wanted to touch on was the effect of IVF on both a woman's body and how she views herself.

In December 2017, I felt like I had sold my body. Actually, that's not quite right: like I had paid someone a lot of money to take it from me. This was when Jonny and I started IVF.

In the last two years I have given birth to Mackenzie, breastfed her, grieved her death, endured eight IVF stimulation cycles, seven egg collections, one round of deep vein thrombosis, one medical interruption of a pregnancy and countless chemical pregnancies. I have had around two hundred blood tests and injected myself over four hundred times.

Starting this process, I was a size 10 but curvy. I had a scar on my lower stomach from the emergency caesarean and a scar on my forehead from the malignant melanoma. I ate well, exercised often but also treated myself with chocolate and wine when I felt like it. I wasn't perfect but I was mostly happy with myself, and when I looked in the mirror I saw me.

The first couple of rounds of IVF were okay, but after that I slowly lost myself. The stress of the last two years has seen lines creeping across my face faster than I can believe to be normal. The bags under my eyes were heavier from the lack of sleep caused by the hormones.

I continued to be careful with what I ate and even at times I went to extremes if I thought it might help IVF. I tried fertility diets, green vegetables, no coffee, no alcohol and limited sugar, but the number on the scales kept rising. I was told a healthy BMI would help us conceive so I began intermittent fasting to slow down the weight gain. I ate protein bars, limited carbs—you name it, I tried it. But then I would have guilt that my body was going through enough—shouldn't I nourish it, not starve it?

No matter what I did, my hormones had other ideas. I put on weight, particularly in the ever-flattering mum pouch on my stomach. I struggled to find clothes in my wardrobe that fit, but I didn't want to buy new clothes and give in to the weight gain. My garage filled with plastic tubs marked 'Skinny me clothes' and left in my wardrobe were baggy pants and sweatshirts.

Suddenly the me in the mirror looked wrinkled and tubby, dressed in oversized clothes. For months and months I had not got my hair done or my nails painted for fear of the toxins affecting my IVF. I slowly critiqued the body in the mirror, from my head down to my toes, but then I remembered what that body had been through and quickly apologised for turning on the woman I saw there.

It felt like what once made me feel sexy and good about myself had been taken away. I was still me on the inside, albeit slightly broken—I still needed love, hugs, kisses and, yes, sex. But if I couldn't see myself as a woman, how could others? I was just a walking, talking, needle-sticking, drug-taking, hormone-riddled, baby-making (trying) machine.

I guess I was lucky to have never truly been angry at my body for failing to do what we wanted it to. But instead of anger I felt pressure. My husband, my family, my friends and my community were all anxiously waiting for me to get pregnant. So much pressure for one uterus, although I knew that the most pressure was being created and applied by me.

I so desperately want see myself in the mirror with a big pregnant belly again, but will that ever happen? Will I ever again see a body that responds to my own actions, be that exercising or eating well? Or am I this now, an IVF woman who doesn't own her body?

I believe deep down that this will pass. I will get my body back one day, but right now it feels so far away and I know I won't ever be the same again. For now, all I can do is learn to be kind to myself. I can put aside time and money to get my hair coloured, my nails painted and have the occasional massage. To do things for me.

I'm not going to fool myself—there will still be crap moments. It's upsetting that some of my best years are being spent feeling this way, but it is up to me to try to change the one thing I can— my mindset. Only I can make this better.

Great, another thing to add to my 'To do' list!

Then there are the mental effects—the jealousy, anger and comparisons you make with others. Jealousy is the most useless feeling when it comes to IVF. I am jealous of people who get pregnant naturally so easily, I am jealous of those who only need one round of IVF to get pregnant, and I am jealous that other people's lives are moving forwards while we stand still. I compare my situation to others, both people I know and those I don't. I compare their journey to our own, their struggles to ours. I hate it but I compare our pain when I hear people struggling with things that are one hundredth of my own. I know I shouldn't, but a part of me does.

Comparison is the thief of joy. IVF is all consuming. But would I change any of my decisions? Do I regret IVF? No, every single moment, every injection, every kilogram gained will be worth it when I hold our baby in my arms. But if you know someone going through IVF, give them a hug.

Is there hope?

'It's fine to feel a little heavy, and it's just fine to sit here and catch my breath, and it's just fine to be a mess at times, and it's just fine to be relatively normal sometimes, it's just fine to miss them. It's just fine to let it all hit me, surrendering and succumbing. And it's just fine to remember that grief has no rules, and that really, it will in many ways last as long as love does. Forever.'

Lexi Behrndt

In June 2019, I was finally due to finish the two injections a day of blood thinner I was having to give myself. Two ultrasounds showed that the blood clot had gone and finally the haematologist gave me the all clear to resume IVF. We went back for our eighth round of IVF stimulation and potentially our last.

The IVF round was the same as all the others, but this time we kept it simple: just the IVF medications, no additional supplements. All our little traditions and superstitions had gone out the window. We no longer sat together in Mackenzie's room doing the injections with hope and anticipation. Instead I would get up before work, stand in the kitchen and jab myself. Of course we had some hope, otherwise we wouldn't be doing it, but too much hope just meant more pain when it didn't work, so instead we went through the motions and hoped for the best.

At the first ultrasound they estimated we would have seven eggs at the most, our worst collection ever. Jonny kept being positive and said it was all about quality, but I began feeling defiant about looking on the positive side, putting as much distance between this round and my heart as possible.

At the egg collection I took in Mackenzie's bunny, the one Kath had brought to the hospital for her when she fell ill. It was the last toy she every touched and now sat on my bedside table. We went through the now familiar process. The gown went on then we spoke to the anaesthetist, embryologist and Dr Gee before I was wheeled in and put into a sleep. When I woke up, they had collected three eggs.

Three eggs. Only three.

There was no hope. I felt that already—this round was a failure.

Over the next week as I recovered from the egg collection, we got our almost daily updates. All three of the eggs fertilised which was incredible, but I knew that didn't mean success. There were so many more hurdles to face. I was in a negative headspace based on experience.

Each day we heard the embryos had kept going, and on day five they called to say one had made it to biopsy and had been frozen while the others were still going. Oh my god, we had got one to testing!

The next day they called to say a second one had been biopsied and frozen and the final embryo, while it couldn't be tested, had been frozen. Two to testing! How was that possible? We couldn't believe it. And the third couldn't be tested but was strong enough to freeze.

We waited two weeks and five days to find out if either of the two embryos that were tested would be healthy and clear of SMA and chromosomal issues. When the call finally came I felt the breath leave me.

Both embryos were healthy. Both! One was clear of all SMA and the other was only a carrier.

How was that possible? We had previously had twelve eggs collected and none had come back clear. Now we had two from three and the third frozen as a possibility? Wow! Suddenly I thought maybe we would be happy again. Maybe we would even have another two children like we had been dreaming about.

This news was incredible, but it wasn't quite like I had imagined it would be. Jonny felt the same. We didn't break down like I had always imagined—in fact, I had to almost fake emotions on the phone to the embryologist. I felt strangely flat. We were happy, I knew we were, but it was almost like life had robbed us of the ability to be truly happy without looking for the trick. We knew not to get our hopes up, that this didn't mean we would have a child. There was still so much to get through. We had previously had the rug pulled out from underneath us so many times that we were now so careful where we stepped.

The one thing I did let myself feel was less pressure. Until that moment I hadn't realised how much pressure I felt at only having one embryo. The idea of transferring that embryo without any others frozen as backup felt terrifying. I had my own expectations, Jonny's, our families, friends, our Instagram family and what felt like everyone else sitting heavily on this one embryo and my uterus. It was overwhelming.

Now that we had three healthy embryos and two frozen non-tested embryos, we decided to take the plunge. Our first transfer.

Each transfer has around a 50 per cent chance at success. I wish it was higher, but there it is. The first step was the usual dildo cam to measure the endometrium lining; over 8 millimetres thickness is more receptive to an embryo implanting. I also needed to start blood tests again to check my hormones and try to identify when I ovulated. This was because the embryo needed to be transferred five days after ovulation as technically that is how old it was before it had been frozen. I think I had six blood tests in eight days, getting up early to have each one done before work. But I didn't mind, I wanted them to get it right.

On the day of the transfer our beloved Dr Gee was unfortunately unavailable, but luckily the head of Genea, Professor Mark Bowman, offered to do it. We had met Professor Bowman before; he was lovely and supportive of our work with Mackenzie's Mission. As I drove us into the Genea carpark, Jonny played the theme song from *Rocky* to get us in the headspace. It has always been important for us to keep our sense of humour and Jonny made that easy.

Inside I got into the usual gown and made sure I had a full bladder, ready for the transfer. The embryologist told us that the embryo had thawed well for the transfer and was all ready to go. She explained that they grade the outside of the blastocyst, which would become the placenta, and the inside of the embryo, which would become the baby. Our embryos all looked like good-quality bubs, so we started by transferring the non-carrier embryo.

Professor Bowman took us into the room where the transfer would happen and once again I laid back with my legs in the stirrups and everything on show. I was used to having no shame. With me were Jonny, the embryologist, a nurse and Professor Bowman, and up on the screen was our embryo. We took photos of it and wished it luck.

The embryo was put into the catheter by the embryologist, then the nurse used an external ultrasound on my uterus to guide Professor Bowman. After inserting a scapula to expose my cervix, Professor Bowman guided the catheter into place before the embryologist pressed the button to release the embryo into my uterus. We saw it go in, tucked away safely. In ten minutes we were done. Ready to go home.

Jonathan: Eventually we transferred our first embryo back into Rachael and I tell you, it's a weird feeling to sit in that room, voluntarily watching another man try to impregnate your wife.

As we left the room the team wished us luck, and there were tears in the embryologist's eyes. That meant the world to us.

For the next ten days I did a pregnancy test every single day—they say don't but how could I not? Some days I felt pregnant. I had bloating, twinges and nausea but I knew this could have been the progesterone pessaries I was required to insert each night. I felt so hopeful and knew this was the one thing in the world I wanted. But it was odd because I felt scared about it working too.

I had spent over a year convincing myself that my life could be happy if I didn't have children. What in my life would I have to say goodbye to when I got pregnant? It wasn't that I ever stopped wanting children. I wanted them with all my heart, but I also had to protect myself so that I would be okay if it was negative.

Every day I took those tests, waiting for two lines that never came. I did the calculations and told myself it was too early, there was still time, but with each day passing that became less true. The day before I was due to get my pregnancy blood test with Genea, I got my period. It was over. Not pregnant.

We had waited so long for that transfer. I had good lining, the embryo didn't have SMA, it was chromosomally healthy and I had carried pregnancies before, so surely it would work, I had told myself.

I couldn't believe this was happening. Why couldn't the world just give us this one thing? Then it could just ignore us and leave us be. We only had two tested embryos left.

After the first embryo failed to implant, we were naturally devastated and scared to transfer the second embryo. We had no idea why the embryo didn't implant, and without this knowledge we couldn't really do anything differently. So we crossed our fingers and ploughed ahead. We were happy at least that the second transfer was being done by Dr Gee—we very much liked Professor Bowman, but Dr Gee was our doctor and we had a special relationship with her.

On the day of the second transfer, we got up early and headed for acupuncture. Lying there trying to relax and picture a sticky little embryo, I called it my 'Hubba Bubba baby' and hoped it would stick like gum. But then I suddenly had a thought that maybe the embryo wouldn't even thaw properly—maybe we would turn up ready to go and our embryo would have already stopped developing and died. Suffice to say the rest of my acupuncture session was not so relaxing.

At 8 a.m. we arrived at Genea. Once again I went through the paperwork and was taken to a room to get changed into the ever-flattering dressing gown and shoe covers. Again I took Mackenzie's little toy bunny to hold. We met with the nurse and Dr Gee, and the gorgeous embryologist, Nuria, told us that the embryo looked as close to perfect as possible. It was fully hatched and had thawed beautifully. We were ecstatic.

Into the surgery room and once again I was popped in the chair with my legs up in the stirrups. On the screen was the embryo we had nicknamed Frosty, because it was the first embryo we ever froze so it had been chilly for a long time. The catheter with the embryo in it was inserted through my cervix and into my uterus. I remember at one stage looking down and seeing the faces of Nuria, the nurse and Dr Gee concentrating, three accomplished women all working hard to get us pregnant. The image was so strong and powerful, it felt right. Surely this was it.

After the transfer, Jonny showed me some funny videos, because studies showed that women who laughed after a transfer had more chance of ending up with a live birth. From there we went to Bills cafe in Surry Hills for a lovely post-transfer break-fast, then it was back to acupuncture. As I lay there covered in needles, all I could think about was my Hubba Bubba baby.

During my first six stimulation cycles I had tried every sugges-tion I found on the internet, even those that seemed pretty out there. But despite this, the cycle that had been the most successful was the last one when I relaxed and threw it all out the window, even having a glass of wine every night. So after my first transfer I just acted normally, not resting and just getting on with life. When that transfer didn't work I decided to go the other way and try everything for the second transfer. I started each morning with hot lemon water; ate pineapple core (yes, it has to be the core), punnets of blueberries and exactly two Brazil nuts a day; drank bone broth at night and took all sorts of supplements. I was prescribed progesterone pessaries both morning and night and I had to give myself a daily injection of the blood thinner Clexane just in case I developed another blood clot. For the next two days I just lay on the couch watching television and relaxing. I was determined to do whatever I could to make this one stick.

Four days after the transfer I finally caved and took a home pregnancy test. It came back with a very faint positive. It was a good start, but we had many faint lines that disappeared the next day, so we weren't getting excited. For the next two days we continued to get lines and they were getting darker, so we started to have some hope. I began testing obsessively, and an afternoon test that day was so much darker, indicating more HCG in my body. The following morning I tested again and the line wasn't as dark as the afternoon before, which freaked me out, though I clung to the possibility that the progesterone from the night and that morning had affected the test. Anxiously I waited four hours and tested again, and the line was darker again—thank goodness! This process of testing can play with your head, but not testing is just as bad.

The lines continued to get darker until I was due for my first beta HCG blood test. The Genea nurses called me in the afternoon to say that the HCG came back as 38. This meant I was pregnant but the HCG was low; the count they wanted to see was around 80-100. But with HCG the most important thing is that it doubles about every 48 hours.

I went in for another blood test the next day. After a few more hours of anxious waiting they called with the result: my HCG was now 65. This was still not high enough but it had almost doubled in 24 hours, so that was brilliant.

I finally felt like we were heading towards happiness, although until we had numbers they were happy with I wouldn't feel 'pregnant'. I did start to daydream, though, about how would we announce it and listening to the heartbeat.

Two days later we had another blood test. I was so nervous and willed my body to flood with HCG. It felt like the nurses took forever to call, and eventually I emailed them saying I was super anxious. The nurse called soon afterwards and broke the news that my HCG had only gone from 65 to 68. It wasn't a viable pregnancy. I should expect to miscarry in the next couple of days.

A minute ago I was pregnant but in this minute I was not.

That was now two of our three embryos gone. It had taken us two years of our life to make those embryos and two months to lose two. Gone, just like that.

The pain I felt in that moment was excruciating. My body was searing hot and I broke into a sweat. I ran out of work and drove home through the tears that were streaming down my face. As I drove, I screamed so loudly I am surprised the windows didn't shatter into a million pieces like my heart was. A piercing, primal, horrible scream that I couldn't believe was coming from my mouth.

I called Jonny. He was clearly shocked and devastated. I asked him to come home but of course I didn't need to ask, he was already going to.

I was desolate once again. You'd think I would be used to it but I will never get used to my heart breaking. At home I got into bed, fully clothed and shoes still on. My tears and snot stained Jonny's pillow which I hugged until he arrived home to hold me. I screamed into the pillow with all my might.

Why? What had I done wrong? Why not just give us a baby? When would this end? I needed to be a mum—would I never be a mum again? My fears were real. How much hope could we keep having? How much pain could I take before I broke? How many times could we stand up again?

Jonny got home and once again he held me. He didn't know what else to do. I was broken, sobbing hysterically and no longer caring how I looked or if I would ever come back from this. Eventually I calmed down and we planned how we would continue. What else could we do?

I didn't want to be strong anymore. I didn't know how to find the positive in this situation anymore. I didn't want to scrounge around wondering how we would afford to keep going, or to rely on the kindness of others to make our life complete. I didn't want to wonder when I would have to make the next hard decision or be broken forever. I wanted to be happy. I just wanted to be happy. In that instant I hated this world.

That night we did our normal pathetic, sad routine and lay on the couch, ordered pizza and had a drink. I cuddled my hot-water bottle in one arm and Jonny's leg with the other until it was finally time to go to bed. My face was swollen from crying, my eyes bloodshot, and my nose blocked up. I looked how I felt on the inside.

The next day I got up and I went to work. What else could I do? I didn't tell anyone. No doubt people were sick of my pain so I kept it to myself until I would be able to tell people without breaking down and scaring them. No one can truly know the pain of a failed IVF round until you go through it yourself, the ups and downs, the constant anxiety. But we have to keep going.

Our follow-up appointment with Dr Gee was a week later. There was no known reason for the two failed transfers, but this in addition to a few natural chemical pregnancies suggested that there might be something else at play, like natural killer cells or endometriosis. She suggested we have a laparoscopy and a hysteroscopy with biopsy—basically, they needed to check my uterus for signs of endometriosis or infection. More operations, more anaesthetics and more money.

The next week I went into Prince of Wales Hospital for the laparoscopy and hysteroscopy with Dr David Kowalski, an extremely talented, generous and lovely man married to a wonderful woman named Lisa. The procedures showed I had stage four endometriosis. Endometriosis is a condition where tissue similar to that in a woman's uterus lining grows outside the uterus. It can cause pain, or you can have no symptoms like me. However, endometriosis can at times cause infertility. It is more common than what is reported, as the main way to diagnose it is through surgery.

This was not what we were expecting. For some people this would be a horrible diagnosis, but it gave us some hope.

Dr Kowalski removed the endometriosis so that now, just maybe, an embryo can implant.

We will keep going. This will not beat us or destroy us. We keep our hope.

Leo

'If I had a flower for every time I thought of you, I could walk in my garden forever.'

Alfred Tennyson

Following the laparoscopy and hysteroscopy with Dr Kowalski, I was sore and quite battered for a few weeks. I had four incisions which needed to heal, along with my uterus, which had been scraped clean of the endometriosis.

Basically, I had a newly renovated uterus. It was never going to look better than it did now, and we had hope that an embryo would stick. So we began ovulation tracking—waiting for the right day to put our embryo back inside me.

The first month my body did something odd. I ovulated very early, on day six. So we missed that month. It was another small blow at the time, but it did give my body more of a chance to recover. We decided that I would have an Intralipid infusion while we waited for my next ovulation. Intralipid is a sterile fat emulsion which is used to treat natural killer cells. Natural killer cells are part of the immune system, but can attack an embryo in the womb, thinking it is a foreign object. We didn't know whether I had these natural killer cells, but we also weren't able to discount it and the infusion had limited risks for me. So I sat for two hours as the white liquid was injected into my veins.

A few weeks later I was back to the draining daily walks to Genea for blood tests to gauge my ovulation pattern. Once that was determined, Dr Gee looked at the best day for our transfer.

On 24 November 2019, a quiet Sunday morning, Jonny and I met Dr Gee in the Genea day surgery. With all our fingers crossed, we transferred our final healthy embryo, and as I lay with Mackenzie's favourite headband wrapped around my wrist, it felt like we were transferring our last hope. Jonny named this embryo 'Charm', as in 'third time's the charm'.

For the next few days we could think of little else, but we stayed strong and didn't do any pregnancy tests. Well ... until day four, when I caved and, terrified, I took a test. Jonny and I spent the next two hours holding the test up to the light trying to see the slightest line. We couldn't be sure, and it was exhausting. Just seeing a pregnancy test caused me anxiety.

The next day, when we tried again, there was a line. We were ecstatic, but as always naturally worried. The excited celebration moment most couples experience had been ripped away from us long ago. A positive pregnancy test usually gave us anxiety and a faint smile rather than a surge of joy.

Each day the line got darker and darker, but that had happened last time too. Finally it was time for the blood test. They wanted my HCG to be over 80—when we got the call, my HCG was 362. They then wanted that number to double approximately every 48 hours. Four days later our HCG was 2611, four days after that it was 10,203 and another week later it was 29,624. We were pregnant.

During these tests we went to Canberra to visit our families. We were still so unsure whether this pregnancy would stick, but we didn't want to have the excited feeling completely taken away from us again. We wanted the opportunity to tell our families and not have that honour robbed from us through fear, especially if we got to keep this baby. So, when we all met for dinner, Jonny and I handed each set of parents a small brown gift bag. Nestled amongst the tissue paper was a positive pregnancy test. I can assure you there were tears.

On 20 December 2019, when we were six weeks and two days pregnant, we went back to Dr David Kowalski. He had generously offered to be our obstetrician through our pregnancy and we were delighted to have him. We knew we were getting the Ferrari of obstetricians. At this appointment he tried to see the heartbeat flicker, which should have been there based on my HCG. He could see something, but it wasn't strong or consistent. My heart raced; I panicked. David could see the yolk sack and the foetal pole but he couldn't see that clear flicker.

David sent us to Sydney Ultrasound for Women. A one kilometre walk from his office. We commenced the walk but I had already convinced myself the baby was gone. As I walked, Jonny had to hold me up. I almost passed out twice and threw up. Eventually we got there and were ushered into the 'quiet room'. I was incredibly grateful for this as I was having a panic attack and needed to lie with my legs in the air, but at the same time I hate those small rooms where you get bad news. I don't ever want to be in one again.

Eventually Dr Greg Kesby and a sonographer came in. They knew our story and led us calmly into the examination room. They put the ultrasound probe on my belly and straight away we saw a little flicker. I burst into tears. The baby was fine, with a healthy heartbeat and measuring as it should. I hugged Dr Kesby and the sonographer and continued to cry all the way back to David's office. Poor David, I could tell he had been stressed too. He couldn't see the flicker for a few reasons: it was quite early, my uterus was retro-verted, and his machine was not as advanced as those at the official ultrasound centres.

During the pregnancy I had to have daily injections of the blood thinner Clexane, due to my prior case of deep vein thrombosis. I was also having a progesterone pessary every morning and night. Neither were fun, but I would have done squats every day for an hour while holding my nose and drinking hot Gatorade if I had been told it would help.

As the pregnancy progressed, I found myself sitting with some really complex emotions. I felt unable to tell people the news with excitement. It became clear that I was waiting for something to go wrong. I guess it was a form of post-traumatic stress disorder, where I always had a sense of impending doom.

I was thinking about Mackenzie more than ever, and hoping I would be able to navigate having a baby in my arms as well as so many lost babies in my heart. I was hoping my trauma wouldn't affect this child, that I would find the space to love all my children and not feel guilty for enjoying life without Mackenzie here.

I also found myself scared about the gender, no matter which way it fell. Of course I just wanted a healthy baby in my arms, but I didn't know which gender would give me most joy, because I felt like all our girls had been stolen from us.

We had discussions about what the birth would be like. I knew I would probably need to have another caesarean. I wanted the safest birth for this baby, but I was also upset at the idea of changing the scar on my stomach that symbolised Mackenzie's entrance into this world.

These were just some of the thoughts tumbling around my head, but I knew my priority in the coming months was to find a healthy way to step through this pregnancy and beyond, for everyone involved.

Everything was going well by all accounts. I had quite bad pregnancy fatigue; I could barely get through the day and some afternoons I just had to go home and sleep. I had some nausea, but nothing compared to some people. Given I had been pregnant multiple times before, my body knew what to do and I gained weight quickly, which made it hard to keep it a secret. Eventually I had to tell people at work, because I could no longer complete operational duties and my clothes were becoming quite tight.

While juggling work and pregnancy, we had some good news about Mackenzie's Mission. In December 2019, Mackenzie's Mission tested its first couples, which led to more interviews and news stories. The day of the first test was a huge day for us.

Over the past two years we have received lots of messages from people who have obtained genetic carrier screening off the back of Mackenzie's story.

We have heard from people who have gone into pregnancy comfortably, knowing that they have been given the all clear from the test; from those who have had scary results but who are thankful that they know the risks and options available to them, and from others who have had unexpected results, both good and bad. One story that I would like to share with you is from one of my Instagram followers.

We were part of a study in Western Australia this year that was pioneered in collaboration with Mackenzie's Mission. We found out some very important genetic information and with additional testing we did as a result, subsequently discovered I'm in Premature Ovarian Failure. Although it was tough, it means that we are now accessing the services we need long before we would have otherwise. It saved us extra years of trying, inevitable heartbreak, impossible decisions and more devastating pregnancy losses like with my first (also like Mackenzie). So thank you. Thank you for everything you do. And thank you, Mackenzie. You're a little star and you shine so brightly for so many people.

Messages like this mean the world to us. Following the first couples' testing, the Mackenzie's Mission website went live. This was HUGE! We are so proud of it, and you can see it for yourself at www.mackenziesmission.org.au.

We felt 'reasonably' comfortable in this pregnancy because the embryo we transferred was an IVF embryo and was genetically tested and healthy. It was PGD tested for SMA—which is said to be 99 per cent accurate—and PGS tested for all chromosome issues, which is said to be 95 per cent accurate. Although these numbers were comforting, we wanted to bring the 95 per cent up closer to 100 per cent. So at eleven weeks pregnant we decided to do the non-invasive pregnancy test (NIPT) to check for chromosome abnormalities.

The appointment went well. In fact, it was lovely. The sonographer and geneticist at Sydney Ultrasound for Women knew about Mackenzie's Mission and could not have been kinder. The scan, which looked at the nuchal translucency at the back of the neck, looked good; the blood test was taken and then we just needed to wait a few days for the results.

The next Wednesday, 29 January 2020, I had gone home early from work feeling unwell. I woke up from a quick nap and saw I had a missed call from David. When I called him back, David told me that our NIPT test results had come back as high risk for a chromosome disorder. My mind froze. I felt the heat creep onto my chest and instantly I began sweating. I stumbled to the bathroom and lay on the cold tiles, still on the phone to David, repeating over and over again: 'This can't be happening.' David said that everyone was confused, given it was a PGD/PGS tested embryo. He suggested that it may be a false positive. But we wouldn't know without further testing.

In complete shock, I called Jonny. Once again I told my love the bad news over the phone while he was at work. His reaction was similar to mine: utter shock. Jonny drove home straight away. We sat holding each other on the couch as we spoke again to David and to the specialists at Sydney Ultrasound for Women to arrange another ultrasound and CVS, like the one we had with Bella. Those tests were to take place on Monday, 3 February 2020, another five days away.

For the next two days I lay in bed crying and reading everything I could in forums, reports and research projects that showed that false positives were possible. I came up with numerous reasons as to why the NIPT was wrong. When there was nothing more to read, Jonny and I got into the car early in the morning and drove all day. We drove to Parkes, Orange, Bathurst, Mudgee and Jervis Bay. We didn't really stop; it wasn't for sightseeing. We just needed to get out of the house. So we just drove.

On Monday we attended our tests. Jonny was convinced that it was a false positive: the ultrasound would look fine, we would have the CVS and all would be okay. I lay down on the bed, exposing my stomach for the ultrasound, and held Jonny's hand tightly. I wanted desperately to run. The next thing we knew our baby was up on the screen, jumping around inside me. Looking beautiful and perfect.

The specialist got straight into measuring the nuchal translucency. This is the space at the back on the neck and is used to indicate chromosome issues. Because of my research, straight way, with one glance, I knew. But for Jonny it didn't sink in until he heard Dr Kesby saying, 'I am seeing things which worry me.' I was watching Jonny when he heard that, and he crumbled. Every muscle in his body gave way and he folded in on himself, head in his hands. I wanted to hold him, to make it better, but I could do nothing. For the first two minutes I was numb, like I had known the result before I walked in the room and had already accepted it.

Dr Kesby and the sonographer began prepping for the CVS, as we needed this diagnostic test to be 100 per cent sure. As they did so, I broke. The two minutes of shock must have worn off. I wailed a heart-wrenching sound and burst into tears. I asked the universe out loud, 'How many children will you take from us?' I sobbed until it was time for the needle to go into my stomach, when I took a deep breath and lay still. I asked for them to turn off the large screen; I couldn't bear to see our baby alive and well when I knew what was coming. I already knew we would not get to keep this baby. I composed myself and just stared at Jonny while the needle was inserted.

I cried as we left. Jonny took me home; I wouldn't let him leave my side even for a second. I suctioned myself to him like a desperate octopus. He was all I had, and I couldn't let him go.

The next day, Dr Kesby called to say the CVS had confirmed a chromosome issue. Jonny and I had already decided that the life laid out for a baby with this issue was not one we were willing to give to our child. We knew we would have to yet again have a medical interruption—otherwise known as a termination for medical reasons (TFMR). Once again, this was a devastating decision for us and not one made lightly. There is so much to consider: what is the condition? Is it lethal? Is it life limiting? What is the quality of life? Are there treatments? What is our financial position? What is our mental health like? What are our values and beliefs? While some people will not agree with our decision, I don't think anyone should be judged either way—for making the decision to keep an affected baby because they love them and want to meet them, or in our case, because we love our baby so much we don't want him or her to suffer. Either decision is brave in my eyes.

I never realised how often TFMRs happen until I started talking about them. So many couples have been faced with this decision, but many don't talk about it for fear of judgement— which I understand. So many feel guilt even years after for what they chose to do, despite knowing in their hearts that they made the right call. It is such a cruel position to be put in.

We had a thousand questions for the universe and for the experts, but the main one was: how did this happen? We had done everything right. This was an IVF genetically-tested embryo. This should have been our happily ever after.

The genetic testing percentages were once again explained to us, but the bottom line was we were exceptionally unlucky. When the embryo hatches on day 5/6, the embryologist takes around five cells from the approximately one hundred cells that are present at that time. The cells are taken from what will eventually be the placenta. It is hoped that the five cells taken are representative of all the cells, including what will become the foetus. Because it is only five cells of one hundred, the test is rated as 95 per cent accurate. PGD/PGS is usually very accurate and contradictory results are rare . . . but it was us, so naturally the worst happened. We felt cursed. We slipped into the 5 per cent inaccuracy. It was literally bad luck. Everyone was in shock—David, Dr Gee, all of Genea and Dr Kesby. It was absolutely devastating, but no one could change what was happening.

David kindly offered to perform the medical interruption. We had formed such a special bond with him, so this meant a lot to us. To know our baby would be handled with love and care gave us some peace of mind.

We were unable to do the surgery until Saturday, 8 February 2020, so once again we faced a wait. I would be pregnant for another four days.

When the beautiful Erin Molan heard about our news, she again reached out to us with love and compassion. She arranged two nights away at the Fairmont Resort and Spa in the Blue Mountains. We were floored by this kindness. We spent two precious nights saying goodbye to our baby, something we will forever be grateful for. It is important to show that these acts were part of our life; that kindness made our world easier to bear. I hope our story encourages others to show that kindness. I know we try to pay it forward when we can.

On Saturday morning, we drove to Prince of Wales Private Hospital. Once admitted, I was shown to a bay and given two tablets to soften my cervix. Jonny never left my side. For a few hours I lay cramping and holding my stomach, but having done this before I knew the baby didn't feel anything but a light sway. David came to visit us, which I knew he didn't do often. He held my hand and told us that we would get there and when it happened, he would be right there with us.

Eventually it was time to be taken down to theatre. Jonny kissed my belly and said goodbye to his baby. I hated seeing the pain in his eyes. As I was wheeled down the hall and through the doors, I kept Jonny in sight for as long as possible.

In the anaesthetic bay, I held my stomach and took one final photograph of my bump. I was given a pre-med anaesthetic to calm me as I was wheeled into the theatre, once again holding David's hand. I remember looking around the theatre, thinking that the best of the best were there, eager to help get us through this in the safest and kindest way possible. I remember thinking that they would be the last people to ever see my baby, and with that I was gone.

Once again I woke up empty.

We were broken. This had really blindsided us.

My beautiful baby, you were wanted with every piece of my being but I couldn't give you that life. I am so sorry.

It took a while for me to be discharged as my blood pressure had dropped, but apart from that my recovery was standard. I was so thankful the procedure went well but emotionally I was a shell. I felt both empty and heavy at the same time.

Jonathan: I had just started to let myself believe we were about to get our happily ever after when Rachael called me at work with bad news about our baby. I was still sceptical, but with Rachael being around twelve weeks pregnant with a tested embryo, and a naïve belief that the dice simply had to roll our way at some point, I was beginning to feel optimistic for our future.

But then our world crashed around us and all we could do was go through the motions. I struggle to think about this baby, and what could have been . . .

I'm now tired and filled with doubt. I look back at myself in my 20s and most of my 30s and find it difficult to connect with the positive, outgoing and extremely social person I once was. Although I haven't been subjected to the multitude of medical procedures required on an IVF journey, it has affected my mental health, my body and my general wellbeing. The toll a difficult IVF journey has on the hopeful fathers is seldom spoken of, and I believe it should be.

Please don't get me wrong, I still believe that Rachael and I will have our child; I believe we will be okay—however after years of this story playing itself on repeat, it's natural to be sceptical, and hold less optimism than we once did. For now, we'll keep working towards our family, and I will do everything I can do to stay positive for the road ahead.

There are physical, mental and emotional ramifications of a TFMR that most people never know of or don't speak about. It is hard to write and hard to hear but I think it's important to talk about the actual physical side of it.

Hormonally, it is hard. When the placenta detaches from a woman's uterus the hormonal system is shocked—it takes time to go back to normal. When a woman is pregnant, she gets a nice surge of oxytocin, which helps her to bond with her baby, so when the baby is gone the woman's body physically and hormonally feels that loss.

During the first part of pregnancy, the body starts preparing the breasts to produce milk. When a woman has a TFMR, the body thinks it has given birth, which means that colostrum (and sometimes milk) begin to be produced after the baby is gone. This is extremely hard. A cruel biological kick.

It is common for women to bleed on and off for a few weeks. They will have a period about four to eight weeks after and in some cases they will ovulate as soon as two weeks after. In terms of other side effects, I personally had cramping, hot flashes, headaches and dizziness.

Finally—and this comforts my heart—during pregnancy, a mother and child exchange small quantitites of cells. This is called microchimerism. It means that every mother has a biological connection with every child created in her womb, at a cellular level, until she dies. No matter whether a baby is born, miscarried, stillborn, aborted or TFMR, this connection endures.

In the many days we spent waiting, between diagnoses and saying goodbye, Jonny and I put our next steps in place. Some people in our position might need time, which I really do understand, but we needed a plan—it was the only way we could get out of bed. Actually, to be frank, even with a plan I struggled to get out of bed. Some days I wish that someone would just put me in a coma and wake me up when it is time for a baby. But without that being an option, we knew we would do another round of IVF in the hope that the results would be better now that my endometriosis has been removed. The only other option is to try naturally and test the baby at twelve weeks, which I don't know if my heart can take again.

Yes, our trust in IVF genetic testing was damaged in this process, but we still know we are lucky to have it as an option. At least with IVF there is less chance for something to go wrong, although it is not a certainty, as we know better than anyone. But we have to try.

From a medical perspective, we were told that what happened was the second-best outcome. If the embryo hadn't implanted, we would have been worried and searching for answers—given I had had the laparoscopy and assuming it was a genetically healthy baby. If my body had miscarried a healthy baby, we would also be worried and searching for answers. But my body had held a pregnancy and it held it well despite the chromosome issue. Now we just needed the right embryo. We tried desperately to hold onto that. Once again I threw myself into research: what else could I try? Essential oils, kinesiology, supplements, reiki?

They say it takes a village to raise a child but for us it is proving to take a village to get pregnant. Despite all the pain we are feeling, we also feel surrounded by strength. We know we are so lucky to have such a strong and dedicated medical team who want to see us succeed.

Going back to life after loss like this is so hard. Painfully hard. You would think we'd be experts by now, but every time still hurts. Cooking dinner, getting groceries, seeing friends, going back to work. It all feels impossible. The worst part is anything that involves people, because we have to deal with their reactions. Sadly, most do not know how to act. Each time I have gone back to work after losing a child I have gone home in tears. Some people respond well, but some people don't. Over the years Jonny and I have had mixed reactions: some good, some bad.

More often than not, people don't come up to us at all—even people who we see every day don't say hello to us when we return to work, let alone mention our loss. Even not saying a word at all—just a hug or a hand on our shoulder—would be enough for us, but unfortunately this kind of acknowledgement is rare. Someone recently gave me a kiss on the cheek and said, 'I just don't know what to say but I am so sorry.' That simple sentence meant a lot to me—it acknowledged my pain. That's all we can ask for.

Trying to turn your brain back on at work is so hard. Some people appreciate the distraction, but my mind is still attached to my baby. I sit at my desk and all I can think is: *I miss my baby*. It feels like the world should have come to a standstill. But each day we get up and try again. And each day it gets a little easier.

Not long after the surgery, David called to check up on us. He also told us the gender of our baby.

A little baby boy.

We named him Leo, our brave little lion.

Roar loudly, baby boy. Roar.

Ever after

'In the depths of winter, I finally learned that within me there lay an invincible summer.'

Albert Camus

I have been putting off writing this final chapter. With every part of me I hoped I was going to be able to finish this book with the much hoped for 'and they all lived happily ever after'. I want to give us that so badly—to give that to everyone we know. But it isn't so straightforward. I am acutely aware that not everyone gets their happy ending.

Maybe when you read this you will look up my Instagram or google our name and you will see me smiling with a big pregnant bump or with a baby in my arms. I truly hope so.

Our journey isn't the average one. This has been a hard pill to swallow at times but ultimately, we just want to continue to be parents. That is all we want. We used to want two more children, but we have come to terms with the fact that we may only have one more, if we are lucky. We have had to compromise on our lives in ways that many will never know.

We may have a child naturally, but most likely not; more likely we will have a baby created in a lab and put inside me by an embryologist and a fertility specialist. Maybe our baby will be from a donor egg or donor sperm, or even a donor embryo. Maybe our baby will be adopted or maybe our second baby will be adopted. I just don't know. What is important for me to express to you all is that no matter how it happens, it will be okay and it will be with love. We will be okay.

I do know that Jonny and I will never give up. Mackenzie made us parents in our hearts and now all we want is a child in our arms again. The pain of giving that up would be far greater than the pain we feel in trying.

Despite all this pain and heartache, we still feel lucky overall. There have been moments when I didn't think I would get through this, but those are just moments. While this book condenses our lives, outlining the depths of our despair, day to day and week to week, more often than not, I have felt strong, lucky and full of love. It is like Mackenzie has given me a strength I never knew I had. She has blessed me with a superpower. I hope that comes across in this book.

Jonny and I are luckier than most: we have a supportive family, wonderful friends and jobs we enjoy. We have experienced the worst of humanity through sharing our story—the scammers, the trolls and the people who judge us and our decisions despite never having gone through the things that we have—but we have also experienced the best. People have taken time out to show my family kindness, and others around the world have wished us luck, sent us gifts to make us smile, prayed for us or told us their stories. Babies die every day, and these babies go unrecognised by most or, worse still, are forgotten by society. But our daughter's name is spoken daily by people around the world. How many people get that? We are lucky.

On the occasions we hold dear, such as Mackenzie's birthday, the anniversary of her passing, Mother's Day and Father's Day, people make cupcakes for her, give blood in her name, donate gifts to local hospitals for sick children; they buy flowers, light candles or plant trees. We are lucky.

Our compensation for sharing our story with the world and exposing ourselves has been kindness. Kindness through words, through gifts, through actions and through financial assistance. People have helped us considerably to pay for IVF that might literally give us our child. So many people don't get that. We are lucky.

We choose to share not for the attention—we would give anything to be a normal couple holding our healthy children. Instead we share to educate others about genetics, child loss and the struggles of fertility. We share in order to help open a conversation that is often closed. To help others feel that they are not alone. My greatest joy is when people write to me and tell me I made them feel less alone.

This is not the life we asked for; this is not the life we expected, but we choose to see the beauty within the pain. We now realise that without this pain we wouldn't have been able to help others, create this book and Mackenzie's Mission would not exist. We choose to keep writing our story. It isn't what we thought it would look like, but we will shape it however we can.

Life is not always kind but as people we can be. This is what has got us through. Kindness rules the world, I am certain of it. If everybody just gave a little more. I encourage you to all try.

When we first lost Mackenzie, we lost belief in our future happiness. But every act of kindness chipped away at the concrete that encased our hearts the day she died. Every supportive or caring word gave us the strength to get through that day, and then the next. I cannot tell you how much these random acts of kindness did for us, for our hearts, for our healing.

Thank you to those who loved us, even when we were no longer fun and happy but instead angry, sad, withdrawn or confused. You let us grieve and didn't put a timeline on us.

Thank you to those who took the time to do something kind for us, no matter how big or small. Every action was seen and felt.

Thank you to those who listened when we wanted to talk, sat with us when we needed silence and company, and distracted us when we wanted to pretend just for a second that we hadn't lost her; that everything was 'normal'.

Thank you to those who continued to let us into their lives and didn't exclude us. It allowed us to have some normality, and let us give back to those who were giving to us.

Thank you to those who showed me that we could and would find joy in life again, who stepped forwards with kind and open hearts.

Thank you to those who have honoured me by sharing your life, your story, and your pain with me. We know we are not alone.

Thank you to all my lovely friends and to my Instagram family who became friends during this time; those who took the time to reach out to us. You saved us more times than you know.

Thank you to our families, who are our rock and our number-one cheerleaders. You made us who we are. We are so lucky to be surrounded by such love.

Thank you to Hope, Bella and Leo; we wish we got to meet you, our beautiful children. We miss you every day. If we had got to keep you and Mackenzie our family would have been complete. But instead you joined your sister so she isn't alone.

Thank you to our future child or children for showing us love and life again. I know we will meet you one day. When that happens, I will do everything I can to create space in my heart for you and to not feel guilty for enjoying you. I will try so hard to remember that my love for you does not reflect a lack of love for Hope, Mackenzie, Bella or Leo. You will give me the strength to keep finding ways to help others and create change as I am not finished yet.

Thank you to my husband. My perfect unicorn man who never fails to make me laugh no matter how much my heart is breaking, whose touch makes me calm and happy, who makes my world complete just by existing. You are my home, my best friend, my love. Together.

Thank you to the little girl who came into this world like a shooting star, so bright yet so fast. Who made thousands of people stop in their tracks and watch her story. The little girl who unwittingly changed the course of the world with her too-short life. To the beautiful little girl who made me a mum and became my greatest gift and my biggest accomplishment.

Our little Mackenzie. You made us the luckiest people in the world. Some people never get to meet their heroes—I gave birth to mine.

Appendix

Ministerial brief
Spinal muscular atrophy and genetic carrier testing
Wednesday, 28 February 2018, 11 a.m.
prepared by Rachael Casella

Attendees

The Honourable Minister Greg Hunt—Minister for Health

The Honourable David Coleman—Assistant Minister for Finance

Rachael Casella—Mother of Mackenzie Casella and genetic carrier testing campaigner

Jonathan Casella—Father of Mackenzie Casella and genetic carrier testing campaigner

Professor Edwin Kirk—Clinical geneticist at Sydney Children's Hospital and genetic pathologist at NSW Health Pathology, Randwick. He is also medical director of the NSW Community Genetics Program, which offers screening for conditions common in people of Ashkenazi Jewish descent.

Professor Kirk is part of an Australia-wide group of scientists and doctors who are advocating for the introduction of preconception screening in Australia.

Doctor Michelle Farrar—Senior lecturer in Paediatric Neurology at University of New South Wales (UNSW) and consultant neurologist at Sydney Children's Hospital, Randwick. Dr Farrar is part of an Australia-wide group of scientists and doctors who are advocating for the introduction of preconception screening in Australia.

Apologies

Professor Nigel Laing—Head of the Neurogenetic Diseases Group at the Centre for Medical Research, University of Western Australia, and the Harry Perkins Institute of Medical Research in Western Australia. He also leads Australian Genomics' Neuromuscular Disorders flagship and is joint lead of its national diagnostic and research network program. Professor Laing is part of an Australia-wide group of scientists and doctors who are advocating for the introduction of preconception screening in Australia.

Professor William Ledger—Head of the discipline of Obstetrics and Gynaecology in the School of Women's and Children's Health, UNSW. He is a senior fertility specialist, obstetrician and gynaecologist. Professor Ledger is part of an Australia-wide group of scientists and doctors who are advocating for the introduction of preconception screening in Australia.

Purpose

The purpose of the meeting is:

To continue earlier discussions with the minister and officials on the genetic disorder spinal muscular atrophy (SMA) and its effects on the Australian population.

More specifically, for attendees to provide an update on the work currently underway, including a number of actions being undertaken at the request of the minister that are aimed at decreasing the prevalence of SMA, and other genetic disorders, through genetic carrier testing and preimplantation genetic diagnosis (PDG).

Background

Spinal muscular atrophy is a neuromuscular disorder characterised by a loss of motor neurons and progressive muscle wasting, often leading to death. In essence, a baby will slowly lose the ability to move, to swallow and, eventually, to breathe. It is a cruel disease as its impacts on both the baby and the family are profound and often tragic. SMA type one babies can be expected to live to about nine months old with a maximum life expectancy of two years. Trial treatments are beginning to emerge, and while these early drug treatments prolong life in some instances, this may only be for a matter of a year or two. There is currently no cure.

SMA is the number-one genetic killer of babies under two; however, despite this, it is largely unknown in the community and, more importantly, few medical professionals apart from specialists have heard of it. Statistically, one in forty people are carriers of SMA. If two carriers of this autosomal recessive gene have a baby there is a one in four chance that their baby will have SMA, and a two in four chance that the baby will be a carrier.

Recent research

New research by the Murdoch Children's Research Institute (MCRI) has shown that the combined affected pregnancy rate of cystic fibrosis (CF), fragile X syndrome (FXS) and SMA is comparable to the population risk for Down syndrome, highlighting the need to routinely offer carrier screening.[1] CF, FXS and SMA are three diseases that have significant health consequences and are among the most common recessive genetic diseases. One in twenty people will carry one of these three disorders.[2]

While these are among the most common recessive and X-linked conditions, there are hundreds of other severe childhood disorders which are individually rare but collectively common. Research conducted in Sydney has shown that it is possible to successfully screen couples for hundreds of different conditions in a single test.[3]

Testing for Down syndrome has routinely been offered for over twenty years, yet most health care providers do not offer screening for other serious inherited conditions to couples planning a

---

1 Murdoch Children's Research Institute, 2017, https://www.mcri.edu. au/news/genetic-carrier-screening

2 'What prospective parents need to know about gene testing such as "prepair"', *The Conversation*, 2017, http://theconversation.com/ what-prospective-parents-need-to-know-about-gene-tests-such-as-prepair-87083

3 Research presented at the Human Genetics Society of Australasia Annual Scientific Meeting in 2016 and 2017; manuscript under review.

family, despite these tests being available since 2012.[4] This is due to a common misconception that testing is only relevant to those individuals with a known family history. In addition, anecdotal evidence suggests that some medical professionals do not even know that such testing exists.

Prevention

While many genetic disorders cannot be cured, most can be prevented. Recent research shows that 88 per cent of couples weren't aware they were carrying mutations for three of the most prevalent genetic diseases, being SMA, CF and FXS. This makes the current practice of screening only those who have a known family history ineffective, costly and dangerous.[5]

Carrier screening is a term used to describe genetic testing that is performed on an individual to check for any genetic disorders they may carry. It is usually carried out through a simple blood test but can also be done through a saliva test. Research shows that each individual is a carrier of three to five lethal recessive genetic mutations.[6]

There are approximately six providers of genetic testing in most Australian eastern states. These offer tests for different sets

---

4   Murdoch Children's Research Institute, 2017, https://www.mcri.edu.au/news/genetic-carrier-screening

5   'What prospective parents need to know about gene testing such as "prepair"', *The Conversation*, 2017, http://theconversation.com/what-prospective-parents-need-to-know-about-gene-tests-such-as-prepair-87083

6   'Explainer: What is pre-pregnancy carrier screening and should potential parents consider it?', *The Conversation*, 2017, https://theconversation.com/explainer-what-is-pre-pregnancy-carrier-screening-and-should-potential-parents-consider-it-79184

of recessive genetic disorders. All five are consumer-pays tests and range in cost from A$350 to A$750, depending on the number of genes tested. The 'prepair™ test' is conducted by the Victorian Clinical Genetics Service (VCGS) and covers CF, SMA and FXS.[7]

The American College of Obstetricians and Gynaecologists (ACOG) has recommended that information about genetic carrier screening for genetic conditions be provided to every pregnant woman or woman planning to become pregnant.[8]

Access to genetic testing

Currently, government subsidies for genetic testing and counselling are only available for couples once they have had a child with a suspected inherited disease or if there is a history for a particular disease in the extended family. This makes the test expensive for some, inequitable and less likely to be undertaken by some couples.

As mentioned earlier, anecdotal evidence indicates that most general practitioners (GPs) do not know about these genetic tests and even discourage those that ask unless there is a family history. In addition, it is not a routine test ordered by private obstetricians and most IVF clinics.

---

7 'What prospective parents need to know about gene testing such as "prepair"', *The Conversation,* 2017, http://theconversation.com/what-prospective-parents-need-to-know-about-gene-tests-such-as-prepair-87083

8 'Carrier screening for genetic conditions', American College of Obstetricians and Gynecologists, 2017, https://www.acog.org/Clinical-Guidance-and-Publications/Committee-Opinions/Committee-on-Genetics/Carrier-Screening-for-Genetic-Conditions

Preimplantation genetic diagnosis

If a couple are identified as being carriers of a genetic mutation which increases the likelihood of their child being born with a genetic disorder, there are options available to them:

1. They can become pregnant naturally and then have pre-natal genetic testing at 10–12 weeks to test whether the foetus has the genetic disorder; or
2. They can undertake IVF and have testing using preimplantation genetic diagnosis (PGD). PGD is a test designed to screen the embryos created through IVF to determine if an embryo has the genetic disorder before implantation.

IVF is an expensive process and is not available to all due to the expense. However, a portion of the costs may be covered by Medicare. Each round of IVF leads to out-of-pocket costs of around $6000. PGD adds an additional cost of up to $5000 for each round, as testing of each embryo (up to five) costs approximately $900. This can result in some rounds of IVF with PGD costing up to $11,000 out of pocket.

For a number of years, Genea IVF has been campaigning on patients' behalf to secure Medicare funding for preimplantation genetic diagnosis (PGD) or genetic testing in order to make sure that this vital scientific technique is accessible to all Australians. Unlike IVF, there is currently no reimbursement for PGD through Medicare or any other state or federal government program. Instead, these costs are covered by couples, which puts PGD out of reach financially for many couples. Recently, Medical Services Advisory Committee (MSAC) considered an application for PGD to be added to the MBS (application no. 1165.1, MSAC meeting 6–7 April 2017). MSAC supported public funding but considered that the MBS was not the appropriate mechanism for this and requested that the Department of Health investigate options for implementation. A decision by the Australian government on this matter is pending.[9]

Cost assessment

Currently the Australian government provides substantial financial support for families who have a family member diagnosed with a genetic disorder, including but not limited to:

- Hospital admissions;
- Ambulance attendance;
- Occupational therapist;
- Physiotherapist;
- Dietitian;
- Nursing;
- Medical specialist;
- Pathology;
- Social work;
- Special education;
- Medicare cover for psychologist support;

---

9 'Campaign for Medicare funding for PGD', 2014, https://www.genea.com.au/my-fertility/why-genea/blog/all-blog/february-2014/campaign-for-medicare-funding-for-pgd?tagid=55 ; MSAC decision, http://www.msac.gov.au/internet/msac/publishing.nsf/content/17BAA5247F22729DCA25801000123C2C/$File/1165.1-FinalPSD-accessible.pdf

- Palliative care;
- Research;
- Centrelink carer allowance;
- Centrelink carer payment;
- Centrelink carer supplement;
- Centrelink carer adjustment payment;
- Centrelink child disability assistance payment; and
- Centrelink pensioner's education supplement.

Genetic disorders are a significant financial cost to the Australian government. These costs could be reduced and funds reallocated for proactive preventative actions rather than on remediation. Further, it would also have the benefit of reducing the severe and lifelong emotional pain involved to families affected by these disorders.

Recommendations

SMA specific

- That the Commonwealth Department of Health create and distribute SMA information packs to registered GPs, IVF clinics, obstetricians and midwives advising about the disease, its symptoms and prevalence and available testing.

Genetic carrier testing[10]

- The federal government should make carrier screening for a large number of severe childhood disorders freely available to

---

10 'Carrier screening for genetic conditions', American College of Obstetricians and Gynecologists, 2017, https://www.acog.org/ Clinical-Guidance-and-Publications/Committee-Opinions/ Committee-on-Genetics/Carrier-Screening-for-Genetic-Conditions

all couples who are considering a pregnancy or are early in a pregnancy;

- In order to implement such a program, a large-scale pilot project should be conducted as soon as possible to determine the operational requirements to offer preconception screening on a population-wide basis;
- Information on genetic carrier testing be sent to all relevant medical professionals;
- Genetic carrier testing be routinely recommended as part of care of pregnant families at all levels by GPs, IVF clinics, obstetricians and midwives;
- Accurate and unbiased information about genetic carrier screening be provided to every couple considering having a family and testing encouraged, bearing in mind that a patient may decline any or all screening;
- Carrier screening should be done and genetic counselling provided, ideally before pregnancy, however, it should be made available to any woman once she is pregnant;
- If an individual is found to be a carrier for a specific genetic disorder, their reproductive partner should be offered testing and genetic counselling about potential reproductive outcomes. Concurrent screening of the patient and her partner is suggested if the testing is undertaken during pregnancy;
- If both partners are found to be carriers of a genetic condition, genetic counselling should be offered to discuss options (i.e. prenatal genetic testing, termination or no further action);
- When an individual is found to be a carrier for a genetic disorder, they should be encouraged to inform their relatives, who are also possible carriers of the same mutation, of the risk and the availability of carrier screening;

- Carrier screening for a particular condition generally could be performed once in a person's lifetime, and the results could be documented and available in the patient's health record; and

- Both prenatal carrier screening and newborn screening be undertaken for genetic disorders as both have benefits.

Genetic carrier testing cost

- The cost of genetic carrier screening be covered/subsidised by the government.

Preimplantation genetic diagnosis cost

- The cost of PGD to be covered/subsidised by the government for those identified as being carriers of genetic disorders.

Together, we can save babies from dying. Change for Mackenzie.
—Rachael Casella

Acknowledgements

The people we need to thank in this book are so important to us that they have been woven throughout the book—but it just doesn't seem enough.

To the team at Genea, led by Associate Professor Mark Bowman and Dr Alison Gee, the words 'thank you' do not express our true gratitude. You have stood by our sides for two years now without wavering. You have made IVF possible for us with your kindness, compassion and professionalism. Without your generosity we would never have had IVF as an option. It is clear that you wanted to help us, cared about our story and wanted to see our dream come true. A particular thank you to Dr Alison Gee—you have never given up on us and I truly believe that you will be responsible for changing our lives forever. You are so special to us. It is also important to thank Mr Rick Forbes, for your support and for cheering us on in the background.

To Dr David Kowalski and Lisa Kowalski, you are the ultimate obstetrician dream team. You held out a hand of compassion and love when we needed it so desperately and we have never looked back. David, we look forward to the day that you are the first person to hold our beautiful son or daughter.

To every medical professional who gave us support, expert medical care, kindness, compassion, and in some cases, love. We know that in many instances our appointments were squeezed in, our fees reduced, and our test results rushed just that little faster. We saw each of these actions, even in our darkest times, and appreciate you all. To every medical professional who dropped their guard and showed us their human side, thank you. I know some people are unsure about crying in front of families for fear of seeming unprofessional, but those who cried tears for Mackenzie, Bella or Leo showed us you actually care. A particular thank you to those who work at Royal Hospital for Women, Sydney Children's Hospital, Prince of Wales Private, Genea and Sydney Ultrasound for Women.

To the beautifully strong women who honoured us by reading this book first and provided us with endorsement quotes—Mia Freedman, Erin Molan, Marcia Leone and Libby Trickett—thank you. Women who lift other women up are priceless. A particular thank you to Marcia and Erin, who through their kind acts have raised me out of darkness more than once.

How can I possibly express the thank you required to those who have made Mackenzie's Mission a possibility? The biggest thank you goes to Minister Greg Hunt—without your under-standing and desire to stop other families going through the pain we felt, Mackenzie's Mission would never have happened. You are a kind, honest and wonderful man and we feel honoured to know you. To the many other members of parliament who made this happen, in particular Minister David Coleman and

Prime Minister Scott Morrison—thank you. Finally, to Briony Hutton, who was Minister Hunt's assistant at the time, your continuous encouragement, love and support never went unnoticed.

To the lead investigators of Mackenzie's Mission: Professor Edwin Kirk, Professor Nigel Laing AO and Professor Martin Delatycki. You are exceptional humans. Australia owes you all a debt of gratitude and most will never know. You inspire me and have a place in our hearts forever.

To the other steering committee members for Mackenzie's Mission: Professor Kathryn North AC, Tiffany Boughtwood and Jade Caruana, as well as the dozens of people who currently work on Mackenzie's Mission. You are changing the world in our daughter's name, creating her legacy, saving lives and protecting families. You are incredible.

To Dr Michelle Farrar and your team, who looked after Mackenzie with such love and care, how can we ever express our gratitude? You were there at every step, both while we had Mackenzie and after we lost her. You will always have a place in our family.

This book would not have been possible without the work of those at Allen & Unwin. A huge thank you to our publishers Claire Kingston and Elizabeth Weiss, who saw value in this book and who wanted to support us in sharing our story, in the hope that it could help other people. To Tessa Feggans, who worked so hard as the editor of this book, streamlining my words—because I could have kept writing forever. To Simone Ford and Aziza Kuypers for their time and editorial expertise.

To every single person—friend, family, workmate, acquaintance or stranger who took the time to reach out to us. We read every word and felt every kind act. You have no idea of the strength you gave us. Thank you.

To our friends, thank you. We are lucky in that there are too many of you to acknowledge, but our hope is that you know who you are. However, I cannot help but mention Kath, my beautiful pillar of strength.

To our parents, Wendy Banham, David Banham, Linda Casella and Ross Casella, you have shown us how to be who we are today. We will be proud if we can be half the parents you are. You are our heroes.

I struggle to put into words the thanks we need to give to our family, as you have been through every step with us. The pain, the laughter, the heartache, the loss and the hope. We love you dearly Chris Banham, Alison Banham, Alara Banham, Henry Banham, Rachel Gately, Michael Gately, Ethan Gately, Sienna Gately and Sophia Gately.

To my husband, co-author, soulmate and father of my children, Jonathan Casella. My goodness, you are my everything. No matter what happens in my life, you make me feel lucky, and most importantly you make me happy. I love you. Together, always.

Mackenzie, Hope, Bella, Leo and all the other beautiful children who are in our hearts but not in our arms, please know you make my life better. You are pieces of my soul. One day I will be with you and I will be whole again.

Helpful services

Child loss, in-vitro fertilisation (IVF), genetic conditions, fertility issues, grief and termination for medical reasons are difficult areas of life to navigate. This book is an account of my personal experience, which I hope people will find helpful. However, as I state throughout the book, I am not a medical expert.

There are many charities and support groups available should you find yourself on a challenging path. They can offer information, support and advice. I have included a list of resources that help people going through any of these issues, as well as some organisations who have helped or had an impact on us, should you wish to show them your support.

Genetics:

Mackenzie's Mission—Genetic reproductive carrier screening:
 <www.mackenziesmission.org.au>
Australian Genomics: <www.australiangenomics.org.au>

Other genetic testing if unable to take part in Mackenzie's Mission: <www.mackenziesmission.org.au/other-options-for-carrier-screening>

Child loss:

Pink Elephant—Miscarriage support network: <https://miscarriagesupport.org.au>

Red Nose—Sudden Infant Death support/Child loss and grief support network: <https://rednosegriefandloss.org.au>

Sands—Stillbirth and newborn death support: <www.sands.org.au>

Redkite—Childhood cancer charity and support network: <www.redkite.org.au>

Charities we support:

Ronald MacDonald House: <www.rmhc.org.au>

Bear Cottage: <www.bearcottage.chw.edu.au>

Starlight Children's Foundation: <https://starlight.org.au>

Make A Wish Foundation: <www.makeawish.org.au>